Educational
Linguistics

Educational Linguistics

MICHAEL STUBBS

Basil Blackwell

© Michael Stubbs 1986

First published 1986

Basil Blackwell Ltd
108 Cowley Road, Oxford OX4 1JF, UK

Basil Blackwell Inc.
432 Park Avenue South, Suite 1503,
New York, NY 10016, USA

British Library Cataloguing in Publication Data

Stubbs, Michael, 1947-
   Educational Linguistics
   1. Language and languages—Study and teaching
   2. Applied linguistics
   I. Title
   407   P53
   ISBN 0-631-13898-6

Library of Congress Cataloging in Publication Data

Stubbs, Michael, 1947-
   Educational linguistics.

   Bibliography: p.
   Includes indexes.
   1. Language and languages—Study and teaching.
   2. Applied linguistics. 3. English language—Study and teaching.
   I. Title.
   P53.S886 1986 418'.007 85-28702
   ISBN 0-631-13898-6

Typeset by DMB (Typesetting), Oxford
Printed in Great Britain by TJ Press Ltd, Padstow, Cornwall

Contents

Acknowledgements

Ron Carter made detailed comments on initial proposals for this book, and has discussed a number of the topics in it with me over several years. Gabi Keck provided a teacher's perspective, and allowed me to explain some things many times until they were a little clearer. Karin Klett helped with the typing, displayed an unconcerned attitude to non-standard dialect, and only spoke to me in the standard language because I was linguistically incompetent. Brigitta van Rheinberg helped with the references, but this only seemed to confirm her belief that linguists cannot agree about anything. My debt to the work of Michael Halliday is discussed in detail in chapter 1. The book was completed during a summer semester in 1985, when I worked in the University of Tübingen in south Germany. I am very grateful to the English Department for providing me with a pleasant term's teaching, and to Pauline and David Reibel for the use of their beautiful and peaceful flat.

The book is based upon articles which were written between 1979 and 1985. Chapters 1, 5 and 10 are entirely new. The other chapters have all been previously published, though some in rather obscure places; they have all been revised and updated here, sometimes extensively. The author and publishers are grateful for permission to reprint this material: the original place of publication is acknowledged after each chapter.

Notational conventions

The following conventions are used frequently throughout the book. Readers are reminded of them where they become particularly relevant. A few other abbreviations and conventions are introduced in individual chapters where they are necessary.

'single quotes'	for quotes from other authors.
"double quotes"	for the meanings of linguistic expressions.
italics	for linguistic forms; e.g. *feline* means "to do with cats" or "cat-like".
*asterisk	for ungrammatical, ill-formed or anomalous forms, which native speakers would not produce under normal circumstances.
Standard English (SE)	written with capitals, this is a technical term discussed in detail in chapter 5.

Relevant Models of Language

1

Introduction: relevant models of language for teachers

All the chapters in this book discuss, in one way or another, what view of language is useful for educationalists, mainly teachers in the classroom, but also researchers. I argue that there is much in contemporary linguistics, broadly conceived, which is of use in formulating such an educational view of language.

The assumptions of the previous paragraph are, of course, widely questioned. It is questioned whether any 'model' of language can be of use for such purposes: reality, it is argued, is too complex to be captured by any model, and it all ultimately depends on the skill of the individual teacher in the classroom. Many educationalists are certainly suspicious of linguistics as a source of understanding about language. I will try and answer some of these objections in this introductory chapter, and hope that the remainder of the book will answer them in practical detail.

Relevant models of language for teachers

Much of the work in this book has been influenced, more or less directly, by Halliday's work on language in education. In 1969, Halliday published a famous article entitled 'Relevant models of language', in which he discusses what would be an adequate definition of language to guide teachers in their work. This is a constant theme in his writings. In a more recent formulation, he discusses whether it is possible to give 'a succinct account of the essential nature of language in terms that are truly relevant to the educational process' (1978: 207). He argues that a course in general linguistics for teachers is essential, but 'not a sort of watered down academic linguistics course - something new, designed and worked out by linguists, and teachers, and teacher-trainers' (1982: 13). This theme of collaboration between linguists and teachers is central in Halliday's view of language in education.

Halliday's writings are in fact one of the most substantial bodies of work available on language in education. I do not have room here to give a thorough review of this work, although such a review is lacking. I hope, however, that this chapter and the book as a whole will provide at least partial answers to Halliday's questions above. He has also written (1978: 12) that it is a fundamental failure of schools not to recognize the relations between language and society and that the 'whole theory and practice of education' depends on the relation between language and people as social beings. One of his basic concerns in education is to extend the functional potential of the child's language. He sees the ability to control varieties of language as fundamental to education (1978: 28); teaching Standard English is teaching a new register in which the child can do new things (1978: 210, 234; and cf. chapter 5 below); and teaching literacy is also extending the functional potential of language (1978: 100; cf. chapters 11 and 12).

Different models for different purposes

Halliday also holds a functional view of linguistic theories: that 'the value of a theory depends on what use is to be made of it, and [that] a model is tested by its effectiveness for specific purposes' (Halliday, McIntosh and Strevens 1964: 301), which might be machine translation, foreign language teaching, speech therapy or teacher-training. He goes further, however, than simply asserting the value of theoretical pluralism. He also argues against the wholesale rejection of everyday forms of linguistic knowledge. Linguistically untrained people, including young children, have their own folk linguistic models. These are one kind of model, are inevitably functional, and should be taken into account by linguists (cf. chapter 14). Halliday argues (1967: 2) that theoretical models are, in any case, less different from folk models than we would often like to admit. Halliday's main statement in this area is an article entitled 'Syntax and the consumer' (1964). He argues that since descriptions of language are required for very different purposes, different models coexist and do not contend for the same goal. Models can be evaluated only in the light of goals, and we can have only private opinions about such goals: there is no one to judge the judges.

The view that different theories cannot be directly compared with each other is a plausible one, although Halliday does not provide any very strong arguments in its defence. Clearly, if things are to be compared, they must be similar in some way. In fact, things must normally be very similar indeed in purpose to be sensibly compared. All vehicles are rather similar in the universe of things, but it still makes little sense to compare a bus with a tractor, or a family car with a racing bike. They must serve different purposes and are good at doing different things. However, we can sensibly compare the merits of two family saloon cars.

In favour of the view that theoretical diversity is good, one might argue that diversity is healthy, whereas uniformity inhibits intuitions, stifles the imagination, prevents speculation along different lines, and encourages unthinking conformity. Language is too rich, complex, subtle and 'messy' (Halliday, 1978: 38, 203) ever to be captured in a single theory. A demand for a single theory implies a simplistic view of the world, and we might not expect it from a linguist such as Halliday, who emphasizes language in the social world with its social, political and educational implications. Such points, however, are not really arguments: they are merely lists of emotive terms such as 'rich and subtle' and 'healthy diversity'. The argument against pluralism also uses emotive terms. Rather than healthy diversity, one might see disarray, opportunism, relativism and compromise. Such terms, however, would also seek to dismiss a view by classifying it in a value-loaded catch phrase.

Halliday also points out (1964: 24), however, that the whole problem can be exaggerated, since there is a 'vast store of knowledge that is just linguistics and common ground to all linguists'. This has been demonstrated in detail by Hudson (1981), in his article on what all linguists agree on. There has now been 50 years or so of agreement about a 'core' of topics which must be included in any serious study of linguistics. This core must include phonetics, phonology, morphology, syntax and semantics; the interrelations between these levels of linguistic description; and the relation between a language so conceived and its use by individual speakers or by a society. Linguistics must arguably include more than that, but the main point is that it must include at least this core.

Amongst many educationalists, there is particular suspicion of structural or formal analysis: that is, description of linguistic forms - variously referred to as grammar or syntax, but in principle including also phonology, morphology and forms of discourse. There is a fear that this represents a step back to a sterile and mechanical parsing of sentences, or to a formalistic kind of syntax which ignores meaning. There are two main answers to such fears. First, discussion of forms does not exclude discussion of meanings. Second, there are meanings transmitted by the forms themselves; by the way the content is conveyed. If teachers and pupils cannot analyse such forms, they cannot analyse many of the ways in which language is manipulated, for example, by the media. And important kinds of cultural analysis are closed to them.

This means that in the context of teacher-training, there is a major problem with the different-models-for-different-consumers view. It can be used to justify concentrating on the anecdotal margins of socio-, psycho- and hyphenated linguistics, and neglecting the central organization of language: grammar in the widest sense and methods of description and analysis.

Arguments against (and for) linguistics

Many arguments are in fact put forward against linguistics in teacher-training, and they have to be answered directly and thoroughly. There is no point in ignoring the fact that linguistics is now just as much of a turn-off for teachers as grammar used to be. And there is no point in talking if no one is listening. Some of the arguments are as follows.

1 'Linguistics has been no help to teachers so far.' This is a major point, since any attempt to introduce linguistics into teacher-training has to fight against a long history of promises and disappointments. The main answer to

this criticism is that past attempts have often been based on unsuitable, purely formalistic models of language which are out-of-date in theoretical linguistics in any case.

2 'Linguistics is too difficult for teachers.' This view risks being simply patronizing. Teachers are scholars and deserve to be able to continue their own professional education. On the other hand, there is no doubt that beginning to study linguistics can seem very daunting. The outcome cannot be foreseen and considerable commitment is necessary before anything worthwhile can come of it. In addition, it is only full-time professional linguists who could be expected to have the overview to select out what is clearly irrelevant to teachers in contemporary linguistics. As a profession, linguists have the social responsibility to make such selections, and to present the findings of modern linguistics in an accessible way.

3 'But simplified linguistics is no good either.' This, as Sinclair (1982) points out, is catch-22. If we simplify the product, teachers may learn without proper understanding, and a little knowledge is a dangerous thing, so it is better not to start at all. The logical fallacy in this argument was well known to the ancient Greeks. A more recent statement is: Even a journey of a thousand miles must start with a single step.

4 'Teachers are practical, down-to-earth people, who don't need all this theorizing.' Halliday (1982; 15) has dismissed this view as 'mental laziness': if teachers do not have a grasp of the general principles, they are condemned to mechanical copying, mistaking examples for orthodoxy in a myopic and superficial way. But this is partly an *ad hominem* (or *ad feminam*) argument. A more powerful argument is that all teaching is based on some theory, whether this is Piagetian or behaviourist or inexplicit staffroom folklore. All teaching is theory-loaded, and all theories are value-loaded. There should therefore be explicit discussion of what these theories are, and of what would be the best theory for the purpose.

There is also a much more general rejection of the need for systematic analysis, and this too needs to be explicitly argued against. Teaching itself is often seen as an intuitive skill, with each classroom encounter unique and not amenable to objective analysis. Even the possibility of objective or replicable criteria of success in teaching may be rejected. Amongst teachers of English literature in particular, there is the view that analysis destroys literature (cf. chapter 7). This view, however, is a rejection of only certain types of analysis, since it forgets that traditional literary criticism uses terms such as *metaphor, synechdoche, trope, genre*, etc., which are just as much jargon to outsiders, as are *phoneme, syntagmatic structure* or *sociolinguistic variable*.

The general point is that we have to deal with entrenched professional positions. All speakers have their own deeply held personal models of language, which the mainstream education system and teachers' organizations selectively develop. We are dealing with the practical sociology of knowledge. No knowledge is neutral, but is always interpreted in the light of already held opinions. The additional complication with language is that the need for explanation is often not seen at all.

In this area, then, as in many others, a lot of energy is spent with pots and kettles calling each other black. Each side accuses the other of being reductionist, of simplifying things and ignoring what is really important. Educationalists accuse linguists of ignoring the unique social context of each classroom, and of wanting things neater than they are. Linguists accuse educationalists of taking linguistic features out of context of the organization of a language, and of looking for a direct and simplistic relationship between isolated features of language and sociological categories, picking and choosing features of language in a piecemeal fashion. (I develop this argument in detail in chapter 13.)

Further, the pots and kettles debate often hinges on the moral issues which are tackled. Teachers of English argue that a main value in studying great literature is that it introduces the discussion of moral issues, and thus leads to the psychological and moral development of pupils. But a study of modern English language and linguistics can also introduce social, political and moral issues (cf. chapter 4). Halliday (1982) argues in fact that linguistics is *uncomfortable* because it destroys fondly held myths about language, and *subversive* because it forces us to come face to face with unpalatable truths about social inequalities in contemporary multicultural societies. Such issues are not hypothetical, as in literature, but are precisely the topics debated by government select committees. They have to do with the role of English as a world language, and with historical and social forces on minority languages and dialects. Teaching a language or teaching about language is therefore a social and political act, and this should be explicit in the teaching. It has to do with changing people's attitudes, not merely with imparting another body of knowledge.

The merits of a syllabus on linguistics for teachers is that it can combine a discussion of social and ethical problems with a clear intellectual content; and not only a body of factual knowledge, but also a training in critical thinking and analysis. (It would be wrong, of course, to make inflated claims here. Subjects such as history and biology equally study the relationship between human beings and their environment, and train students how to weigh complex evidence in reaching rational decisions on morally important issues.)

Theory and practice

Much of the trouble arises from a suspicion of theory per se. But as Lawton (1981: 7-8) argues, teachers need to do the right things, to do them for the right reasons, to be aware of what they are doing, and to be able to explain to others what they are doing. If they cannot make clear to themselves and others why they do what they do, then they are condemned to unprincipled imitation. In addition, they will be unable to counter criticisms of their practice, and teachers are regularly under attack from many quarters. They will be vulnerable to crude calls for accountability and for visible, but superficial 'results'. Some things *can* only be explained in theoretical terms. For example: Why were traditional grammatical parsing or drills wrong? How is talk related to learning? Why are non-standard dialects not merely 'bad' English? How does the English spelling system work? Why is oracy not parallel to literacy?

One of the problems in studying language in education is the wide range of types of facts about language which have to be considered. For example (as I show in detail in chapter 5), the concept of Standard English can only be understood by a combination of linguistic description (e.g. of its syntax), of a theory of linguistic variation (it is an intersection of dialectal and functional varieties), of the ways in which it has been deliberately codified and subjected to language planning over centuries, and of the political and ideological implications of its use.

Similarly (as I have also discussed in detail elsewhere: Stubbs 1980), literacy can only be fully understood by study from several different directions. We need descriptive linguistic information on how the spelling system works, and this requires technical linguistic concepts including phoneme, morphophoneme and morpheme (cf. chapter 12). Reading must also be seen as a psychological and perceptual process. But it must also be seen sociolinguistically, as an activity which has different social functions in different social groups (cf. chapter 11). And it must be seen ideologically as part of the social practices by which social control is maintained. Street (1985) provides a particularly clear discussion of the differences between a view of literacy as a neutral technology or skill, and a view of literacy as a set of concrete social practices which are understandable only within political and institutional settings. He also points out that a linguistic approach might be thought superficially to support the 'technical' model, although in fact it undermines it. My only criticism of Street is that he neglects the more technical aspects of speech-writing relations. Both the technical and the ideological understanding is required.

I think it is possible to show that any linguistic topic of interest to educationalists must be approached in three ways, which we can crudely label for initial convenience as: description, theory and practice. Here are some further examples.

1 Suppose our general area of interest is *regional and social dialects*. First, we require descriptive information; for example, how exactly they differ from Standard English. Second, we require a theory of how dialects relate to social class or ethnic group and to speakers' identities. And third, we need to discuss what account educational policy should take of such dialect diversity: for example, what is the role of dialect, if any, in the classroom?

2 Or suppose our interest is in the *ethnic minority languages* spoken in the UK. We need descriptive information about the language actually used by speakers: for example, on code-switching or language mixtures. We need information on who speaks which languages, and theories of bi- and multi-

lingualism: for example, whether it affects cognitive development. And we need to know what practical provision to make for teaching English as a second language or teaching the ethnic community languages.

3   Or suppose our interest is in *child language acquisition*. We require descriptions of the difference between children's and adults' language. We require theories of how children acquire language: is it basically genetically programmed or environmentally determined? And we need to know how all this relates to policies of teaching English as a mother tongue in schools, or to the language of school subjects more generally.

My claim is that any topic concerning language in education must logically be approached from at least these three points of view. Description and theory are interdependent. Both must be formulated with the educational practitioner in mind. But also practical planning and policy are untrustworthy, if they are not firmly based on systematic information.

In chapter 4, I have developed this three-way division into a way of organizing a whole syllabus on English language, and have given many more examples and illustrations. The main points here are as follows. By the shorthand term *description*, I mean ways of analysing any piece of actual language in use: educationalists require ways of commenting systematically on the linguistic forms which occur in any piece of language they come across. By *theory* (even more shorthand), I mean theory of linguistic variation: what kinds of diversity are expected in languages, their correlation with social class and other social groups. Basically we require a theory of the relation between language and human beings in society. Both description and theory should be non-prescriptive. They describe people's linguistic behaviour, without trying to prescribe what people ought to do. By *practice*, I mean here applied policy-making at all institutional levels, including governments, publishers, educational systems and ultimately individual classrooms. Here, any discussion is inherently prescriptive: but it should be *informed prescriptivism*, based on the preceding description and theory.

Each of these three main divisions can of course be discussed at much greater length. For example, in chapter 2 I begin to develop what a descriptive sociolinguistic theory of language variation would have to look like. It would have to distinguish between dialects and diatypes (varieties of language defined according to use). For example, regional and social dialects are spoken in different geographical regions and by different social groups. Diatypes vary according to the use of language in formal or informal settings, as in writing or speech.

Cultural analysis

I do not intend to imply in any of the above that it is possible to have pure description which is independent of theoretical or ideological assumptions. I have phrased things in the way I have, however, because the opposite danger is too evident in education: there is ideological discussion with no attempt to provide the descriptive basis for it.

I would take the view that all educational research is, and all school curricula should be, forms of cultural analysis, and are therefore inherently ideological. This view is developed very clearly by Lawton (1983). Most of this chapter has been about the knowledge which *teachers* should have about language. But this knowledge can be the basis of what teachers select for their *pupils*. Lawton argues that a school curriculum is a selection from a culture, and that it should contribute to pupils' understanding of social norms and practices: for example, the social, economic, moral and belief systems of the culture. Clearly an ability to analyse linguistic and other communication systems is central to understanding the society in which we live, the ways in which it is run, and its dominant social and political values. (Cf. especially chapters 4 and 5).

There is one common confusion here. Teachers who raise such ideological issues with their pupils are often accused of political bias or indoctrination. This is a basic misunderstanding. Teachers who give their pupils the methods to understand better the culture in which they live are giving their pupils the tools to make their own analyses and arrive at their own interpretations. It is teachers who do not question the status quo who are biased. They take for granted the present order, as though it was 'natural' or inevitable, with no possibility of change, and as though it was possible to report things neutrally. Pupils must be given the analytic tools to analyse purportedly 'neutral' reporting and to analyse the ways in which reality is socially constructed. This is why they must be able to analyse forms of language as well as content.

The aims of this book

My aims in this book are therefore as follows. First, to provide descriptive information and precise ways of talking about aspects of language which are of interest to educationalists. Examples which I discuss in detail include: the English spelling system; the vocabulary of English; the syntax of Standard and Non-standard English; the semantic and pragmatic organization of casual conversation, literary language and the discourse of language-disordered children.

Second, to provide concepts for discussing variation within language and the relation between such variation and language use. I discuss in particular: dialectal versus diatypic variation; standard versus non-standard language; written versus spoken language.

Third, to show how such descriptive and theoretical discussion can be of practical value to teachers. I discuss in particular: the planning of a school syllabus in English language; the teaching of literature; the teaching of spelling; the place of Standard English in schools; the diagnosis of children with language disorders. I do not, of course, claim to discuss any of these topics exhaustively. However, I do try to show, with reference to detailed examples, how systematic description and theory can provide a principled basis for school curricula and classroom lessons; and therefore to show with reference to particular examples how classroom lessons can be based firmly on theory, while remaining eminently practical.

Fourth, to discuss the ideological implications of the description, theory and practice, and to show how an understanding of language variation can contribute to a cultural analysis of the society in which the teachers and pupils live. Topics which I discuss in some detail here include: the role of English as an international language; the nature of literacy; the role of Standard English in maintaining the dominant social and political values of society.

FURTHER READING

Halliday, M. A. K. (1978) *Language as Social Semiotic*. London: Edward Arnold.

ACKNOWLEDGEMENTS

This chapter is published here for the first time. Some sections are based on parts of an article published as 'Relevant models of language for teachers', in M. Spoelders, F. van Besien, F. Lowenthal and F. Vandamme (eds), *Language Acquisition and Learning: Essays in Educational Pragmatics*, vol. 2, Leuven/Amersfoort: Acco, in collaboration with Communication and Cognition, Ghent, 1985.

I am grateful to Gabi Keck for comments on a previous draft.

2

Understanding language and language diversity: what teachers should know about educational linguistics

Introduction

This chapter develops several of the ideas introduced in chapter 1 about a relevant model of language for teachers, and proposes several ways of organizing people's thinking about language. It provides ways of thinking about language diversity: both the range of languages and dialects used within Britain; and also the range of language varieties, dialects and styles used within English. It also begins to discuss a way of analysing the central linguistic organization of English.

Teachers and (other) experts

Teachers must often feel that they are under siege from academic experts on all sides, and that they are expected to assimilate an increasing amount of knowledge quite apart from the actual subjects that they teach. They are increasingly expected to know about different methods of teaching and examining, about the physical and psychological development of children, about the effects of social class or ethnic group on educational attainment, and so on. As well as all this knowledge about pedagogy, educational psychology and educational sociology, they are also increasingly expected to know about educational linguistics. Ideally, all teachers (not only teachers of English or foreign languages) should know a great deal about language, since all teachers in contemporary Britain, America and elsewhere constantly come up against problems in at least some of the following areas: child language acquisition, including pathological language development; literacy, including teaching reading, writing and spelling; non-standard dialects in the classroom; immigrant languages, and therefore teaching and testing English as a foreign or second language. They ought, ideally, to be informed about the current debates over language deprivation, language across the curriculum, community languages in schools, and so on.

There is no doubt at all, however, and no point in ignoring the fact, that many teachers are suspicious of academic expertise in general and of linguistics in particular. Rosen's ironic description must ring many bells: 'those sinister figures in the wings, faintly contemptuous, armed with the paraphernalia of expertise and tapping ominously their research findings' (1978: 55). There are many reasons for such distrust of linguistics: the disillusion which has followed many past attempts to use unsuitable, over-specialized models of language for pedagogic purposes; the consequent trivialization of linguistic insights; the partly justifiable feeling that much theory is mere theorizing with no practical pay-off. However, it is important not to be discouraged by previous bad selections and inappropriate applications of theoretical work.

Many teachers are also understandably discouraged from undertaking their own study of basic issues in language and education because they recognize the practical problems involved in implementing new ideas. There is often enormous inertia to be overcome within schools, and the defences which all institutions can set up against change usually mean a long time-lag between a theory being formulated and applied. In addition, many teachers simply find that their focus is very diffuse. In addition to teaching their particular subject, they generally have pastoral duties, and are concerned also with the design of new materials, syllabuses and curricula.

As far as suspicion of theory is concerned, one myth is, however, more easily disposed of. There is a widespread belief that contemporary linguistics is so divided and incapacitated by basic theoretical disputes and disagreements that it is in no position to contribute to important social and educational problems. This view, that any such practical application of linguistics is at best premature, has been put forward by some linguists themselves. It is, nevertheless, exaggerated. There are, it is true, many debates and disagreements within linguistics, but they tend to be on relatively technical matters, and do not affect the kinds of issues discussed in this book. The large number of basic facts, concepts and principles which all linguists agree on has been set out in explicit detail by Hudson (1981). The list is specifically designed for educationalists interested in the place of linguistics in schools. It covers the basic principles of descriptive linguistics; the differences between languages and dialects; varieties of language; language change; children's language acquisition; pronunciation; writing; vocabulary; grammar and meaning.

The problems for teachers in Britain

The rest of the discussion in this chapter (and most of the chapters in this book) assumes the perspective and problems of a teacher working in the UK, and therefore working with English as the most widespread language in the education system. Many of the general points are valid for other countries and languages, but this cannot be assumed. Attitudes towards different languages and different varieties of language vary considerably between different language communities, and usually cannot be predicted by an outsider. This is itself a general sociolinguistic principle: the linguist must pay attention to the beliefs and attitudes of the local language community.

Teachers in Britain need to have knowledge about the following aspects of language, if they are to be able to make informed and rational decisions about the wide variety of language problems that arise in schools and classrooms.

Language diversity within Britain

This includes knowledge about different accents and dialects of English; and knowledge about languages other than English which are spoken in Britain, including indigenous languages such as Welsh, and languages such as Punjabi or Italian, now widely spoken here due to recent immigration.

Language diversity within English

This overlaps with the first aspect of language, since the variation includes regional and social accents and dialects. However, it also includes what is often called stylistic variation; that is, different styles or varieties which are appropriate to different purposes, topics, social contexts, and so on.

Practical language planning

The two areas of language described above involve theoretical and descriptive knowledge about the dimensions of diversity: what kind of diversity can be expected in principle and what actually occurs in practice. This knowledge should provide the basis for the many value judgements and policy decisions which have to be taken constantly by teachers. These include such questions as: Do non-standard dialects of English or ethnic minority languages have a place in schools? If so, what? Should schools have integrated policies of language across the curriculum?

A model of language itself

It must also be said that much teacher-training flirts with external aspects of the sociology and psychology of language, but avoids the issue of the central organization of language itself. Any language or dialect is enormously complex, involving sounds, words, sentences and texts. Any serious study of language must involve a study of this phonological, lexical, syntactic and textual organization. Although all languages are complex, some of the organizational principles are nevertheless very general, simple and intuitively obvious once they are pointed out, and can therefore be explained fairly rapidly.

Quite apart from its practical use to teachers, such a course of study, especially the final aspect, the model of language itself, has its own autonomous educational value.

A succinct pedagogical account of language

Such a four-part framework may seem very ambitious, but it begins to seem rather more manageable if we outline the main criteria it has to fulfil:

1 It must be possible to set out the main features of the framework fairly simply and rapidly. The study of language in any serious way requires a very considerable investment of time and effort. It is therefore important for students to be able to see from the beginning approximately where they are heading. Few people are willing to invest great effort on intellectual blind dates, particularly when similar enterprises have led to disappointments in the past. It does not follow, however, that the framework has to be superficial: indeed, it must not be.

Another justification for some initial over-simplification is this: if an idea is to have any hope of making a practical impact, it must be possible to express it simply. One has only to think of educational slogans which have been swallowed whole in the past to see how unfortunately true this is. We require, then, a framework which can be quickly grasped in its essentials, but developed in as much detail as is required.

2 The framework must be firmly based in recent work on language and language variation. However, it must not be biased too strongly in favour of any particular model of language which is currently fashionable. In fact, it must be based on both traditional and recent insights into language. Much in people's views about language is very traditional, and these views must be developed, not simply disregarded. Traditional insights often have considerable merit, if they are carefully selected, and in any case modern linguistics is often less innovatory than some superficial accounts might lead one to believe.

3 The framework must be realistic, sociologically and psychologically. It must be able to tell us about real language in use, and it must be able to organize thinking for very practical purposes, such as preparing teaching materials and language planning in schools. I will attempt to provide just such a framework – at least a reasonably comprehensive checklist of features of language which cannot be ignored by teachers. Many facts and details will then be filled in by the chapters that follow. This is, then, both a framework for interpreting the rest of the book; and also for organizing any other knowledge about language as it becomes available. Even if such checklists are crude, they can be useful aids to systematic thinking. They need not be unprincipled just because they are coarse grained. And they can be made more delicate once the broad overall principles have been grasped.

The aim, then, is to provide a coherent view of language which is designed for teachers: a succinct account of at least part of the essential nature of language which is truly relevant for teaching purposes. If that sounds a difficult, or even slightly foolhardy undertaking, then this is deliberate. This must be the explicit aim. If we fail, then at least we know what it is that we have failed at. Too much writing about language for teachers has been fragmentary and incoherent, not to say patronizing, as though teachers were capable only of grasping a few of the more superficially interesting facts about language, but not of assimilating a systematic and serious approach.

Language diversity in Britain

Britain is a country which gives a superficial impression of being monolingual, since 'everybody speaks English'. It is true that almost everyone does speak English in Britain, and even that most people speak only English. However, this is a statement about individual monolingualism: most individuals are monolingual in English. A moment's thought shows that there are, nevertheless, very large numbers of individuals who are not monolingual; and that as a country Britain is societally multilingual.

It is often useful to take the boundaries of a country or state as a unit for linguistic investigation. There are obviously no necessary correspondences between countries and languages (although governments and groups of people often think there should be, hence the separatist movements in places such as Quebec and the Basque country). It is evident, on the contrary, that many languages are spoken in Britain (certainly over a hundred are in common use); and that, conversely, English is spoken in many other countries. However, it is state boundaries that are used to determine political decisions about which languages are to be used in education, government, the legal system and so on. The term *Britain* is therefore, in this context, not accurate enough. We have to distinguish between both the UK and the Republic of Ireland (where Irish Gaelic has official status), and between England and Wales (where Welsh has official status, for example, in courts of law), and between Wales and Scotland (where Gaelic has no such official status).

Within the UK there are two main dimensions of language diversity. Languages spoken may be either *English* (including various dialects of English) or *non-English* (including Welsh, Turkish, Cantonese, etc.). And languages may be either *indigenous* (in the sense of having a long history of hundreds of years' use in the British Isles, such as Welsh), or *non-indigenous* and now used here due to historically recent immigration (such as Caribbean creoles, Turkish and Cantonese). These basic dimensions are schematically represented in table 1, although the terms used are shorthand mnemonic labels. The diagram is crude, but it shows immediately that all four logically possible combinations of the two dimensions of diversity occur in present-day Britain. One hundred or even fifty years ago, categories 2 and 4 were not significant in terms of numbers of speakers.

Comments are required immediately on terms such as *indigenous, British, English* and *immigrant*. The term *indigenous* in this context refers to languages which have a long history of use in the British Isles. The only languages in this category are English itself, including various dialects, and the three Celtic

Table 1   Dimensions of language diversity in the UK

	English language	Indigenous to Britain
1 British dialects of English (e.g. Cockney)	Yes	Yes
2 Other dialects of English (e.g. Caribbean creoles)	Yes	No
3 Celtic languages (e.g. Welsh)	No	Yes
4 Recent immigrant languages (e.g. Punjabi)	No	No

languages, Welsh, Scottish Gaelic and Irish Gaelic. The Celtic languages were in fact spoken here before English, although they have been pushed continually further west and north by English over the past 1000 years. *Indigenous* therefore contrasts in this context with languages spoken in Britain due to recent immigration. The main waves of immigration – for example, from the Caribbean and the Indian subcontinent – occurred in the 1960s, and as a result the range of languages used in certain areas of the country (especially London and cities in the English midlands, such as Birmingham, Nottingham and Leicester) has changed sharply in a short period of time. Terms such as *British* and *non-British* can sometimes be used instead of *indigenous* and *immigrant*, but this can, on occasions, be unnecessarily confusing. It is evident that the question of someone's nationality is in principle quite separate from the language he or she speaks. Many recent immigrants to the UK speak a language other than English, but have full British nationality. Their children may also speak this language, although they were born in the UK, are British and have never been outside the country.

We also have to beware of such terms, since they express the viewpoint of the white Anglo-Saxon majority. They may seem to other groups to be irritating white liberal euphemisms, which express the standpoint of mainstream culture. Minority groups may prefer different terms to express their perceptions.

The term *English* is used in the table to refer solely to language, and therefore includes Standard English and Non-standard dialects. The term *dialect* is defined more fully below, but can be left with its everyday meaning for the present. Note simply that some non-British dialects of English (including Caribbean creoles) are recognizably related to English, but very far from what we normally mean by English, and incomprehensible to most speakers of Standard English.

I can now fill in a few more details on the categories 1-4 in the rows of the table. The category *British dialects of English* refers to varieties such as Standard British English, and regional dialects such as Cockney, Geordie and Scouse. *Other dialects of English* include varieties which have their own characteristic accent, vocabulary and grammatical features: for example, Indian English. The main dialects involved here are, however, Caribbean creoles. There is considerable variation here over terminology. The term *Jamaican creole* is frequently used, but although the Jamaican influence is often the strongest, due to the number of immigrants from Jamaica itself, there are in fact different varieties of creole from the various West Indian islands. Speakers themselves often refer to their language simply as *patois*, although this term is also used to refer to French-based creoles: for example, from St Lucia. Another complication is the variety now sometimes referred to as *London Jamaican* or *British Black English* (Sutcliffe 1982). This has developed from Caribbean creoles, but has developed in Britain, and is now distinctly different from varieties of language in the Caribbean. Again, it is clear that a British versus non-British distinction is an over-simplification.

There are three *Celtic languages* used in Britain: Scottish and Irish Gaelic are very closely related, and Welsh is slightly more distantly related to both of them. Scottish Gaelic has around 80,000 native speakers, with main concentrations in the extreme north and west of Scotland, especially in the Hebrides. Irish has around 40,000 native speakers, but they are mainly in the Irish Republic, in the extreme west and south. Welsh has around 650,000 native speakers, unevenly distributed throughout Wales, with higher proportions in the north. (Both Irish and Welsh have many more non-native speakers.) Manx and Cornish were also Celtic languages, but are now both extinct and survive only as cultural hobbies. The last native speaker of Manx died in 1974, and Cornish died out in the 1700s.

Finally, a term such as *recent immigrant languages* is descriptively accurate in historical terms, although not very satisfactory. The Bullock Report (DES 1975), refers coyly to 'families of overseas origin'. The term *ethnic minority* is also used: it is usually clear enough in practice, although it sometimes serves as a euphemism for black, and sometimes is taken more widely to include, say, Italians and Greeks. There is more confusion in talking about the *mother tongue* of ethnic minority children. The language of their parents or grandparents may be, say, Urdu; but their own native language may be English with Urdu serving as a *community language* – that is, a language with particular literary, cultural and religious functions in the local ethnic community.

It is very difficult to give accurate statistics for immigrant, ethnic minority languages in the UK, since the government simply does not collect such figures. The census form used in England in the last 1981 Census, for example, contained no questions at all about language, or even about country of origin. The government feared the racist implications of such questions, although it is difficult to see how any serious planning can be done for education, housing and the like, without accurate information on the languages spoken, dates of arrival in the UK, place of residence and so on. Even with information about, say, parents' country of origin, it is difficult or impossible to estimate the language spoken when many countries, such as India, are multilingual. And even with information about languages spoken, this gives no indication about how, if at all, such languages are actually used in the UK. However, the commonest languages in terms of numbers of speakers are those from the north of the Indian subcontinent: Punjabi, Urdu, Bengali and Gujerati. These are followed by European languages - German, Polish, Italian, Greek and Spanish - and by languages from south-east China - Cantonese and Hakka. Another hundred or so languages could be added to this list. It is also worth mentioning that as well as having many pupils in a school who are bilingual, there may also be many who are biliterate and familiar with a writing system other than that used for English. This may be one of the scripts used for northern Indian languages, or Arabic, Chinese, Greek or Hebrew. (For detailed information on the languages spoken in Britain see Rosen and Burgess 1980; Linguistic Minorities Project 1985; Trudgill 1984b.)

Although all my discussion here assumes the point of view of a teacher working in Britain, the framework can be adapted in fairly obvious ways to situations in other countries. For example, in the USA, the category of indigenous languages would comprise native American Indian languages, and Spanish would be one of the languages with high numbers of speakers due to relatively recent immigration. In Australia, the indigenous languages are Australian Aboriginal, and there are now large numbers of speakers of immigrant languages from Europe and elsewhere. In both the USA and Australia, there are distinctive non-standard varieties of English: Black English vernacular in the USA, and Aboriginal English in Australia. In France, indigenous Celtic languages are represented by Breton, and varieties of Arabic are significant amongst immigrants from north Africa. And so on.

Language diversity within English

There are two main types of variation within English: *dialectal* variation (which has a widely understood everday meaning, and simply requires to be refined somewhat) and *diatypic* variation (which is often rather loosely referred to as different styles or registers). The discussion in this section again assumes the perspective of British English. Many of the general principles discussed are valid for other countries and languages. On the other hand, there are many facts about the pronunciation, vocabulary and grammar of Standard British English, and its relation to styles of formal spoken and written English, which are peculiar to British dialects and not the same for other languages (see chapter 5).

Generally speaking (and disregarding for the moment the caveat above about mother tongues), any individual has just one language variety which he or she regards as his or her native language or dialect or mother tongue. This may be Standard English, an indigenous regional dialect such as Scouse, or a Caribbean creole. Such varieties are *dialects*. They are permanent and are difficult to change, even if speakers want to change their dialect for strong social reasons. Admittedly, some speakers are bidialectal, and can switch between a regional dialect and Standard English, but it is unusual to feel equally at home in two dialects. It is usual to distinguish between *regional* (geographical) and *social* dialects, although many dialects give information about both the geographical and social background of speakers. For example, if someone speaks Scouse, this implies not only that he or she comes from Liverpool, but that the speaker is also probably working class. Middle-class speakers may have a recognizable Liverpool accent, but will generally avoid more extreme local dialect forms. A defining characteristic of Standard English, on the other hand, is that it is not geographically restricted. There are minor differences between the Standard English used in England and Scotland, although Scottish speakers are generally recognized by their accent rather than by vocabulary or grammar. It is possible also to distinguish *historical dialects*, such as Old English, Middle English or seventeenth-century English, although these do not concern us directly here. Given information about a speaker's dialect, then, it is possible to fix him or her regionally and/or socially.

Although, generally speaking, individual speakers have native command of only one dialect, they have command of many different *diatypes* – that is, they change their language according to who they are talking to, what they are talking about, where they are, and so on. The most general dimension which determines the diatype used is the formality of the social context: intimate, casual or more formal. Also, whereas a dialect is more or less permanent, speakers go on acquiring competence in more diatypes throughout their lives. Few of us are competent in varieties of legal English, but we could acquire competence in such diatypes given the need and the training.

In summary: a dialect is a variety defined according to user; a diatype is a variety defined according to use; dialects are relatively permanent; diatypes are inherently variable and change from situation to situation.

It is possible to specify more precisely the dimensions of diatypic variation. *Field* refers to the topic being discussed: for example, football or history. *Tenor* refers to the formality and social relations between the participants: for example, pupils in the playground versus teacher and pupil in the classroom. *Mode* refers to the medium of transmission, usually speech or writing. The field, tenor and mode clearly affect the kind of language used. (See Gregory and Carroll 1978, for a discussion of this model of language variation.)

In summary, I have so far in this section made the distinctions in figure 1. Dialects and diatypes are, of course, not independent: any dialect shows diatypic variation. In addition, there are complex relations between particular

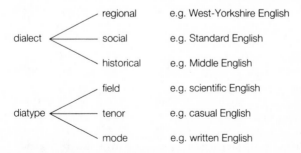

Figure 1   Dialectal and diatypic variation

dialects and particular diatypic uses. One of the most important is the very powerful social convention that Standard English is the appropriate social dialect for almost all formal (tenor), written (mode) uses. (See chapter 5.)

Levels of language

So far, I have rather seemed to imply that a dialect or diatype can be described as an undifferentiated whole, but this is impossible. Any statements we make will be about particular aspects of a language variety. We might, for example, make statements about: the vocabulary of Cockney (the lexis of a regional and social dialect); the vocabulary of legal English (the lexis of a diatype defined according to field); ways of forming plurals of nouns in Caribbean creoles (the morphology of a dialect); grammatical differences between Scottish and Irish English (the syntax of regional dialects); vowels in Scouse (the phonology of a regional and social accent); question-answer exchanges between teacher and pupil in the classroom (the discourse organization of a diatype); and so on.

In other words, it is possible to describe language varieties at different levels. The precise divisions and also the terminology differ according to the particular school of linguistics, but roughly speaking we have to distinguish between linguistic units of different sizes, such as sounds, words, sentences and texts. The following terms are fairly standard, although (for reasons which do not concern us here) linguists disagree to some extent on the exact relationship between the levels: *phonetics* and *phonology* (the organization of sounds); *morphology* (word structure); *lexis* (vocabulary); *syntax* (grammar or sentence structure); *semantics* (meaning); *discourse* (the organization of texts above the sentence). *Phonetics* and *phonology* refer, by definition, only to spoken language: we therefore require also the term *graphology*, to refer to the organization of features of writing systems, spelling and the like. We can therefore think of English varying in two dimensions, as in figure 2. Discussion of exactly what is meant by each of these levels of language would amount to a substantial course in linguistics. But the overall point should be clear: it is possible to think in principle of a thorough and systematic description of varieties of English, even though any such comprehensive description of even one particular variety would be an enormous undertaking and probably impossible on practical grounds. The aim of giving such a framework is not, however, to propose that teachers attempt such descriptions, but so that they have a way of precisely locating any partial and fragmentary description they come across, and placing it within a general view of the organization of a language.

There are many examples in this book of precisely such partial descriptions of aspects of dialects and diatypes. For example, chapter 6 discusses lexis in detail, with particular reference to diatypic variation. Chapter 12 discusses aspects of the graphological organization of written English. Chapter 5 discusses the phonology and syntax of Standard English and non-standard

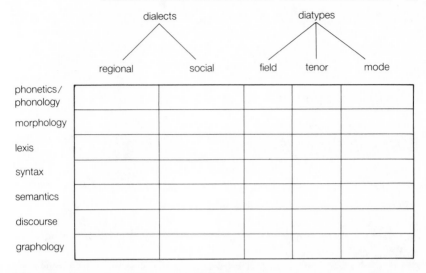

Figure 2 Dimensions of language variation
Any language can be described along two dimensions: different varieties, dialectal or diatypic; and different kinds of units, such as sounds, words and sentences. We can therefore talk of any instance of language in terms of these two dimensions, and make statements about, for example, the phonology of a regional dialect, or the lexis of a diatype.

dialects. And chapters 3, 8, 9 and 10 discuss aspects of the discourse organization of written and spoken English.

The basic concept is, then, that language is inherently variable. Languages are not uniform, homogeneous things or objects: they are enormously complex organizations, which vary in multidimensional space. There are, nevertheless, certain major dimensions of variability which can be stated and which can allow us to systematize our thinking about them.

Theory and practice

In summary, I have provided a way of thinking systematically about basic kinds of language diversity. The fundamental distinctions are set out in figure 3. This provides a descriptive and theoretical framework which is general, comprehensive and powerful, but which is also precise enough to be applied to specific features of language in use. However, the framework is entirely descriptive and theoretical: it provides a way of setting out information about language diversity in a convenient way. It does not in itself tell us how to solve practical, political, social and educational language problems. This is not my immediate aim in this chapter; the aim is to provide a systematic basis for thinking rationally about such problems.

So far I have discussed some questions of the sociology of language in Britain, and some aspects of the use of language for different purposes in

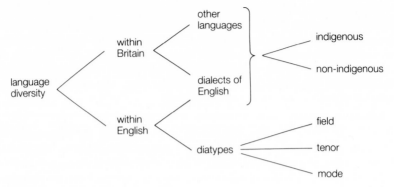

Figure 3 Language diversity in Britain

different situations. I now have to move to a discussion of the organization of different aspects of language itself.

A traditional model of language

There is a traditional model of language, which is defective in some ways, but which again provides a useful way of organizing our thinking: see figure 4. *Spoken* and *written* refer to the two main diatypic modes discussed above.

Chapters 8-12 are divided between discussion of these four aspects of language. This is a convenient division, and provides a way of checking that we are not neglecting any basic aspect of language in use. Traditionally in schools, for example, much more attention has been paid to written than to spoken language; indeed there are good reasons for this. But sometimes 'literate' has been used more or less as a synonym for 'educated'. Conversely, some recent educational thinking has emphasized 'talk' (something of a vogue word in some quarters) at the expense of other aspects of language use, and has devoted great attention to discussing teacher-pupil talk, children's exploratory talk, and so on. It is only relatively recently that attention has been paid to listening comprehension outside the foreign-language classroom, and that attention has been paid to pupils' spoken production (see chapter 8). This emphasis on spoken language is valuable as a counter to previous neglect of it, but what is really required is a balanced view of the relation between spoken and written language. The relation between spoken and written English is

	spoken	*written*
production	speaking	writing
reception	listening	reading

Figure 4 A traditional model of language

very complex (for detailed discussion, see Stubbs 1980), but some of the most important facts are as follows. Spoken language is basic, in that it is learned naturally before written language, and is massively more frequent in occurrence. Written English has a special prestige and place in the formal educational system. There are also special relations between written, formal and Standard English, that is, between mode, tenor and social dialect (see chapter 5).

On the other hand, the traditional four-way division conceals several things. It might be taken to imply that speaking and writing are active, whereas listening and reading are passive. This is not so, and listening and reading involve active interpretation. It might also imply that listening and reading comprehension are essentially different, whereas they have much in common (see especially Brown 1978).

In order to develop these last points, we require a model of language which is based on the concept of interpretation and prediction, and this is the topic of the last section of this chapter. We require a model of language which can help in understanding essential characteristics of listening and reading comprehension; teaching written composition; teacher–pupil discourse; children's exploratory talk and writing; teaching English as a mother tongue, as well as teaching English as a second or foreign language. We require a model, in other words, which is immediately applicable to practical teaching problems. Yet it must also be theoretically well based. It must be simple to explain in its most essential features, yet capable of interesting theoretical elaboration. Again, this may seem like a hopelessly ambitious and foolhardy aim. And to talk in this connection of a 'model' of language is probably too ambitious. What I will discuss is just one concept which can, however, be explained rapidly, and which is of considerable help in organizing our thinking about language in use.

Predictions and expectations

For any such model to be relevant for teaching purposes, it must be a model of how language is interpreted in real-life situations, however simplified and idealized it may be in some respects. It must place centrally the search for meaning which characterizes any use of language. It is a basic finding of linguistics that people always attempt to make sense of language which they hear or read. They even do their utmost to make sense out of apparent nonsense, a fact exploited by politicians and advertisers amongst others. They make predictions about what is likely to occur, and interpret what does occur in the light of these predictions.

Such predictions and expectations operate with respect to the kinds of dialectal and diatypic variation discussed above. There are very powerful social conventions and expectations, for example, about the kinds of English it is appropriate to use in *The Times*. These expectations concern both dialect and diatype (standard, formal). The expectations are relaxed somewhat, but by no means entirely, for various tabloid newspapers. It is well known that both Conservative and Labour politicians (Margaret Thatcher and Harold Wilson, for example) have received professional training in losing and acquiring different characteristics of accent, due to the expectations people have and the inferences they draw from ways of speaking. And unless we are familiar with a regional dialect or subcultural style of speech, we have difficulty in making the correct predictions which allow us to understand it fully.

The concept of prediction can be illustrated more precisely as follows. Consider, as a very simple example, this unfinished sentence:

I travelled down from Edinburgh to London by ————.

Possible completions will already have occurred to you. But consider which of the following words are possible:

train, car, bicycle, camel, myself, Tuesday, lunchtime, table, happiness, up.

Some of these words are likely, whereas others are impossible. Some are more likely than others. For example, 'train' may have occurred to you immediately, rather than 'lunchtime' or 'myself', although all three possibilities are grammatical and make sense. In addition, the possibilities depend both on linguistic knowledge ('train', not 'happiness') and also on real-world knowledge ('train' not 'camel'). That is:

I travelled down to London by camel.

is perfectly meaningful, but bizarre given our everyday knowledge about the transport system in Britain. Whereas:

I travelled down to London by happiness.

is arguably not interpretable at all. Could you, for example, explain to someone what it means?

The basic concept involved in this model of language is already explained: in any normal use of language we can always predict, at least partly, what is coming next. This does not mean that language use is deterministic. We can only sometimes predict with total certainty what is coming (in English q is always followed by u). And expectations can be broken - although if we recognize broken expectations, then this implies that there were expectations there to be broken. The power of this concept of language is that it operates at all levels of language. The example above involves predicting single words on the basis of the preceding isolated sentence. Normally we would also have more help from the preceding discourse and the non-verbal context.

We can also make predictions at the level of letters (and at the level of sounds, although this is simply more awkward to illustrate on the printed page). Real-life examples of such expectations in operation occur with typing mistakes. Often these do not disturb our comprehension, since there is enough information in the surrounding text to know what was intended. We assume meaning and search it out. We are dealing, in other words, with two sides of the same coin. Speakers make predictions, and they can do so because language contains redundant information.

Another way of approaching the central concept is to ask: how far can language be distorted and still remain intelligible? How can we make sense of the very elliptic language of the telex and newspaper headlines, or of the language of young children and foreigners, or of Stanley Unwin? (see chapter 4 for an example of Unwinese.) We clearly do not require 'perfect' English in order to make sense of utterances, but equally there are limits on how far language can be distorted and still make sense. What are the boundaries of comprehension?

The same principle again operates in discourse sequences. Suppose you hear:

There were these two theoretical linguists and they were stranded on a desert island . . .

then you immediately predict that a joke is coming. In general, I am proposing an *expectancy model of language* that emphasizes the use of language in connected discourse. Such a model is developed at great length for teaching purposes by Oller (1979), and I have also discussed such a model in more detail in chapter 3.

I now have to illustrate briefly why such a model of language is useful in teaching, and how it emphasizes aspects of language which are central in listening and reading comprehension. Consider, first, reading comprehension. In preparing reading primers for teaching initial literacy, it is now a basic principle that the language used should be in line with young children's expectations. Much ridicule has been poured on books which use sentences of the type: 'Run, Spot, Run! See Spot run, Jane.' Such 'primerese' does of course make a laudable attempt to control the language used for teaching young children. The idea is correct, but based on a faulty concept of simplification. Words are chosen because they are short or display regular letter-sound correspondences, and not because they contribute to a meaningful story. So we end up with strange sentence structures, and cannot use predictions about what is normal language in a story. The simplification may actually make it more difficult to follow the story (see Perera 1980).

In real-life uses of written language, discourse is always interpreted for a purpose: enjoying a story, searching for information in a telephone directory, or in a textbook or on a can of beans. In teaching children to read, we teach them explicitly (although often inadequately) about spelling conventions. We teach much less about the grammatical differences to be expected between spoken and written language, and we teach hardly at all about the different discourse organizations to be expected in narratives, instructional language, explanations, lists, and so on.

The basic concept involved is that reading is what Goodman (1982) has called a 'psycholinguistic guessing game'. We use our knowledge about what is normal language and normal text to predict what is coming next, rather than reading every letter, word or sentence individually. This principle has common-sense, everyday validity. It is common for someone to report that a novel was 'difficult to get into', but was very enjoyable once they were past the beginning. This is only to be expected. At the beginning of a story, a reader has only the most general expectations, based on what stories are usually like, and perhaps more specialized knowledge of particular authors, and what kinds of characters, places and plots they use. But once the story is fully under way, the reader has very specific predictions about what kinds of things will happen, and this eases comprehension.

It is probably obvious enough that similar points could be made about listening comprehension. It may be less obvious that the same concept of prediction is also applicable to the development of writing skills. A lot of attention has been paid recently to the notion of exploratory or first-draft writing. It is pointed out that children are often expected to produce final-draft writing in essays or reports, but are not given the chance first to develop their ideas in note form. It is evident, however, that rough notes, made for the writer's own benefit, will be very different in organization from material intended to be read by others. Basically, notes are not required to contain enough information to enable others to make the correct predictions which make comprehension possible. Such issues are central to an understanding of the essentially verbal and textual nature of Western education, which is centrally concerned with, and might even be defined as, a training in making things explicit.

Consider, in summary, some major features of the model of language that I have proposed in this last section.

1   It is very general and very simple, and therefore has considerable overall coherence. The basic concept of prediction can be explained in a few minutes with simple examples.

2   Nevertheless, it can be developed over years of study into a very detailed model of linguistic organization applicable to all levels of language: sounds, syllables, words, sentences, paragraphs, and so on.

3   Although it is very general, it can be made very specific and applied to precise details of language.

4   Although I have here presented it in an informal way, it can be formalized if required. We have to recognize here, incidentally, a very strongly held prejudice in many people against formalism. This is unfortunate, as formalization is often an extremely useful technique, although like anything else it can be abused. Such strongly held feelings must nevertheless be taken into account.

5   It tackles aspects of the central organization of language, whereas very often teacher-training flirts only with peripheral aspects of language use and never actually analyses language itself.

6   It is very practical and can be applied immediately to preparing teaching materials of various kinds. Material for guided reading, writing and listening can be based in rather obvious ways on the concept of making sense via making predictions.

Linguists are familiar with many problems in the kind of model of language structure which I have discussed briefly here. Certainly it captures only one aspect of linguistic organization, and needs to be augmented with other models. However, it does capture an aspect of language which is particularly relevant to teaching. On the one hand, we have to bear in mind that linguists and teachers may require models for different purposes. On the other hand, I have not emphasized – although it is perhaps evident – that I have presented the concept of prediction here in a way appropriate to teachers. At least some of the ideas are adaptable, given suitable presentation, for teaching pupils themselves about language. The concept of prediction leads in rather obvious ways to the preparation of teaching materials for listening and reading comprehension, for example. In fact, many teachers may feel that they are already doing many activities of the type I have suggested.

There is always a danger in such discussions of telling teachers what they know already, in superficially different words. In this instance, I would be happy if this is the case. A major aim of applied linguistics is to make explicit good practice, which may be unconscious, and to provide therefore a principled and systematic basis for activities which may otherwise remain unrelated, inexplicit or fragmentary.

Concluding comments

Introductory chapters to books come in various shapes and sizes. Some, for example, attempt to place the chapters which follow in a historical or social context: to explain the reasons for the current debate about language in education. Others attempt to provide a detailed commentary and interpretation of the following chapters. I have not tried to do either of these things.

I have tried instead to provide a general interpretative framework which will allow readers themselves to make better sense of the book. For, although the chapters are often superficially rather different in content and style, they are all based on the assumption that language and languages can be understood in a principled and systematic way – and that this understanding is essential for teachers and pupils. And they all try to contribute to our understanding of the languages and dialects used in Britain, the diversity of styles and uses of English, and the ways in which language is interpreted in use.

The interpretative framework which I have provided is admittedly rather coarse. However, it can be tested against the many facts about language and language use in the chapters which follow.

FURTHER READING

Stubbs, M. and Hillier, H. (eds) (1983) *Readings on Language, Schools and Classrooms.* London: Methuen.

ACKNOWLEDGEMENTS

This chapter is a revised version of an article first published in M. Stubbs and H. Hillier (eds), *Readings on Language, Schools and Classrooms*, London: Methuen, 1983, pp. 11-35.

I am grateful to Margaret Berry, John Broadbent, Jean Bleach, Mike Byram, Walter Grauberg and Mary Willes, who all made detailed comments on a previous draft of this article.

3
Applied discourse analysis and educational linguistics

Introduction

This chapter develops several of the ideas of chapters 1 and 2: about the relations between theoretical linguistics, applied linguistics and teacher training; about the relations between description, theory and practice in language study; and about how much description and analysis is appropriate on language courses for educationalists. It also develops from chapter 2 the concept of a model of language use which is based on linguistic expectations and predictions. Some aspects of this chapter are rather more technical than chapters 1 and 2, and it provides a fairly detailed survey of the applications of discourse analysis to educational linguistics, with a large number of references. However, it also provides several detailed suggestions for practical teaching activities.

This chapter continues discussion of the question: what should teachers and students know about language? I will attempt to give one possible answer to the question posed in the following quote from Halliday (1978: 207):

> I am often asked by teachers if it is possible to give a succinct account of the essential nature of language in terms that are truly relevant to the educational process. It is not easy to do this, because it means departing very radically from the images of language that are presented in our schoolbooks and in the classroom . . . We have to build up an image of language which enables us to look at how people actually do communicate with each other . . .

My general argument will be that a model of language relevant to educational purposes should focus on language in use in connected discourse. I will review some general issues concerning the relation between linguistics and teacher-training, and then discuss two very different in-service teacher-training courses which I have prepared, discussing the theoretical rationale behind the courses, which lies in recent work on discourse analysis. Finally, I will review some applications of discourse analysis in teaching both the mother tongue and foreign languages.

In considering discourse analysis and education, there are two logically possible areas of application. One could (1) study the discourse of teaching itself, as part of a study of institutional language. Alternatively, one could (2) teach about discourse and communication, as part of the content of a foreign language or mother tongue syllabus. There are two main topics for (1), a study of classroom discourse. One is spoken classroom interaction between teacher and students, and this has been a major research area in the social sciences since the late 1960s (see chapter 13). The other is the study of the discourse organization of written teaching texts, primarily 'textbooks' and related material. Education in Western schools and higher education is, in these senses, predominantly verbal and textual (cf. Van Dijk 1981: 2), and a study of teaching itself therefore demands a study of its written and spoken discourse. Possibility (2), teaching about discourse and communication, could also have two rather different emphases. The main aim might be to increase students' communicative competence, by giving them more ability in a wider range of discourse types, and therefore increasing the functional potential of students' language (cf. Halliday 1978: 57). Alternatively, one could teach directly the theory of discourse analysis, as part of a course on language or linguistics. Teaching about language in the education system usually means teaching about either grammar or literature, with only unsystematic discussion of the wide variety of non-literary discourse.

This framework of possible applications of discourse analysis underlies this chapter, although not all four areas are equally discussed. The framework is similar to one proposed by Van Dijk (1981), in a very useful survey article on discourse studies and education. Van Dijk admits, however, that his article is entirely speculative and programmatic: I will try here also to give more concrete examples.

I will not attempt to give a comprehensive overview of the applications of discourse analysis. It would not be practicable to attempt a survey of such a recent and open-ended field, which draws on several different academic traditions, including linguistics, cognitive psychology, sociology and artificial intelligence. It is probably more useful to try and tackle a few more specific questions with reference to particular examples. In educational linguistics, this means discussing particular syllabus proposals and teaching strategies. Amongst other possible applications of discourse analysis which I will not be able to discuss here are: a view of psychotherapy as conversation: (e.g. Labov and Fanshel 1977); an approach to developing the communicative competence of mentally retarded patients (e.g. Price-Williams and Sabsay 1979); training doctors, either native or foreign speakers, to interact more efficiently with patients (e.g. Candlin et al. 1977); and social skills training (e.g. Hargie, Dickson and Saunders 1981), including the vast literature on effective communication in business and management. The applied study of discourse in these and other areas is, however, concerned with training professionals of different kinds to understand better the rules and conventions underlying spoken and written discourse. Again, it may be more useful to avoid bland overviews, and to develop most of my points specifically with reference to teachers, making points relevant to other professional groups by implication. I have preferred therefore to be mildly original, rather than to attempt a comprehensive survey, and my bibliographic references are intended as representative, but in no way exhaustive.

Milroy (1984) provides one general alternative approach to a socially responsible applied discourse analysis, in her discussion of the theoretical and practical issues raised by communicative problems. In particular, she discusses the kind of cross-dialectal communicative problems which are likely to have serious social consequences when professionals and clients from different social groups and with different dialects meet in school classrooms, doctors' surgeries, courtrooms and other comparable settings. For case studies which analyse the discourse in such settings, and discuss such cross-dialectal communicative problems, see Harris (1980) on magistrates' courts and Malcolm (1979) on school classrooms.

Definitions and terminology

There is considerable variation in the use of the term *discourse analysis*, so I had better insert a brief note on what I mean by it. First, I do not intend to draw any important distinction between *text* and *discourse*. As these terms are normally used, they often imply only a difference in emphasis, but nothing of theoretical importance need hang on the distinction. A distinction is sometimes implied between written text and spoken discourse. Alternatively, discourse refers to interactive language *versus* text as non-interactive monologue, whether spoken or written. For example, one can talk of the text of a speech. Another distinction is that discourse implies length, whereas a text may be very short. Halliday and Hasan (1976) define a text as a semantic unit and point out that complete texts include *Exit* and *No smoking*. Some scholars have used the two terms to label theoretically important distinctions, but since I will not be concerned with those distinctions here, I will ignore them.

Similarly, I will favour the term *discourse analysis* over other terms for reasons of convenience rather than theory. The term *text analysis* would do equally well, except that it usually implies a particular European tradition of text linguistics. The term *conversational analysis* might also serve, except that it almost always implies work which derives from ethnomethodology. It is also too narrow in that it implies a restriction to conversation, and the exclusion of more formal discourse, although there are problems in the analysis of discourse which are common to formal and informal, written and spoken language - for example, the analysis of lexical and grammatical cohesion.

By *discourse analysis*, I mean therefore the linguistic or sociolinguistic analysis of naturally occurring discourse or text, spoken or written. This does not deny the validity of other approaches: a full understanding of discourse is necessarily interdisciplinary. It merely restricts my topic here to manageable limits. (This definition of discourse analysis is developed at length in Stubbs 1983b).

Discourse analysis in teacher education

Linguistics in teacher-training: some general points

The main question to be discussed in this chapter is: what kind of understanding of language is relevant in teaching the mother tongue or foreign languages, or in teaching in general? Which linguistic concepts should be presented to teachers and how? What therefore is the relation between linguistics and teacher-training? Language is complex, so some simplification in the presentation is inevitable; but how can the simplification be managed without distorting the material or patronizing the audience? These questions are not often discussed explicitly by linguists, although it is only professional linguists who have the necessary knowledge and full-time commitment to linguistics which would allow them to select what is relevant to teachers, or to any other professionals. Educationalists could not be expected to do this for the simple reason that there is so much in contemporary linguistics which is of no direct relevance to education. It is arguably a social responsibility of linguists as a profession to present to non-linguists in an accessible way the aspects of knowledge about language which are of important practical value.

The complexity, breadth and specialization of contemporary linguistics has itself meant that educationalists have often rejected linguistics *in toto*. Not being able to see the wood for the trees, they have jumped to the conclusion that linguistics comprises jargon and formalism, and discusses only a model of language which is of no use to teachers and pupils, since it avoids real language behaviour. Descriptions such as linguistics is 'scientific', 'mathematical' or 'abstract' are often used to refer in a slightly confused way to such feelings. There is no point in ignoring the problem that linguistics is now as much a turn-off for many teachers as grammar used to be. This may be a superficial reaction, but it must be countered. It follows that questions of presentation are crucial.

There is often a suspicion in teacher education of anything that practising teachers might not understand immediately, and linguistics has a reputation for conceptual difficulty. Many teachers have an image of themselves as practical and down-to-earth folk, having to cope with everyday life at the chalk-face, in the blackboard jungle, and as taking a sensible stand against the impractical theorizing of linguists, sociologists and psychologists of education, and all the rest. There is doubtless much justification in such a sceptical attitude towards theory, and it has to be taken into account in preparing training courses. If the clients are not interested, they will not learn anything. And they are often justifiably sceptical after past promises and disappointments. Teachers are under constant pressure from new ideas and information, not only from linguistics, but also from psychology, sociology and other disciplines, and under constant pressure to respond to what often turn out to be short-lived fashions.

However, the view that teacher-training must have the practical short-term goal of making them better teachers in the classroom tomorrow may be short-sighted and dangerous. It is short-sighted since there are other longer-term, and possibly more interesting and ambitious goals. And it is dangerous since it implies that teachers have no need for, or are incapable of continuing their own general education or engaging in their own scholarly study about their subject or about their own professional behaviour. Teachers *are* scholars. However, some recent educational thinking has retreated into well-meaning, but ultimately sentimental concern with children, sometimes disguised as a practical stance against abstract theorizing. This has sometimes led to teacher-training courses which flirt with the peripheral aspects of academic disciplines. It must be admitted, for example, that some courses focus almost exclusively on psycholinguistic and sociolinguistic aspects of language, but avoid any detailed analysis of language itself. Carter (1980: 228) has likened this to the absurdity of a mathematics course which avoids doing too much mathematics. However, it has to be demonstrated that training can provide interesting intellectual challenges, of inherent interest to teachers as educated people. Also, it must be admitted that a real problem with teaching linguistics is that it requires a very considerable initial investment by students before they begin to see the general value of what they are doing, and can use their understanding to prepare their own teaching materials. Studying linguistics is like going on a blind date.

A danger of an overly practical, short-term view is that without principles teachers are condemned to follow techniques superficially, without being able to adapt them for their own particular circumstances. They may take particular examples as orthodoxy, mistaking them for unchangeable prescriptions, and be unable to invent new examples. Finally, of course, an insistence on a practical approach may conceal a basic misunderstanding, if it is taken to imply that teaching can be theory-free. All teaching takes place on the basis of some theory (whether Piagetian, audio-lingual, or whatever, or simply classroom folklore), and this should be made explicit. As I have begun to indicate, discourse analysis can itself begin to analyse the assumptions underlying classroom dialogue and written texts.

There are further problems related to how abstract and analytic teaching about language and linguistics should be. It is plausible that a functional view of language in use will be of more direct relevance to teaching practice than a purely abstract view of language as system and structure. A view of language in use also starts from everyone's everyday experience of language. However, it is difficult to introduce samples of real language in use, without immediately decontextualizing and trivializing them. It has often been pointed out that the search for authenticity in language teaching materials is an illusory one. If an authentic text (that is, a text originally written for some real purpose, without the linguist's intervention and not specially prepared as teaching material) is taken out of its context, and used for something else (teaching), it is thereby made inauthentic. However, this is simply to note that all teaching implies some contrivance, which may be more or less extreme.

A more basic problem may be that, even if it is accepted that a functional orientation is of more interest to teachers, this functional view may appear hopelessly vague if there is no formal analytic model to support it. If one starts with functions, one often never gets (back) to forms. To argue in a Hallidayan fashion, for example, that language is as it is formally, because of the functions it serves, assumes a sophisticated prior understanding of forms: of concepts such as rank-scale, and the mapping of one layer of structure onto another. More generally, one might argue that the valuable thing which is to be gained from a study of linguistics is not the details of particular formal arguments, but the style of argument itself: the nature of the data used, the attention to evidence of different kinds, the concept of a counter-example to a clearly formulated statement, and so on. However, this kind of argumentation can only be properly demonstrated on detailed examples, and has been fully developed only in descriptions of phonological and syntactic forms. Again, at least some analytic work seems necessary.

It is important, in summary, to distinguish between language in education and linguistics in education: they are potentially very different. (Cf. the papers in Carter 1982b, which make this distinction very clearly.)

Although these questions of selection for pedagogic purposes are not often explicitly discussed in print by linguists, they are probably constantly discussed in the course of meetings over syllabuses and examinations, and they have to be faced in one way or another by any linguist who has to select topics in preparing a lecture course or writing a textbook. Probably all teachers have to adopt a policy of diminishing deception: starting with plausible, but strictly speaking unsound and over-simplified arguments, to get students used to the style of argument and the basic subject matter. This starting matter is then gradually refined and replaced by something better. Different teachers will take different decisions on how much initial distortion is defensible. However, some is inevitable, and if anyone feels unhappy with the situation, it can be pointed out that the process of diminishing deception is in any case what happens in anyone's intellectual development, and what happens at a much slower pace in the whole history of intellectual progress. As Feyerabend (1978: 156) has pointed out, an argument does not necessarily reveal the true beliefs of the arguer. One may, for example, adopt and express arguments which one believes to be false, in order to persuade an audience. This is a common pedagogic tactic, since false arguments may have to be followed through to their logical conclusion, before being revealed as false.

Although all teachers are familiar to some extent with such decisions, their interest here is that they constitute a possible definition of applied linguistics: the selection or development of theories for different purposes. However, the view that applied linguists interpret and mediate linguistics for practitioners is only one possibility. There has been considerable debate recently over whether applied linguistics is (1) a body of linguistic knowledge which is applied to practical problems (i.e. linguistics applied), or (2) a quasi-independent body of knowledge and specially developed theories (i.e. applied linguistics). For example, Widdowson (1979c, 1980a, 1980b) provides a series of arguments which represent his own changing views about the degree to which applied linguistics should develop its own theories independent of theoretical linguistics. He argues in later papers (e.g. 1980a) that models developed by theoretical and applied linguists are incompatible, since there is a radical difference between analysts' and users' models of language, and applied linguistics has to take account of the latter. (Cf. chapter 14.)

One also has to be careful about the general rationale which is proposed for linguistics in teacher-training, or indeed more generally. It is often argued that language is peculiarly central in human society, that humans are *homo loquens*, that human society would be impossible without language, that a detailed understanding of language can tell us how the human mind works, and so on. In studying language, therefore, students learn about essential and defining characteristics of their psychological and social environments. These arguments may all be true, and they are convincing rationales for studying linguistics. However, they do not clearly distinguish linguistics from other traditional academic disciplines, including biology, physics, geography, history or mathematics. All these disciplines and others tell us about the relationship between human beings and their environment. They also have much to teach students about valid forms of argument, different ways of evaluating data and evidence, and so on. And, in any case, the relationship between an abstract knowledge of language (or any other subject) and behaviour is indirect.

There are, then, several general problems concerning the presentation of linguistics to educationalists, and by implication to other professionals. These problems are inseparable from the more specific problem of formulating 'a succinct account of the essential nature of language in terms that are truly relevant to the educational process' (Halliday 1978).

Other problems do arise, however, from the admittedly special relationship between speakers and their native language. Everyone has a native language, and this is a great advantage in such teaching, since this implicit linguistic competence provides an enormous resource to draw on in teaching an explicit and conscious knowledge of language. However, it is also a disadvantage, since language is so notoriously open to misunderstanding and myth. Language is so central to everyone's life that it is surrounded with mystique. It is difficult to see any need for explanation at all. Either it all seems natural and is taken for granted without the need for explanation being seen at all. Or speakers assume that just being a native speaker makes them experts, especially if they have been further sensitized by some language study: for example, a training in literary criticism or learning a foreign language. Carter (1981) therefore argues that teacher-training must explicitly tackle misunderstandings about linguistics as the systematic study of language, since the attitude of mind required in linguistics is often believed to be contrary to the sensitivity required in literary study. It is almost certain, for example, that any course will have to tackle the common prejudice against formalism, idealization and explicitness, held by many students with literary training. Linguists are regularly accused of wanting to have things neater than they are, and of idealizing away just what is interesting about instances of language in use. Since linguists themselves differ in their view of how much idealization is permissible or useful, this provides a major source of confusion for students. So any course therefore starts from a certain necessary demystification: some students find it exhilarating to have their assumptions challenged; others find it uncomfortable and destructive.

To discuss here any further the issues involved in the dissemination of information about language and linguistics would take me too far from my main theme, so I will make just a few concluding comments central to any application of sociolinguistics. Information is never neutral: it is always transmitted in the face of prevailing expectations, preconceptions and entrenched professional interests. Any serious discussion of such problems would have to examine the way in which such prevailing views are supported and legitimated by institutions. In Britain, this would involve, for example, a study of the role of NATE (National Association for the Teaching of English) and its journal *English in Education* in forming the ideas of teachers, teacher-advisers and other educationalists. Or see Gordon (1980), Stubbs (1980: ch. 7) or Atkinson (1985) for discussions of the way in which Bernstein's ideas have often been distorted and simplified in their transmission to teachers and their subsequent application. To take a more general example: sociolinguistics is the study of language variation. It argues, contrary to much recent theoretical linguistics, that language is inherently heterogeneous. When they have written on educational issues, sociolinguists have therefore tended to stress the value of diversity, and have seen bidialectalism, bilingualism and biliteracy as positive resources which teachers can use and encourage. By and large, however, the educational system, and government itself, has seen such diversity as a problem. For such reasons and others, applied sociolinguistics cannot avoid consideration of the practical sociology of knowledge.

Discourse analysis and foreign language teaching

It has often been argued by both linguists and teachers that theoretical linguistics has little or nothing to offer the practice of language teaching. For example, one extreme statement is by Sampson (1980: 10): 'I do not believe that linguistics has any contribution to make to the teaching of English or the standard European languages'. Sampson admits that linguistics may contribute to the teaching of exotic languages, but only in so far as it provides descriptions which are not otherwise available of such languages. Sampson's statement clearly recalls, in an even more extreme fashion, a famous quote from Chomsky (in Lester 1970: 52). It may be, however, that such beliefs are due to looking for the contribution of linguistics in the wrong place. Sampson's and Chomsky's view appears to be that theoretical descriptions of syntax have nothing to offer teachers, who have their own more appropriate pedagogic descriptions. However, what I will now argue more directly is that recent work in discourse can be very helpful in constructing an appropriate and coherent pedagogic description of language.

On the face of it, the most obvious application of discourse analysis to foreign language teaching is to help to construct the kind of model dialogue common to so much language teaching material. Role-playing, drama and simulated conversations are one established method in foreign language teaching (e.g. Maley and Duff 1978). It is therefore plausible that a better understanding of real dialogue should lead to better dialogues for teaching purposes. However, it is obvious that a close transcript of a real conversation is very far from what is normally required for teaching. Any conversation will contain many characteristics which are relevant only to its original context of occurrence. The indexicality of everyday conversation has been the particular study of conversational analysis, which derives its theoretical impetus from ethnomethodology. (Cf. Atkinson 1981, for a discussion of ethnomethodology and applied linguistics, and the argument that situational and notional syllabuses are both rather crude attempts to apply sociological ideas.) If real conversations are used as the basis for pedagogic material, they will have to be carefully adapted to be at the right level of generalization. Davies (1978) compares in detail differences between an audio-recording of a real family breakfast and a foreign language textbook representation. He discusses the several different kinds of idealization required, if one is to be turned into the other. (Cf. also Burton 1980, for a detailed comparison of real discourse and simulated dialogue in playscripts.)

Another problem is that both teachers and students are, in general, ignorant of the structure and functions of conversations: discourse has simply not been studied in the educational system in the way that grammar has been for hundreds of years. Roulet (1981) therefore argues that foreign language teaching must be supported by mother tongue teaching, in which conversational analysis based on authentic documents is taught. Such suggestions are made within the more general context of suggested *rapprochements* between foreign language and mother tongue teaching which are currently (in the early 1980s) being debated (cf. chapter 14).

If one is thinking of the direct applications of discourse analysis to language teaching, then this could mean also several other things. In general it suggests teaching language as communication (cf. Widdowson 1978; Brumfit and Johnson 1979), and communicative syllabuses rather than grammatical syllabuses (cf. Munby 1978). Teaching English for science and technology (EST) or for other academic purposes (EAP) or, more generally, teaching English for special purposes (ESP) imply teaching communicative competence, since the aim is generally to teach adults a foreign language for some specific, real, possibly quite restricted purpose, not for the artificial purpose of passing an examination. Applied linguistics has to recognize that language is studied for different reasons. Often the study of language is instrumental:

not an end in itself, but a means to an end. The concept of notional or functional syllabuses is closely related here (Van Ek 1975; Wilkins 1976): that is, the view that the syllabus can be constructed round a list of speech acts, communicative and semantic categories, rather than the traditional grammatical organization of most syllabuses. Although a communicative syllabus would necessarily be partly functional, it has been pointed out, however, that a notional syllabus may be a list of isolated functional categories, and not take fully into account the sequential organization of connected discourse (Widdowson 1979d). In fact this important criticism has been levelled against speech-act theory itself: that it studies isolated acts, although often the illocutionary force of an utterance can only be interpreted from knowledge of its place in a discourse sequence.

More narrowly still, applied discourse analysis might imply teaching something which has been neglected in the past, but about which we now have information due to recent research. For example, Brazil, Coulthard and Johns (1980) propose teaching discourse intonation. Or one can teach directly other interactional skills, such as teaching students to interrupt politely. In general, discourse analysis is beginning to provide information at the level of contrastive pragmatics. Different speech communities differ in their rules for turn-taking, expression of politeness, amounts of talking, use of ritualistic formulae and the like, and such information is of potential use to the language learner. Textual conventions similarly vary in different languages: written Arabic, for example, makes little, if any, distinction between sentences and paragraphs, and punctuation conventions therefore differ considerably between Arabic and English. Detailed contrastive analyses of specific speech events have begun to appear: for example, Godard (1977) compares behaviour on the telephone in France and the USA by analysing sequential rules for openings. On the other hand, such work clearly has a long way to go before comprehensive contrastive descriptions are available. It has frequently been pointed out that much of the work on speech-act theory and conversational maxims is Western European in its assumptions. For example, Ochs Keenan (1976) criticizes Grice (1975) on these grounds, showing that not all of Grice's conversational maxims hold in Malagasy.

The papers in Sinclair (1980) provide other views on applied discourse analysis and foreign language teaching.

There are, however, alternatives to these kinds of direct application. One alternative is to try to convey to teachers a general view of language, which constantly takes into account its use in connected discourse in different social contexts. This is the topic of the next section.

Discourse analysis and training EFL teachers: course description and discussion

The course material described here was part of an intensive eight-week course taught in China in 1980.[1] The course material filled about 90 hours of lectures and seminars: 8 weeks of 6 days each and roughly one lecture and one seminar each day. Another one or two hours each day were generally filled with other related topics in modern English language, language teaching methodology, cultural background, films, and so on.

The students were over fifty Chinese lecturers in English at institutes of higher education, including universities and teacher-training colleges. They came from all over China, some from high-prestige institutes in Beijing (Peking) and Shanghai, others from small institutes a long distance from main centres. Their command of English varied from near-native-speaker competence to some students who had almost no useful comprehension of normal spoken English at all. Many had, of course, no opportunity to hear native speakers: none had ever spent any period of time in an English-speaking country; and some had recently been 'turned around' from teaching Russian. The break in Sino–Soviet relations came in 1960, and from 1966 to 1972 all universities in China were closed during the Cultural Revolution, and the study of foreign languages was stopped. In general, the students' comprehension of written English was much better, and many of them were in fact teaching intensive or extensive reading. Their knowledge of descriptive linguistics was in general restricted to traditional grammar. Quirk et al.'s (1972) grammar was well known, although in many cases students had clearly not understood the linguistic principles on which it is based. The students were also very familiar with the International Phonetic Alphabet and with broad phonemic representations of words, as this is standardly marked in even elementary EFL textbooks in China. The 50 students were divided into three groups on the basis of a cloze passage and a listening comprehension test, plus subsequent minor adjustments to the groups. The course described here was given to the 'top' group of 16 students. On the oral testing procedures used by the Foreign Service Institute (Oller 1979: 320), these students would have been at points 3 or 4 on the 5-point scale:

3 Able to speak the language with sufficient structural accuracy and vocabulary to participate effectively in most formal and informal conversations, on practical, social and professional topics.

4 Able to use the language fluently and accurately on all levels normally pertinent to professional needs.

The aim of the course was to teach neither EFL nor TEFL, but to teach descriptive linguistics with reference to modern English language and to TEFL. It attempted to provide a coherent approach to describing English, which was particularly appropriate to TEFL, with the underlying theoretical coherence coming from work in discourse analysis, text analysis, narrative analysis, cohesion, speech act theory and related areas. In other words, the course was predominantly theoretical, but was theory explicitly geared to teaching practice. This would hopefully: (1) improve the students' own communicative competence in English; and (2) allow them to improve their own teaching and testing techniques, by (3) teaching them about linguistic description. Hopefully, this would be both of practical value and also intellectually interesting. As the course progressed, I realized how important requirement (2) was. Since we knew next to nothing about actual teaching conditions in Chinese higher education, we could not impose actual teaching methods, but only provide the underlying principles in the hope that our students would then be able to adapt our ideas to their own circumstances.

There were several constraints on the course, which may seem extreme, but which doubtless have parallels elsewhere. These must be taken into account, since there is little point in providing students with impractical ideas. First, a communicative approach to foreign language teaching requires, to all intents and purposes, native-speaker competence in the teacher. It is worth remembering that the communicative approach was developed very much through courses in ESP, where native English speakers were developing basically study-skill courses for improving reading ability to handle written academic English (EAP). There are considerable dangers in having non-native speakers produce texts for teaching purposes. For a teacher who has less than native-speaker competence, the safest method may well be to base teaching firmly on given texts. Much teaching in China is very traditional and text-based, for this and other reasons. Many of the ideas in the course therefore aimed to provide students with ways of manipulating naturally occurring texts.

At the outset, I had intended a course fairly evenly balanced between spoken and written discourse. However, these various practical constraints led to a concentration on written texts with some work on listening comprehension: the less than native competence of the students; the need to start from and develop the traditional text-based methods already used by the students; the lack of books and the need to exploit available texts to the maximum effect; the difficulty of using native models of spoken language; and the fact that many of the students were explicitly teaching extensive or intensive reading for EST or EAP. Given the general isolation of the students (and *their* students) from native English speakers, there was in any case no direct motivation for attempting to develop their competence in spoken English. Teaching communicative skills in spoken English was therefore not a direct aim, although during the course they heard a lot of spoken English in lectures, seminars and more informal conversation.

One basic decision was that all materials used should be authentic texts. I have already admitted above that the search for authenticity is illusory, since material is taken out of its original context if it is used for teaching. (Allwright 1979 proposes one way round this problem, albeit in a very special situation.) Given the students' need to exploit texts to the maximum effect in their own teaching, I relaxed the authenticity criterion to allow the manipulation of texts for teaching purposes. (I give examples below.) Nevertheless, here authentic texts means material originally produced for native speakers, and not produced for teaching and designed for learners. There are several very useful collections of such material from a wide variety of written styles (e.g. Levine 1971; Maley and Duff 1976) and collections of short stories (e.g. Cochrane 1969; Dolley 1967). This decision leads inevitably to other consequences. It follows that all work was on analysing and interpreting connected text. It also means that no linguistic feature or content will ever be introduced for its own sake. This point applies both to syntax ('Today we learn the passive') and also to function ('Today we do polite requests'). Texts may be selected because of some central or recurrent feature, but that feature will always be contextualized in other features. The choice of materials also makes it fairly easy to avoid both linguistic correction and linguistic aid (e.g. supplying words), if this is thought desirable. All theory and practice was, therefore, explicitly related to this aim of handling real connected text.

The general model of language underlying the course, and put over more or less explicitly at different stages, was as follows. Learning a language is essentially learning to make correct predictions. As soon as something is said, one can make predictions about what is likely or unlikely to be said next. Expectations may be broken, predictions may be wrong, and people say unexpected things. However, unfulfilled predictions show that there were predictions made, and whatever does occur is interpreted in the light of what was expected. If something is not expected, this surprisal value is part of its meaning. These points can be reformulated in terms of redundancy: if an item is predictable, then this means that it is redundant. Linguists are fully familiar with this information-theory approach to language and meaning. And they are fully familiar with the way in which it is equally applicable to all levels of language: phonology, graphology, lexis (e.g. collocations), syntax, semantics and discourse. It is also evident to linguists how this concept may be reformulated into a concept of structure as constraints on linear sequence. In one way or another, all modern linguistics is based on the concept that language is polysystemic: that is, there are always constraints on linear sequence, and different paradigmatic choices are available at different points in the sequence.

From a theoretical point of view, these ideas are very powerful and general, although of course they run into all kinds of difficulties as a theoretical model, and these are well known. However, what we are concerned with here is their appropriateness as a model for understanding foreign language, and for producing coherent and interesting language teaching materials. They relate well, for example, to the influential view of reading as a psycholinguistic guessing game (Smith 1973), with all its implications for teaching reading. Learning a foreign language is seen, therefore, as acquiring predictive competence. Halliday (1978: 200) points out that there are certain things which are particularly difficult for a speaker of a foreign language. These include: (1) saying the same thing in different ways; (2) hesitating and saying nothing much; and (3) predicting what the other person is going to say. These aspects of linguistic competence are all closely related; they all have to do with understanding and producing language in discourse under the constraints of real time. They all also concern ways of exploiting the redundancy of natural language in use.

The expectancy model is a good one for foreign learners for very practical reasons. First, when they are listening to spoken language, learners are often worried when they do not understand every word. They miss a word, wonder what it was, and miss the next few words. However, native speakers do not listen to every word: they exploit the redundancy of any piece of language, make predictions and then check their predictions by sampling. It can be good for foreign learners' confidence to be made aware of this. And the principle immediately suggests ways of preparing listening comprehension materials (cf. Brown 1978, and below on 'helping the listener'). Learners have to listen like a native, as Brown puts it. A comparable point holds for reading comprehension, where it is sometimes difficult to break learners of the habit of looking up every unfamiliar word in a dictionary. Again, this leads to many obvious reading exercises involving guessing word meanings from context and the like (e.g. see Clarke and Nation 1980, for many suggestions). It is worth also pointing out to students, that in order to find the meaning of a word in a dictionary, this assumes that part of the meaning has already been guessed from context. All words are ambiguous in isolation, and dictionary users have to select the relevant dictionary entry. Students can therefore gain a more sophisticated theoretical understanding of both word meaning and of the organization of dictionaries. The general aim of the model of listening and reading comprehension is to make students independent: of dictionaries, teachers and so on. This might be proposed as the whole aim of education: to make students independent of teachers. This was certainly an important consideration on the present course, where students were used to very formal teacher-centred classes, and lacked any confidence in their own ideas.

Taking now one topic on the course in a little more detail, a major component was classic structural lexical semantics. However, this was taught as a way of analysing texts, and therefore proposed as one kind of discourse analysis. At one level it was presented as a way of teaching directed reading: by forcing students to identify key-words in arguments, and by identifying hyponyms, antonyms and synonyms, to identify the outline of the argument. At a more theoretical level, this led immediately to a discussion of lexical cohesion. This, in turn, was taught both as a technique of linguistic description, and also as a further method of intensive reading, with particular reference to the stylistic analysis of literary texts. This led further to a redefinition of such lexical relations in terms of relations between sentences: entailment, paraphrase, contradiction, presupposition, and so on – and hence to other ways of analysing the organization of texts. (Chapter 7 discusses these concepts in detail.) It is also possible to relate structural semantics directly to language teaching strategies. For example, Blum and Levenston (1978) have proposed that there are universals of lexical simplification which include the use of superordinate terms, synonymy, paraphrase and the like, and therefore principled ways of making do with less words: precisely what a language learner often has to do. Hudson (1980: 93-4) also puts forward the suggestion that in hierarchic lexical taxonomies such as sets of terms for plants or animals, there are maximal information levels. To take a simple example, a term such as *mammal* is less useful than *animal* for most everyday purposes, and *collie* will less often be useful than *dog*. (Chapter 6 discusses this topic in detail.)

This aspect of the course involved practical work on intensive reading, summarizing, note-taking, explaining and reformulating. All such activities involve understanding the semantic structure of texts, both in their local and global organization. As well as these aspects of lexical cohesion and logico-linguistic relations, the theory also covered narrative structure (cf. Labov 1972c) and speech act theory, as well as communicative competence in general. Such practical activities blur the distinction between EFL and study skills. This means that language is not being taught in an intellectual vacuum, but as a tool. It also blurs the distinction between EFL and mother tongue teaching, since many such analytic activities are also useful with native speakers.

I have room here to give only a few practical examples of the kind of classroom activities which were based on such a view of semantic organization and discourse predictions.

1   The technique of cloze passages is well known. Passages are specially prepared by deleting words; students have to make predictions from context and complete the gaps. Such exercises are linguistically principled, but nevertheless involve artificial preparation of texts. A real alternative which I used was to take a newspaper article in East African English which contained a large number of Swahili loan words, incomprehensible out of context to an English speaker. These loan words provided real lexical gaps for students to translate into English.

2   A common situation in which hearers have to predict large parts of a conversation occurs when they hear one end of a telephone call. It is usually possible to predict much of what is said at the other end of the line. It is easy to tape record a telephone call, and to delete one speaker's contributions from the transcript to form a discourse cloze passage.

3   A short story can be divided into sections and fed to students one section at a time. Their task is to predict what will happen next, and to write the continuation of the story. Again, this involves some manipulation of a text, but forces students to make explicit their expectations in a way which is essentially similar to that involved in an intelligent first reading of a literary text. Any such exercises can provide material for subsequent more formal analysis of the students' own predictions. This will inevitably involve comparison between different students' predictions, and between these predictions and the original. This will inevitably lead also to an analysis of the grammatical and lexical cohesion in the passages, of semantic relations such as paraphrase and entailment, as well as of the macrostructure of narratives and other discourse types. (In chapter 7, I discuss in more detail some aspects of the semantic organization of a literary text and give other examples of such classroom activities, suitable for mother tongue teaching in secondary schools.)

It might be argued that the model of language proposed here is not specifically linguistic, and that the concepts of predictability and redundancy are applicable to many aspects of psychological activity (e.g. memory) and social behaviour. Nevertheless they are particularly clear when applied to language, and the theory has been most explicitly developed with reference to linguistic examples. Furthermore, as the concern with autonomous linguistics mellows, it may be useful to start looking for a basis of linguistic organization in wider psychological and social competence. It is not entirely plausible that linguistic competence is as distinct from other cognitive abilities as some linguists have proposed.

Discourse analysis and analysing classroom language

The view of teaching which has been widely held in the West for centuries is a predominantly verbal one. A teacher does things such as lecturing, explaining, asking questions and telling students to do things. Students have a largely complementary role of listening, understanding, answering and basically responding to the initiative of the teacher. Many people also hold some version of the view that people learn things by expressing them in their own words. This is why we distrust students' work if it is copied verbatim from a book. And it appears reasonable that 'talking through' a problem can often clarify it. A widely held and often taken for granted view of classroom behaviour is therefore based on some version of teacher–student verbal dialogue, with a high value placed on the public, explicit, verbal expression of knowledge. This view of education, with its equation of teaching and talking, is, of course, culture-specific. Not all cultures take it for granted that the verbal channel is the primary channel for learning, but believe that learning occurs through silent observation, participation, self-initiated testing, experience, and so on. In addition, the Western model of teaching has often been attacked by educational theorists, but it has proved remarkably resistant to such criticism. In a culture such as ours, which assumes a close relationship between teaching, learning and talking, an obvious application of discourse analysis is to analyse the teacher–student classroom dialogue itself. This *is* the educational process as it is experienced day by day by most students. It is important that teachers have systematic ways of analysing their own daily professional behaviour; and such reflection on the process of classroom interaction itself is becoming a standard component of teacher-training courses. For example, micro-teaching is now a common teacher-training technique. Such training is also becoming increasingly common for doctors, managers and other professionals.

A very substantial body of work on classroom interaction has been published since the late 1960s. There is no room to review this work here, and it is in any case fairly well known. The work varies according to how it draws on linguistic, sociological, anthropological and psychological methods, but broadly speaking there have been three influential kinds of study of classroom language. Type 1 could be called insightful observation. This involves detailed study and commentary on recorded lessons. It is valuable in that it demands close attention to be paid to the details of real language, but is inevitably limited, since it is restricted to impressionistic and selective commentary. The best known British work is probably that of Barnes, Britton and Rosen (1969). There is no doubt that many teachers find Barnes's work very helpful: it has made them aware of all kinds of things they had never noticed before and Barnes is a very sensitive observer. This is precisely one of the problems; there is no method or guiding principle for those of us who are not as sensitive and full of insight as Barnes. Such work can be made more principled and theoretically secure by using field-work methods developed in sociology and anthropology, and by relating the observational data to an explicit theoretical framework such as symbolic inter-actionism. Type 2 involves the use of coding schemes: that is, sets of categories designed to code or classify large amounts of language, usually as it happens in real time. This may be valuable in allowing broad trends to become visible and in making gross comparisons between different teachers, different school sub-jects, even groups of teachers in different countries, and so on. However, it inevitably means that close attention is no longer paid to the actual language used. This approach derives from work done in the 1950s by the American social psychologist Robert Bales. The best known work on classroom language is by Flanders (1970). (Cf. chapter 13.) Such coding schemes are frequent-ly used in micro-teaching, when this is used as a teacher-training technique. Type 3 could simply be called discourse analysis. The aim here is to describe spoken discourse as a linguistic system in its own right: to discover what the units of analysis are, and how these units relate into sequences.

There are various applications of such linguistic analyses of classroom discourse. Several researchers have studied teacher–pupil interaction to investi-gate whether teachers and pupils understand each other. Willes (1978, 1981, 1983) and Holmes (1983) report on miscommunications between teachers and pupils in infant classrooms in Britain and New Zealand respectively. Malcolm (1979) reports on communicative interference between teachers and Aboriginal pupils who speak varieties of Non-standard English in Western Australia. He also goes further to propose how such sociolinguistic study can lead to action research, involving teachers and Aboriginal classroom aides.

I will not be concerned here further with such direct applications of studies of classroom discourse, but will discuss whether it is possible to combine an in-creased understanding of teacher–pupil interaction with an increased under-standing of language in general. Ideally, a linguistic approach to classroom discourse would: sensitize teachers to the complex, but orderly nature of class-room dialogue; improve their teaching via this increased sensitivity; provide them with a firmer theoretical basis for understanding their own professional behaviour in the classroom; and provide them with a theoretically interesting account of an important aspect of language. This is undoubtedly too tall an order to be fulfilled on many teacher-training courses, and in the next section I will discuss what might be possible with reference to part of a second in-service training course which I have prepared.

Discourse analysis and classroom language: course description and discussion

The material which forms the basis of discussion in this section is published as Stubbs and Robinson (1979). This is part of an Open University course on

Language Development. Other material on the course covers phonetics and phonology, lexis, syntax, semantics, communication and context, assessing children's language and the language curriculum in schools. The course is designed as a post-experience course for schoolteachers. The course is reviewed by Carter (1980), which is in turn criticized by Czerniewska (1981).

At the beginning of the material on discourse, we express the objectives as follows (Stubbs and Robinson 1979: 9):

> After studying (this part of the course) students should (a) have a broad view of different approaches to analysing classroom language; (b) have had experience in the problem of transcribing natural spoken language from classrooms; (c) be able to describe classroom lessons using one particular system of analysis; (d) understand some general limitations on all systems for describing language behaviour; (e) have several ideas for ways of exploring the language of their own classrooms; (f) have an increased understanding of the study of discourse as a level of linguistics, as are phonology, syntactic study and semantics; (g) have a set of criteria to think about the work they read on classroom language; (h) have a way of talking precisely about their own classroom language, and of studying aspects of it.

In my discussion here, I will concentrate on the objectives which have to do with an appropriate approach to analytic techniques and theory, and their relation to practice, which I have commented on above. Note that the objectives do not hold out the promise of improved teaching, and we add also the following caveat (Stubbs and Robinson 1979: 13-14):

> We are concerned at every stage with the details of real language in classrooms, and for some readers this may lead to an assumption that such work is directly and obviously relevant to teaching practice. However, while we do see such work as very relevant, such an assumption needs qualification. There is no reason, for example, why increased insight into teacher-pupil discourse should in itself lead to better teaching. It may do or it may not (it depends on the *educational* decisions and action that the teacher takes) . . . Nor is there any special value in the analysis of classroom discourse for its own sake, and it would be wrong of us to promise that there is.

The material summarizes and criticizes different approaches to classroom language: insightful observation and coding schemes (pp. 16-26); defines criteria for linguistic descriptions of discourse: descriptive categories should be finite in number, relatable to data, comprehensive in coverage, and restricted in their possible sequential combinations (pp. 26-31); discusses problems of transcription (pp. 32-3); discusses differences between grammar and discourse (pp. 33-4); discusses the nature of teachers' questions (pp. 34-9); and then presents a summary of Sinclair and Coulthard's (1975) analysis of classroom discourse in enough detail to allow students to analyse their own data (pp. 39–55). This analytic approach is also the subject of an accompanying television programme by Willes.

One major problem concerns the amount of analytic skill which students should have at the end of such a course. As I discussed briefly above, this is a general problem for any course in linguistics. How much should students be expected to be able to apply the description in the narrow sense of applying its categories in a replicable way to data? An emphasis on textual analysis means concentration on one descriptive framework, ignoring or playing down its limitations, and neglecting alternative descriptions, whereas a lack of detailed description may mean vagueness. With reference to the grammatical sections of the course, Czerniewska (1981: 38), one of the Open University staff who prepared the course, says: 'Our decision . . . was merely to provide students with an awareness of a descriptive approach . . .' However, merely to be aware that pupils' language requires to be seen systematically, for example, is surely not adequate for an in-service course for teachers. Mere consciousness-raising can lead to a course which is 'all bricks and no foundations' (Carter 1980: 226).

Another problem is how such a course can be evaluated in general. Czerniewska (1981) accuses Carter (1980) of judging the course by inappropriate criteria, those of academic linguistics, and, in commenting (1981: 39) on the whole course, says that 'the real test is its usefulness to teachers'. In fact, she defines (p. 37) an in-service course in an even narrower fashion as 'one that will lead to improved classroom practice'. The claim that applicability to the classroom teacher in this sense is primary is a common type of argument, which I have already discussed. This is only one test. Others are accuracy, consistency, clarity, interest, academic and intellectual value. Furthermore, the relation between analysis (e.g. of discourse) and behaviour (e.g. in classroom interaction) will rarely be direct.

The main question is one of the practical educational value of analysis. A major part of the material is concerned with analysing characteristic teacher–pupil exchanges, which have a structure initiation–response–feedback (IRF), for example:

Teacher   Now what can you tell me that all reptiles do, all reptiles do it.
Pupil   Lay their eggs on land.
Teacher   Good, lay their eggs on land, lay their eggs on land.

There is a danger that such descriptions may be taken as prescriptions. They might either be taken as a model of good, clear teaching, confusing what is a norm with what ought to be a norm. Or they might be taken as a warning of what should be avoided as restrictive teaching practice. However, the question of whether such exchanges are pedagogically good or bad is a separate question from their analysis. Presumably they are good for some purposes (e.g. checking factual knowledge), but hopelessly restricted for others (e.g. discussing literature). What such analyses can do is to provide a firmer basis for such interpretation and value judgements, by providing a precise way of talking about recurrent patterns in classroom discourse. This is analogous to the role of linguistic description in stylistics. Linguistics can provide more evidence and a firmer basis for a literary interpretation, but the analysis is not an interpretation. (Cf. chapter 7.)

The fact that people make this kind of interpretative leap is itself interesting, however, and suggests another educational use of discourse analysis. It is almost impossible to avoid such value considerations in doing such analyses. Ideological questions are thus opened up by any critical analysis of institutional discourse, whether between teachers and students, magistrates and defendants, doctors and patients, and in general between professionals and their clients. In such areas, discourse analysis can provide ways of studying the language of social power and control, prestige, status and deference, manipulation and misunderstanding, and can provide evidence for discussion of the moral, ethical, social and political questions which arise. This is a modern study of rhetoric.

Related work which manages a skilful integration of descriptive theory, methodology and practical educational concerns is by Willes (1978, 1981, 1983). (Willes 1978 is part of the set reading for the Open University course.) She has studied the teacher-pupil interaction in reception classes in British infant schools. Her descriptions are based on Sinclair and Coulthard (1975), but the descriptive system is not mechanically applied. It is put to practical exploratory use in an innovative and imaginative way. She uses Sinclair and Coulthard's description of classroom discourse as a theoretical statement about communicative competence in classrooms. She argues that not all classroom discourse fits the IRF pattern which they have identified (a descriptive point); and she investigates the different rates at which pupils learn to conform to this pattern (findings based on the description). But she also discusses the social and educational value of the IRF pattern, and argues that teachers should try to depart from it (a pedagogical point). She also uses the descriptive framework to develop other research methods. For example, some children seldom speak in the classroom, and their communicative competence cannot therefore be directly observed. Willes devised a discourse cloze procedure to test their competence: a story about classrooms with blanks in the teacher-pupil dialogue for the children to fill in. Such an integration of theory, methods and practice is rare, but provides a model study in applied discourse analysis.[2]

Discourse analysis in classroom practice

Introductory points

It is traditional to consider language under separate headings of reading, writing, listening and speaking. There is obviously much to recommend these distinctions, although they are often artifical. For example, there are processes of linguistic comprehension common to both reading and listening, despite the often used divisions of reading comprehension and listening comprehension, and foreign language or mother tongue courses designed to teach one or the other. In addition, the division into two productive and two receptive aspects of competence must clearly not be taken to imply that speaking and writing are active, whereas listening and reading are passive. Listening and reading comprehension clearly involve active processes of prediction, for example. Given these caveats, I will use the traditional distinctions to structure the following sections, although the categories will sometimes overlap. So far, I have discussed discourse analysis in teacher-training. The remainder of the chapter discusses the content of syllabuses for students, whose aim is either to develop students' communicative competence or to teach them about language and linguistic theory.

Helping the reader: literacy and stylistics

It is now commonplace to assume that the written language used in basal readers should be adjusted to the spoken language of the learner. Otherwise the beginning reader has to learn a new style or dialect at the same time as learning to read; and it is assumed best to learn one thing at a time. Thus, much scorn has been poured on 'primerese' of the type 'Run, Spot, run. See Spot run, Jane'. Such primerese does of course make a plausible attempt to control the language presented to the beginner, but the basis of the selection may be wrong. Lexical items are chosen for their regular sound–letter correspondences, shortness, and so on, rather than for their contribution to meaningful connected prose. More recently, it has been argued that an approximation of reading primers to the spoken language of beginners should also involve discourse organization. This is important, given the general failure of attempts to break reading down into discrete subskills, such as vocabulary recognition, identifying key ideas, and so on. Both local and global textual organization appear to contribute to reading comprehension, and to be inseparable.

A useful summary statement of discourse factors to consider in preparing literacy materials is by Longacre (1977). He argues that discourse is the primary unit of linguistic structure, in the sense of being the unit which people are aware of. Examples include functional units at the level of speech acts and speech events: story, explanation, request, giving directions, and so on. If literacy materials are to approximate to the actual usage of spoken language, the choice of discourse genre is crucial. The general argument is that materials should be in line with learners' expectations. This general approach fits well with the Goodman (1982) and Smith (1973) model of reading as a psycholinguistic guessing game, although Goodman and Smith have not developed their model at the level of discourse. An active, interpretative search for meaning takes place at all levels of language. (For more general reviews of the contribution of sociolinguistics to literacy teaching, see Gudschinsky 1976; Stubbs 1980.) Much discourse-oriented work on the preparation of literacy materials has been carried out by linguists working with the Summer Institute of Linguistics. As a result, there is much work which is predominantly concerned with Bible translation into exotic languages (e.g. Callow 1974).

A different academic tradition which has contributed a great deal to the structural analysis of prose passages is psychological work on the cognitive processing of discourse. Both the overall macrostructure of narratives, descriptions, explanations and the like, and also the micropropositional development of texts from sentence to sentence, are seen as cognitive schemas which play an important part in the comprehension and production of texts. Mandler and Johnson (1977) and Van Dijk and Kintsch (1978) provide useful reviews of this work. Examples of applied educational studies are provided by Stein and Glenn (1979), who investigate young children's comprehension of stories, and by Waters (1980), who provides a case study of a single child's written production over a year. Much of this work is within the cognitive psychological approach to studying memory, which is defined as the ability to recall the semantic content of texts. This derives from the classic work of Bartlett (1932), who showed that remembering a story is not mere repetition, but an active process of interpretation and reconstruction based on familiar structures and standard story schemas.

Such work turns out to be very compatible with work which sets out to specify the discourse structure of academic textbooks and articles. Such analysis has often studied science texts, both because they are highly structured in some rather obvious ways, and also because of the importance of such texts to foreign learners of English in EST and EAP courses. The aim of such work is to identify discourse plans such as: problem-solution; assertion-justification; exemplification-clarification-conclusion. (See Roe 1977; Hutchins 1977 on science books; and Tadros 1980 for similar work on economics textbooks.) Montgomery's (1977) work on the discourse structure of science lectures also contributes to this approach to EAP. Academic lecturing is characteristically a mixed mode: partly spontaneous spoken language, but based on written notes. Montgomery's work could also be considered under listening comprehension below.

Such work is of theoretical interest to linguists, since it is concerned with the semantic organization of texts. It has obvious applied interests in helping students to understand academic materials. The basic pedagogical rationale is clear enough. We try at least to teach students explicitly about the organization of written language at the level of graphology, although our teaching may often be inadequate. We do less well at the level of syntax, since there is as yet inadequate description of the differences in grammar between spoken and written English. But systematic teaching about semantic organization (including cohesion and paraphrase) and discourse (e.g. narrative structure) is almost non-existent.

Such work is therefore beginning to have an educational impact. Work is beginning to be done on the way in which pupils in British schools actually use textbooks in classrooms, and this involves both observational studies of school classrooms and also analyses of the textual structure of school textbooks (Lunzer and Gardner 1978). In foreign language teaching, it is now common to have courses designed specifically to promote reading ability in relatively well defined academic areas. Typically, for example, students of chemistry or music might require a reading knowledge of German, students of art might require a reading knowledge of Italian, or students of history or law might require French. There are now several ESP textbooks on the market which aim to develop skills of effective reading in the sense of understanding textual organization and finding sense relations in texts. (See Allen and Widdowson 1974 for an example of such material; Widdowson 1975b, 1979a for discussion of the underlying discourse theory; and Von Faber and Heid 1981 for a description and discussion of several specific courses.)

It might be thought that such work on written texts is rather far from the analysis of spoken discourse or conversation, since written texts are not interactive. However, as Sinclair (1981) has pointed out, a written text could in principle consist only of strings of propositions with logical connectors. Anything else is interactive, including: predictive structures, discourse labelling, cross references, and so on. Any such organizational features serve to present the text interactively, by taking account of the readers' likely knowledge and reactions at different points in the text. Thus, to take a rather obvious example, I began this paragraph by writing 'It might be thought that . . .', in order to take into account an objection to my argument which I predicted at this point from some readers.

As far as an educationally relevant model of language is concerned, it is also important that this view of reading, as coping with the textual organization of books and articles in order to read for meaning, is compatible with the increasingly accepted view that we learn to read and write by using language. In real life, discourse always has a reason for being interpreted. With written discourse, these reasons range from passing a pleasant hour with a detective novel to retrieving a specific bit of information in a scientific article or telephone directory. It does not occur to us as fluent adult readers to confuse such different functions of reading. However, there is increasing evidence that many children have problems learning to read because they never understand what reading is for (Stubbs 1980: 98ff.). So, to emphasize the main theme of this article, such a view of reading contributes to a coherent overall view of language. It must be admitted that this view is not yet well defined or very explicit, but it may be explicit and coherent enough for practical educational purposes.

At a more analytically sophisticated level again, from the students' own point of view, stylistics can be regarded as a training in close reading, and work on discourse has also begun to influence analysis here. Stylistics is usually taken to mean the linguistic analysis of literary texts: a study of how literary effects are created and how readers' intuitive reactions to texts can be explicitly accounted for. In so far as stylistics uses descriptive linguistic techniques to explain literary effects, it is already applied linguistics. There are many problems in such a view of stylistics, which attempts to take such a linguistic account of texts as a theoretically adequate account of literary effects. For example, it is arguable that a systematic linguistic analysis will necessarily concentrate on superficial features of linguistic form, that it can only provide comprehensive accounts of short, and possibly minor, texts, and that any analysis only provides the literary critic with more data, but does not in itself lead in any rigorous way to an interpretation. These problems do not directly concern us here. However, as Widdowson (1975a) argues in detail, stylistics can also be a useful teaching strategy. Techniques which force students to pay close attention to linguistic features of texts can provide a way in, which can help students to understand the organization of complex texts and therefore help in the interpretation of literature.

Recently many studies have drawn on work in discourse analysis and speech act theory. Pratt (1977) proposes a speech act theory of literature. Searle (1975) discusses the logical status of fictional discourse and what kinds of speech acts literature is performing. Carter (1979) uses discourse concepts in an analysis of Auden's poetry. And in chapter 7 of this book I use the concepts of conversational implicature, following Grice (1975), in an interpretation of a Hemingway story. Stylistics and literary criticism in general have often been restricted to prose and poetry, and drama has been neglected. It is dramatic dialogue which provides an obvious area of application of discourse analysis. Burton (1980) provides a detailed study of short plays by Ionesco and Pinter, and a general discussion of the relationship between theatrical dialogue and natural conversation, both using discourse analysis to develop literary theory and also using the insights of dramatists as data for the description of natural discourse. (See also Short 1981). A related body of work studies narrative structure: this includes work by scholars such as Propp (1928), Todorov (1969) and Genette (1980). Some of this work is predominantly literary criticism; other work on oral narrative is more obviously sociolinguistic (Labov, 1972c). All of it uses basically linguistic-structural techniques of description to provide a more explicit account of the local and global structure of literary texts. Where literary criticism previously discussed related questions at all, it was often restricted to rather superficial commentary of, for example, differences between spoken and written language (e.g. Page 1973 on the uses of direct speech in novels).

Helping the writer: written composition

Teachers are often understandably at a loss when required to correct students' written compositions. First, there is often no clear dividing line between coherent and incoherent text, as there typically (or at least often) is between grammatical and ungrammatical sentences. A text in which surface lexical or grammatical cohesion is faulty may often seem unclear or in bad style, rather than obviously 'wrong'. Second, our intuitions about grammatical well-formedness have been sharpened by two thousand years of explicit syntactic study. Comparably explicit work on discourse organization is only now start-ing to appear. (For a detailed discussion of how far the concept of well-formedness applies to discourse, see Stubbs 1983b: ch. 5.)

The tradition of teaching written composition is mainly confined to schools in Britain, and almost unknown at university level, although there are occasional courses in report writing for engineers and the like. The American tradition of teaching rhetoric in the form of freshman composition tends to be derided (in Britain) as remedial English, and its often vague aims satirized as 'a course in existential awareness and the accurate use of the comma' (Bradbury 1976: 111). This is precisely the kind of observation which has kept linguists away from discourse analysis in the past: the fear that discourse either involves questions of mere surface style; or that discourse is impossible to delimit, and that there is no way to prevent semantics, pragmatics, culture and the world from flooding in. The plot in several campus novels resolves around the frustrations of teaching freshman composition in American colleges (e.g. Bradbury 1965; Lodge 1975; not to mention Pirsig 1974). However, an excellent recent British book on writing to a directive which could be used on such courses is by Nash (1980). He aims to strengthen students' intuitions about structures in discourse, and discusses varieties of rhetorical design and textual cohesion.

There is no doubt that manuals of style such as the famous American high-school text by Strunk and White (1979) discuss important issues of textual organization. What such manuals often lack is any systematic framework within which to discuss such organization, and often matters of information structure or cohesion are described vaguely as questions of emphasis, balance, rhythm, monotony or variety, or simply as good or bad style. Similarly, work by British educationalists (e.g. Britton et al. 1975) has usefully discussed the different functions of written language, such as poetic, expressive and trans-actional. They have also usefully pointed to the unfair demands often placed on school pupils who are expected to produce final draft writing before producing and revising preliminary drafts, arguing for the value of both exploratory talk and exploratory writing. Again, however, such work is often inexplicit in its discussion of form-function relations.

Enkvist (1981) provides a useful summary of some rhetorical applications of text linguistics, which is very relevant here, and suggests how the teaching of both mother tongue and foreign languages could benefit from a more explicit discussion of text strategies, which is now available. In teaching English as a mother tongue, this could make explicit the ways in which language is adapted to hearers and readers. In EFL, such work could provide an explicit basis for explaining the ways in which information may be concentrated or diluted for different audiences: for example, a discussion of how much redun-dancy foreign learners require in a text. One way to 'dilute' a text is to insert existential structures (Enkvist 1981: 199):

There were three books on the table. All fell down.
The three books on the table all fell down.

Such topics have received much explicit discussion in recent work on natural conversation (e.g. Ochs 1979, on left-dislocation structures in casual conversation versus formal or written language).

At a practical level, Keen (1978) and Gannon and Czerniewska (1980) demonstrate ways in which teachers can analyse the textual cohesion in children's writing, and therefore better assess it and correct it.

Helping the listener: listening comprehension

For obvious reasons, listening comprehension has traditionally been a topic for the foreign language classroom rather than in mother tongue teaching, although it should become clear that some of the points discussed here are relevant to both. It is worth while also bearing in mind that the strict foreign language/mother tongue distinction is frequently much less clear than often appears at first sight, especially in the increasingly multilingual classrooms in Britain and the USA, and with the existence of varieties of language such as creoles, which blur the language/dialect distinction. I have also pointed out above that recent courses on ESP blur the distinction between foreign language learning and study skills.

Brown (1977, 1978) has discussed the inadequacy of many EFL tests of listening comprehension, which make demands on learners that are never made on native speakers. Her main general point is that it is inappropriate to judge spoken language by criteria only applicable to written language. For example, a test which requires hearers to extract discrete details of information from casual conversational language, rather than the overall significance of the utterance, may be confusing the forms and functions of written and spoken language. Spontaneous speech is not usually used for transmitting detailed information. Where it is, it is usually backed up with written or visual aids, as in much teaching. Or the propositional information occurs in short bursts, as in giving directions in the street, or giving orders in a shop. Alternatively, hearers will probably record at least the gist of what is said in writing, as in giving complex orders to workmen. It is therefore inappropriate to ask questions about the detailed cognitive content of casual conversational language. Brown's work is based on an examination of both the phonological obscurity (including elisions and assimilations) which characterizes most spoken English (Brown 1977); and also of the differences in discourse organization between written transactional and spoken interactional language. Adult interactional language is characterized by: slow tempo; division into short chunks with a lot of pauses; one-place predicates in which one thing is said about one referent at a time; topic–comment structures; paratactic structures which rarely make explicit logical relations between clauses (cf. Ochs 1979). In general, these features mean that information is not densely structured. Brown points out that when spoken language is intended to transmit detailed factual information, then special discourse structures have evolved. For example, in radio news broadcast, a typical structure allows information to be repeated three times. Brief headlines are followed by an expansion of the news items, which is followed in turn by a repetition of the main points.

Crystal and Davy (1975) have published transcripts of unedited audio-recorded conversations, representing Standard, educated colloquial English usage. They admit, as might be predicted from the arguments which Brown puts forward, that they are 'unclear as to how data of this kind can best be used in a teaching situation' (p. x). A paradox is whether informal language can be formally taught or tested. Such conversational English is important, as it is different from the language presented to learners in most textbooks. Usually students are exposed to formal varieties, although informal conversation must provide some kind of baseline for a description of English, if only because of its massively common occurrence. Crystal and Davy do not suggest teaching the productive use of such a variety of English; they propose a policy of exposure to increase the receptive skills of discrimination and comprehension. Similarly, Brown (1977: 156) does not approve of teaching foreign learners to produce assimilated and elided phonological forms, but only developing students' listening comprehension of such forms.

One of the main teaching points suggested by such work is that there is much more variety in English than is often realized. This is often not realized since spoken language varies much more than written language, but is more difficult to observe. (Cf. Stubbs 1980: chs 5-6 for a more detailed discussion, and also chapters 5 of this book.) This point is relevant to both foreign language and mother tongue teaching.

Helping the speaker: rhetoric and oracy

Traditionally, rhetoric studies the effect of a text, written or spoken, on its audience. Classical rhetoric starts from a belief that audiences are open to persuasion. It holds also that ways of presenting arguments can be taught, and that the validity of these arguments can be analysed. There is therefore much debate on questions such as whether eloquence or style of presentation of an argument can compensate for its faulty logic. The systematic study of rhetoric and the structure of discourse was founded by scholars such as Aristotle in his work on narrative and tragedy. Scholars such as the first-century Roman orator Quintillian wrote textbooks on the art of speaking, discussing the choice of subject matter and the style of delivery appropriate to different speakers such as politicians, attorneys and preachers. It is perhaps not too much of an exaggeration to say that little progress was made between such work and the twentieth century. Indeed, Corbett (1965) uses the categories of traditional rhetoric to analyse famous public speeches. As well as work on narrative structure already mentioned, however, several scholars have recently pointed out ways of developing the traditional concerns of rhetoric in linguistically interesting ways, which draw on contemporary work in discourse, semantics and pragmatics. For example, different approaches are represented by: Nystrand (1983a), which has particular reference to written discourse; Widdowson (1979a), which has particular reference to EFL and

EST; and papers by Sperber and Wilson (e.g. 1983), which have particular reference to semantic and pragmatic theory.

Rhetoric traditionally has to do also with formal spoken language. Work by Sophists, two thousand years ago, on the successful pleading of legal cases is applied discourse analysis of great social relevance. Teaching of spoken language in the mother tongue often means hints on speech making, or training in interactional skills such as interviewing. However, formal spoken language is influenced by written style: spoken legal language provides an obvious example. Many types are in fact mixed: partly spontaneous spoken language, but supported by written notes, such as much lecturing and public speaking. The general topic of the relationship between spoken and written language is too large to discuss fully here, but the following points are particularly relevant. Both written and spoken language show stylistic variation according to the formality of the context of utterance. However, spoken language varies more in form, between casual and formal, than written language does. Furthermore, the more formal spoken English becomes, the closer it moves towards written lexis and syntax. These generalizations are valid for educated Standard English, although not always for non-standard varieties of spoken English, nor for other languages. (cf. chapter 5.) It follows that extending students' functional command of spoken English, by giving them access to a wider variety of styles, means extending their competence in the direction of the standard written language.

As linguists have often pointed out, there are paradoxes involved in correcting or teaching informal language. They would argue that everyone has competence in the informal conversational varieties of their native language: this is simply what is meant by being a native speaker of a language. I have already mentioned some arguments against teaching foreign learners productive competence in informal spoken varieties of language. Much of this section may therefore seem rather negative or to shade into something else, namely teaching written language. However, some of the confusions involved are rife in much educational research, and current work in the forms and functions of written and spoken discourse can make explicit some of these confusions.

Within the education systems in Britain and the USA, spoken language has in any case been largely undervalued until recently. Education has usually been based predominantly on written language: indeed education has often been equated with literacy. These assertions are inevitably broad and rather crude, but the general point should be clear enough. It is relatively recently that educationalists such as Barnes and Todd (1977) have argued for the value of informal small group talk amongst pupils with no teacher present. Such work usefully draws into question the taken-for-granted equation between education and formal written language. However, it may lack both a systematic formal description of the spontaneous spoken discourse in such teaching situations, and also lack a very convincing educational rationale. It is plausible that small group discussions help children to formulate their ideas, for example, but this is a commonsense observation, rather than a firmly demonstrated point about the relation of language and thought.

The term *oracy* is used to mean the ability in spoken language, either spoken production or listening comprehension. If we are thinking of teaching or assessing oral production, then this could involve, for example, getting pupils to tell stories, give explanations or short lectures to the class, criticize and challenge arguments put forward by other speakers, take part in or chair small group discussions, and so on. Such language would then be judged according to its appropriateness to the situation, whether this involves talking in a group of other pupils, or talking to single adult, teacher or examiner. The term 'oracy' is particularly associated with the work of Wilkinson, which began to appear in 1965, with an influential book (Wilkinson, Davies and Atkinson 1965). (Many other books and articles by Wilkinson and his colleagues have since appeared: see chapter 8 for a more detailed review of part of this work.) The concern with assessing spoken English is, however, wider than this. In Britain, CSE (Certificate of Secondary Education) boards are obliged to set an oral component in their examinations, and such examinations characteristically attempt to assess such abilities as fluency, clarity, audibility, liveliness, intelligibility, developing an argument or sustaining an interesting discussion. Work on oracy is at present influential amongst British teachers, although it is not entirely satisfactory. The implication of the term appears to be that oracy is parallel to literacy, but has been neglected because no term happens to have been available in English. However, this implied parallelism is very dubious for reasons I have already discussed. The most general logical problem is that spontaneous behaviour is not intended to be assessed. In fact, the question arises as to whether such aspects of a pupil's life should be open to assessment at all: it is, in practice, impossible to separate a pupil's personality (e.g. his confidence in the test situation) from such language ability. There is a consequent danger that it is the examiner's competence (to elicit effective language) which is assessed, rather than the pupil's competence (to produce it). There is in any case no consensus about what constitutes effective speech appropriate to different purposes. This is because such speech can create and define social situations, as well as defining an individual's membership of social groups. Further, we know very little about language development after the age of about 5 years, and therefore have very little idea of the conversational competence to expect of 10- and 11-year olds.

At the very least, such attempts to assess children's spoken language would have to draw on what we do know about children's discourse and on work on the semantics and pragmatics of natural language. Recent work on child language has moved away from the 'sentence centrism' which characterized Chomskyan work, and studies the acquisition of communicative competence in social contexts. Bates (1976), Ervin-Tripp and Mitchell-Kernan (1977) and McTear (1985) are representative of what is now a very extensive literature, although it is largely concerned with the language of young children of up to about six or seven years. In turn, such approaches to child discourse have clear implications for educational research into the differences between linguistic interaction in the home and in school (e.g. Tizard and Hughes 1984; Wells 1984). In addition, any proposals to test children's oracy would have to come to terms with problems such as: the distinction between sentences, utterances, propositions and speech acts; overt and covert meanings, including concepts such as presupposition, entailment and implicature (cf. chapters 7 and 8). The ability to make such distinctions is precisely what is being tested in the pupils in tests proposed, for example, by Wilkinson, Stratta and Dudley (1974) and it is only fair that the testers should be able to make explicit just what distinctions the pupils are supposed to be able to make.

In summary, there are both educational research studies and also teaching and assessing techniques which ignore the organization of classroom talk as sequential discourse (see chapters 8 and 13).

Teaching about discourse

As part of the content of a syllabus, it is possible to teach directly about different kinds of discourse, such as casual conversation, formal meetings, diaries, songs, legal contracts, and so on: clearly a very long list of such discourse types is imaginable. The aim here would be to give a systematic understanding of discourse organization and structure, the great variety of discourse types in spoken and written language, and the relation between discourse types and social contexts. Such teaching may have different emphases. It may aim to develop students' own communicative competence by increasing the functional range of their language, productive or receptive. Or it may aim to teach linguistic theory directly. With younger pupils an intuitive approach would be appropriate, moving towards more explicit and theoretical approaches with older students. (Cf. chapter 4, for discussion of how such textual analysis could fit into a more general English language syllabus; and Tinkel 1979 for discussion of teaching linguistics in schools.)

There is one aspect of such teaching that I have so far only briefly mentioned, however. This is the use of such analysis to open up ideological questions. Recent linguistics has largely ignored the rhetorical, social and public uses of language which are of central concern to educators, for example: the language of politics, law and religion; journalism and the media; technical language; translating and interpreting; and in general the kinds of socially weighted language used to establish and maintain control in school classrooms, courtrooms, doctors' surgeries, mental hospitals, or by 'experts' and 'science'. There are, of course, isolated exceptions to this neglect (e.g. Bolinger 1980a, 1980b). However, these areas have largely been the province of sociologists, literary critics and others. This is unfortunate, since linguists could offer a great deal to such topics. As Milroy (1984) argues, if socially responsible linguists do not do such analyses, then they will be done, but less well, by others.

A major principle, well studied by linguists, is that people have a very strong tendency to make sense out of nonsense. This is one way in which hearers or readers exploit the redundancy of discourse: they assume that utterances make sense and make predictions about what they think was meant. This applies at all levels, from typographical errors and slips of the tongue to the interpretation of political rhetoric, advertising or whatever. Linguistics has also developed powerful ways of analysing the syntax and semantics of deceptive language. There are different ways of deceiving through language, by smuggling in propositions without explicitly stating them, and this has been a major topic of the current linguistic interest in semantics, pragmatics and discourse presuppositions. There is very considerable theoretical debate in this area, but significant progress has been made in studying the differences between propositions which are asserted, or presupposed or entailed by other propositions, or implicated, but not stated in so many words. The theoretical debate centres not so much on the surface description of such facts, but on how precisely they should be accounted for within linguistic theory: for example, within semantics or in a pragmatic component. Levinson (1983) provides a clear summary of the basic issues.

Much of this work therefore gives detailed definitions of what speakers are committed to in discourse and what they can deny without logical contradiction. Such analyses are directly applicable to the ways, for example, in which news is presented in the media. To cite one very brief example, a BBC radio news programme announced:

Sir Geoffrey Howe explained that the budget measures were necessary, because . . .

The use of the factive verb *explain* assumes the truth of the following proposition, in a way that a non-factive verb such as *claim* would not. Embedding propositions in this way can make them more difficult to identify, and more difficult to challenge. It would therefore be possible to study discussions between political commentators on radio and politicians or other public figures. One could study the propositions to which one or both speakers are committed at a given point in the discourse, whether such propositions have been asserted or are taken for granted, and which propositions are, conversely, under explicit questioning in some way. A detailed study of the syntax and semantics of factive verbs and related linguistic devices is a necessary prerequisite for such a study.[3] (Cf. Stubbs 1986.)

Semantics has not characteristically been applied to practical issues, although it is clear that there are many problems in, for example, the interpretation of legal documents, which are essentially semantic. Linguistics is, however, beginning to provide the tools which would allow such applications in a principled way, and which would therefore answer this complaint from Enoch Powell (1980): 'To sit down to write about "the English of politics now" is to be appalled by the difficulty of finding any objective instruments which would prevent description from being mere whimsy or subjective guesswork.' See Lerman (1980) for one such extended attempt.

A more adequate account of such features of language in use would demand a detailed discussion of work such as Foucault's (e.g. 1972) attempts to define the discourses which constitute such fields as medicine or economics, and Habermas's (e.g. 1979) work on communicative competence and universal pragmatics. Such a discussion is well beyond the scope of this chapter.

However, it should already be clear that recent work in pragmatics has therefore contributed many concepts which can help to analyse such rhetorical strategies. People have many everyday ways of talking about language, but they do not normally have available ways of talking precisely about such aspects of meaning. Again, I have had room here only for the briefest examples of a type which might be developed by a teacher in the classroom. The basic argument is that language is used for social control, but that the mechanisms of such control are describable and understandable, and that some escape is possible. As Bolinger (1980a: 387) argues: '. . . people . . . are bright enough to learn the language of language – with a bit of help from linguists who have acquired a sense of their social responsibilities'.

Conclusions

There is no well-established body of work that represents the applications of discourse analysis. Since discourse analysis is itself not a well-defined field, this is hardly surprising. What I have tried to illustrate in this chapter is the re-emergent interest amongst both linguists and educators in analysing connected discourse in socially important contexts. I have argued that linguistic approaches to discourse are beginning to provide explicit ways of discussing aspects of language which are very relevant to the educational process. I have no doubt that current work in discourse is a very rich source of ideas for educational theory and practice, if it is well selected and interpreted. Good teachers may justifiably feel that it provides only a different slant on what they already do. A general problem with much applied social research is that it tells practitioners, in different words, what they know already, if only unconsciously. However, making explicit the principles of good teaching practice is precisely one important aim of applied discourse analysis. The systematic study of language in use provides many ideas for teaching, from lesson plans to whole syllabuses. Just as importantly, it provides a principled and explicit basis for work that is done, by relating it to a coherent theory. This is what is meant by applied linguistics: theory which suggests and illuminates good practice.

NOTES

1 This course was taught in summer 1980 at the Peking Language Institute (Beijing Yuyan Xueyuan) under the auspices of the British Council. My colleagues on the course were Alan Cunningsworth and the late Cliff Garwood, and I am grateful to them for many valuable ideas. In summer 1984, at the same institute, I taught a second course on broadly the same lines, but also involving the use and detailed analysis of advanced courses on English for academic purposes, which are based on recent work in discourse analysis. I have also used similar material in a much

reduced version of the course taught at the University of Sana'a, Yemen Arab Republic, at Easter 1981. I am grateful to students on these courses for their ideas and reactions.

2 I should also make explicit what is otherwise not clear from my bibliographical references alone, that many of the studies discussed in this article derive from work originally done at the University of Birmingham, England, or are developments of ideas put forward in Sinclair and Coulthard (1975), although in several cases these studies have moved a long way from their origins. These studies are: Brazil, Coulthard and Johns (1980); Burton (1980); Carter (1979); Harris (1980); Malcolm (1979); McTear (1981); Montgomery (1977); Roe (1977); Stubbs (1983b); Stubbs and Robinson, (1979); Tadros (1980), Willes (1978, 1981, 1983).

3 I am grateful to Andrew Gilling (personal communication) for discussion of such analysis of argumentative discourse. My comments here summarize some aspects of his current work in progress.

ACKNOWLEDGEMENTS

This chapter is a revised version of an article first published in Peter Trudgill (ed.), *Applied Sociolinguistics*, London: Academic Press, 1984, pp. 203–43.

For comments on a previous draft, I am grateful to Margaret Berry, Ron Carter and Mike McTear.

English in the School Curriculum

4
What is English? Modern English language in the curriculum

Introduction

This chapter proposes a syllabus for English teaching which is based on a study of English language in the world. This syllabus develops the proposal made in chapter 1 that language must be studied in a way that combines the analysis of actual spoken and written language with a conceptual understanding of language variation, with an understanding of issues of practical language policy, and also with a social and political understanding of the implications of language diversity. I therefore intend the syllabus to be a contribution to the type of curriculum discussed by Lawton (1983), who proposes that *cultural analysis* should be a basic means of curriculum planning. A school curriculum is a selection from a culture. It should teach pupils to analyse the culture they live in, to criticize it and to understand its patterns of power. An analysis of communication systems is clearly central to such an aim of putting pupils in a position to interpret and possibly change the world.

I think there is still a fairly widespread view within English teaching that it is only or predominantly English literature which can raise with pupils funda-mental ethical, social and political questions, and can contribute to the moral development of pupils; whereas teaching about language is inevitably for-malistic and barren, and raises no questions of substance. This stereotype, assuming it is in fact held in some form, is clearly false. As I show in this chapter, a study of English language in the world raises many questions about society and politics, about why English has spread round the world at the expense of other languages, and about its uses in different countries. I think it would also be widely accepted that English teaching has often lost its sense of direction in recent years. There has been particular confusion over whether English teaching should have specific intellectual content, which can be taught to pupils, or whether it is not essentially concerned with developing pupils' creative and expressive potential. I do not wish to question for a moment that English lessons can help pupils to learn to express their own ideas and feelings, but I try also in this chapter to show that English teaching should be concerned with interesting conceptual content and with developing systematic arguments about language. I also try to show that learning about language can be basically fun!

This chapter was originally prepared as a lecture for an Australian audience, and I have kept some of the references to language and education in Australia, since they illustrate the general theme of English as an international language.

In 1979, I was invited to give the keynote lecture to the conference of the Australian Association for the Teaching of English, in Perth, Western Australia. The theme of the conference was *What is English?* Since I was invited all the way round the world to address the conference, you might reasonably feel that I should have answered the question. I did indeed feel under a considerable obligation at least to try and answer it. To answer the question, I would, of course, have had to understand what it meant, but I have to begin by admitting that it strikes me as a rather peculiar question. It seems a peculiarly fundamental question for an Association of Teachers of English to be posing. I wonder if other teachers' associations pose comparable questions: What *is* chemistry? Does mathematics count? Has history a future? Where is geography going?

Perhaps it is simply that all conferences of educationalists appear to end up by debating: What *is* education anyway? Or is English really so different from other subjects on the curriculum? This has been argued: it has often been said that English is the most fundamental subject on the curriculum, since *all* teachers are English teachers. But then this leads to a situation where the English teacher might teach almost anything.

Topics for an English syllabus

Some of the reasons for the question become clear if we simply list some of the subjects which are taught on English courses: literature, grammar, creative writing, drama, the history of English, essay writing, the mass media, 'communication', and so on. Clearly this is a mixed list, and not a coherent basis for a syllabus. Sometimes the brief is even wider than this. One book on English teaching (Stratta, Dixon and Wilkinson 1973) has the apparently formalistic title *Patterns of Language*. The authors claim (p. xi) that 'a growing mastery of language relates to a deepening awareness of self, of others and of the human condition'. This appears to make English teachers responsible not only for the linguistic development of their pupils, but also for their psychological, moral and interpersonal development - and to expect them also to provide a world view and philosophy of life.

The English teacher, it would seem, is expected to raise questions of value and civilization, freedom and responsibility, growth and maturity, sense and sensibility; guiding pupils towards a 'deeper intuitive sense of individual humanness', going beyond 'nihilistic postures' which diminish and deaden, bringing elements from individual experience into a structure that represents life, in 'dimensions of love and trust' - poignant and profound, beyond conventional modes and forms, and as complex as life itself. (The phrases in quotes are from a book which came to my attention because of its title, *English in Australia Now*, by David Holbrook 1973: 125, 120, 199.)

This all seems to me to be most confused. English teaching is not the study of the human condition. It is not even to be identified with The Humanities. English *is* very complex, but not as complex as life itself.

In this chapter I will propose a type of English syllabus which has clear intellectual content, a substantial body of factual knowledge; which involves training in critical thinking and analytic skills; and which involves discussion of problems which are socially and morally important. The syllabus will be based on a study of the contemporary English language.

Definitions

Let me start with a few comments about what can and cannot be achieved by definitions. Then I will discuss the type of knowledge on which such a syllabus could be based.

Definitions only matter when there is some confusion. And confusion only matters when the subject is an important one.

English language is clearly an important topic. First, English is an international language. It is important as an auxiliary language in many parts of the world, and millions of pounds are involved in teaching English as a foreign language. There was an article in the *Times Higher Educational Supplement* (26 May 1972) about private enterprise in Poland, with the headline: 'English teaching the most lucrative enterprise after growing tomatoes'. We are dealing therefore with a practical, economic and political issue. Second, English is important to speakers: witness the current debate over Black English in the USA, British West Indians' identification with varieties of Caribbean creoles, or the violence in Wales over the relation of English and Welsh. People's attitudes are the most important factor in the end, and a major aim of language teachers must be to change people's attitudes, to increase their understanding and tolerance of linguistic diversity. George Bernard Shaw's comment is still true: 'It is impossible for an Englishman to open his mouth, without making some other Englishman despise him.' We are dealing therefore with important social issues.

People have always and everywhere been very sensitive to linguistic differences and have used them as markers of social-group membership. One of the earliest cases on record is reported in the book of Judges (12 : 5-6) in the Old Testament. The Ephraimites are fleeing from the Gileadites, and trying to get away across the River Jordan:

When any Ephraimite who had escaped begged leave to cross, the men of Gilead asked him, 'Are you an Ephraimite?', and if he said, 'No', they would retort, 'Say Shibboleth.' He would say 'Sibboleth', and because he could not pronounce the word properly, they seized him and killed him . . .

Third, English -provides interesting problems for linguists. With the increasing complexity of English, various questions arise. What do we mean by *the English language*? Or by dialects of English? Or by English-based pidgins and creoles? How do languages diversify and change? How much diversification can there be before we can no longer talk of the same language?

So, I see no point in definition for its own sake. Dr Johnson once said: 'Sometimes things may be made darker by definition. I see a cow . . . I define . . . Animal quadrupes ruminans cornutum. But a goat ruminates, and a cow may have no horns. "Cow" is plainer.' But the attempt at definition would be valuable if we discover interesting things along the way, and increase our understanding of the linguistic diversity which a label like *English* represents. I am going to suggest that if we do this, we can in fact provide the basis for a syllabus for teaching English in schools and universities: that contemporary English language is a varied and interesting topic for school children, university students, educationalists and linguists.

English in the modern world

Let me now start to discuss the position of English in the modern world, some of the things that have to be taken into account in studying it, the functions it serves in different countries, and its relation to other languages.

In studying contemporary English language, we have to consider a large number of factors which were simply not considered by traditional language historians, because many of the pressures on English have grown up largely in the last hundred years. These pressures include: an unprecedented number of speakers; its use as an international language with a very large number of speakers of English as a foreign language; mass literacy and the associated massive printing and publishing technology; the mass media; the proliferation of institutionalized varieties of English; the use of English against a background of enormous linguistic diversity; and social developments, including urbanization, social-class stratification, and geographical and social mobility. Let me take these in more detail.

It is usual to distinguish three categories of English in use. First, English as a *native language*. Up to 400 million speakers have English as their native language in Britain, the USA, Australia and elsewhere. Second, there are millions more who use English for everyday purposes as a *second language* in areas such as India and West Africa. Third, there are still more millions who have learnt English as a *foreign language* for some purpose.

One estimate (Potter 1974) is that one person in seven in the world uses English for one of these purposes. No other language has both so many speakers *and* such a wide geographical spread. (Chinese has many more speakers, although the situation is complicated by the number of mutually incomprehensible dialects.) English has twenty times more native speakers than it had two hundred years ago (Strang 1970: 17, 177), with principal communities in the USA (c. 211 million), Britain (56m), Canada (22m), Australia (14m), New Zealand (3m), Caribbean (3m) and South Africa (1.3m). (South Africa has in addition 1.8m Afrikaans speakers, out of a total population of 24m (Valkhoff 1971).) South America is the only continent without a large English-speaking community.

One surprising fact about English is that the national standard languages are very uniform. There are noticeable differences between various national standards: English, Scottish, Irish, American, Canadian, Australian, New Zealand, South African and Jamaican. But despite these differences and considering the geographical spread, the diversity of international written English is very small indeed. A major reason for regarding all the many varieties of English as *English* is that they share this single superposed variety, the international written standard, which has been codified by centuries of dictionary makers, grammar-book writers, printers and publishers, and education systems. The result of this codification is what we mean by a standard language. (Cf. chapter 5).

When we consider English as a second language, there is a danger of prematurely christening new Englishes, but there are developing standards in areas where English is used as an auxiliary language or link language of wider communication. It is now meaningful to talk of South Asian (or Indian), West African, Malaysian and Filipino English. These varieties have developed primarily since the Second World War, due to governments retaining English after independence as a language of world communication. (See Kachru 1969; Platt 1975; Spencer 1971.) The functions of international English add more startling statistics: it has been estimated that 75 per cent of the world's mail, 60 per cent of the world's radio broadcasts and 50 per cent of the world's scientific literature are in English (Strang 1970: 73; Quirk et al. 1972: 4). Varieties such as West African or Indian English may be fairly well standardized, but the competence of individual speakers clearly differs greatly. We have to distinguish between the variety and individuals' knowledge of it. Also, English may be used by a very small percentage of the population. In India, for example, English has important functions in education and publishing, but is used mainly by educationalists and civil servants, and spoken by less than 2 per cent of the population (Das Gupta 1969: 583).

Crystal (1985) argues that estimates of the kind quoted above for numbers of speakers may be far too low (i.e. upwards of 300 million for native speakers, plus 300 million second-language users, plus 100 million foreign-language users, giving around 700 million). He argues that hundreds of millions more people have a systematic awareness of English and some communicative competence in it. This may be due to following lessons: for example, 100 million Chinese watched the BBC television programme *Follow Me*. But also, in the Indian subcontinent, there are very many people of limited educational background, who can use a limited semi-fluent English. There might be a tendency to ignore this, on the grounds that such speakers have only a smattering of English: but Crystal's point is that they have some knowledge of English and not some other language, which demonstrates again the place of English in the world. Depending on how conscious one is of international standards, the total number of users of English in the world would have to be revised upwards to anything between one and two billion.

Another set of factors, which are beyond the scope of traditional methods of language study, is the massive urbanization and associated complex social-class stratification of modern technological societies. Big cities are simply not speech communities in the classic sense, and the resulting urban dialects and social-class dialects cannot be captured by the methods of the traditional dialectologists, such as Harold Orton. The traditional types of dialect atlas, for all their pioneering value, cannot record the linguistic diversity of big conurbations. Inevitably they are primarily records of the dialect of elderly rural men who have not travelled widely: agricultural workers 'with good mouths, teeth and hearing', as the *Linguistic Atlas of England* puts it (Orton, Sanderson and Widdowson 1977).

Another relatively recent pressure on English is mass literacy. In Britain, it was the Education Acts of 1870 and 1872 which made it a requirement for the first time that all children should learn to read and write. A stable tradition of standardized literary language goes back much further than this, of course. In the eighteenth century, the big dictionaries such as Samuel Johnson's were published, and they were recording what was already established practice amongst printers. The long tradition of literacy means, amongst other things, that English has a very large vocabulary. Unabbreviated general dictionaries contain 500,000 entries, although no individual speaker knows anything like that number of words. (See chapter 6.) However, with massive printing technology, and associated systems of libraries, education and mass literacy, the relationship between spoken and written English has changed. There is now, for example, an enormous inertia against any kind of major spelling reform in English, and any reform is impossible for practical reasons for the foreseeable future.

Or consider a very recent pressure on English which has had a small, but significant effect since around 1970: the feminist movement. Certainly this has had an effect on address terms on letters, such that *Ms* is now as common as any alternative, at least in the academic community in Britain and the USA. But the real effect will come via the publishers, and several non-sexist codes of practice for book publishing are now in use. The best known code of practice is probably the *Guidelines for the Equal Treatment of the Sexes in McGraw-Hill Book Company Publications*. Other sets of guidelines are in use by publishers such as Ginn & Co.; Holt, Rinehart and Winston; Macmillan; Random House; Scott, Foresman & Co.; and others (Miller and Swift 1976).

The important point here is that it is the big publishing houses who standardize and codify our language. The first big dictionaries of English, produced in the eighteenth century, took as their model what was accepted publishing practice of the time. Authors and editors now consult dictionaries, and continue the circle. Once this circle is set up, and is further supported by the education system, it is very powerful. (Cf. chapter 5.)

Problems with a historical view of English

A traditional way of regarding English has always been to regard it historically, to see modern English as derived from Old English, which in turn split off from other Germanic languages and so on. Part of this approach involves looking at the origins of words: etymologies.

There are various difficulties in the concept of etymology, however. In the first place, speakers do not, by and large, know the etymologies of words. Etymologies belong to the history of a language, and people do not know the history of their language; therefore etymologies have no direct effect on speakers. Take the stereotypical word in Australian English, *dinkum* in the sense of "true" or "authentic". It seems that the word is traceable to an English dialect phrase from Lincolnshire (where *fair dinkum* means "fair deal"). Or take the ultimate etymological confusion in the word *kangaroo*. Its etymology is uncertain, but it probably passed from an Aboriginal language (where it did not mean "kangaroo" anyway) into English, and then spread from English into other Aboriginal languages. Aborigines thought they were using a European word, and vice versa (Turner 1966: 27, 199).

Or take the example of a suffix which is now fairly productive in English: *-nik* as in *beatnik*. The origin of the suffix is the Slav languages, as in Russian *sputnik*. But as a productive suffix the source is mainly Yiddish-influenced American English, from where we have forms such as *Kibbutznik, no-goodnik* and *alrightnik* (in the sense of *nouveau riche*, if I may offer a French translation). We now have a term used by homosexuals for heterosexuals: *straightnik* (Rosten 1968).

I am also keeping my eye on words ending in *-gate*, as this suffix travels around the world. On an analogy with *Watergate*, the term *Muldergate* caught on very fast. There is now a book entitled *Oilgate*, about the breaking of oil sanctions on Rhodesia (Bailey 1979). And on the day of the AATE conference, someone brought to my attention a headline in *The Weekend Australian* (1-2 September 1979, p. 8): 'The Prawngate scandal down on the farms'. The word *Watergate* was originally unanalysable, but *-gate* now seems to have been detached and turned into a suffix meaning "scandal" or "political scandal".

So the concept of etymology is becoming increasingly complex and sometimes meaningless, due to the increasing variety of English and the increasing contact with other languages. There is internal borrowing, from American to British English, although many Americanisms are not recognized as such in Britain. In addition, an international vocabulary is developing, such that words do not really belong to any single language, and it is rather meaningless to say what their source is. Many words in areas such as science and technology, politics and sport are recognizable in a large number of languages, including English. In other words, the increasing complexity of sociolinguistic relations between languages has changed the concept of etymology. Languages have always used each other as reservoirs of vocabulary, but this common reservoir is growing. The distinction between English and non-English is not as clear-cut as people might think.

The boundaries of English

Now, I am arguing that the distinction between English and other languages is more fuzzy than some people think. But I do not wish to argue that logically black-is-white (Flew 1975: 104). There may be complex differences of degree, with no clear boundaries, but that does not mean that there is no difference at all. Many a mickle may mak' a muckle. As Edmund Burke observed: 'Though no man can draw a stroke between the confines of day and night, still light and darkness are on the whole tolerably distinct.' In other words, don't get carried away by talk of fuzzy boundaries, gradient phenomena, continua, clines, inherent variability. In describing English, we require both the concept of clear-cut categories and also the concept of gradience.

Neither do I wish to argue, however, that the truth is always in the middle. I do not think that moderation should be carried to extremes. Some phenomena in English are truly gradient, but others are categorial. For example, it is an interesting sociolinguistic fact that some varieties of English are very uniform, whereas others are not. International written English is remarkably uniform; and so is Australian English (compared to British English), although it is spoken throughout three million square miles.

Consider another aspect of the boundaries of English: the question of which words are 'in' English, from the everyday point of view of which words get recorded in dictionaries. First, there is the problem of obscene words: should they be included or not? When new dictionaries are published, reviewers always seem to start by looking to see which obscene words are included (Leach 1972). The problem involved is not just one of propriety - but a full-blown logical paradox. Dictionaries are regarded as one of our most respectable institutions. Obscene words are not respectable: that is part of their meaning. But if they are in the dictionary, they must be respectable. In other words, if taboo words are recorded in dictionaries, the very act of recording them will change their meaning. We are dealing with a version of the observer's paradox (Labov 1972d) which affects many aspects of language study. We would like ideally to observe how language is used, when no one is observing it.

Many Australian Aboriginal languages have very complex systems of linguistic taboos, observed in talking in the presence of taboo relatives: so-called 'mother-in-law' language; or used for ritual purposes, at initiation ceremonies and so on (Dixon 1971; Hale 1971); and which provide very valuable semantic data for linguists.

Or there is the problem of obsolescent words. For example, English has a large number of collective nouns. Some of these are still quite current: a *school* of fish, a *pride* of lions, a *swarm* of bees, a *flock* of sheep, a *litter* of puppies. But others have little existence nowadays outside school textbooks in English: a *gang* of elks, a *wedge* of swans, a *drift* of hogs, a *knot* of toads. These are all genuine examples (recorded by Lipton 1977), but known only to a very small number of speakers. Should dictionaries be storehouses of old words? How long should words be recorded? It is difficult to say, since no one has ever seen a word die. Such examples open the way to a nice game, incidentally. I propose as new collective terms: an *anthology* of English teachers, a *conjugation* of Latin teachers, a *nucleus* of chemistry teachers, a *proper subset* of logicians, a *systems network* of Hallidayan linguists, a *drone* of lecturers.

English and linguistic diversity

Contemporary English is therefore subject to many sources of diversity: not only traditionally recognized regional and social variation, but relatively new kinds of variation due to its increasing contact with other languages.

It is a basic principle that the amount of linguistic diversity in a community will regularly be underestimated. The reasons are very simple. Everyone's speech varies according to the formality or casualness of the social situation. But we see only our own close family and friends in a wide range of social settings. We tend to see people from other social groups in relatively formal settings. For example, teachers often only see pupils in the classroom, and it is difficult or impossible to observe them outside school: the observer's paradox again. Teachers may therefore get only a restricted view of the range of language which pupils use. Another reason why language variation gets systematically underestimated is that there is more variation in the spoken than in the written language. And it is, simply, easier to observe written language. It follows that dictionaries will under-record the extent to which English is changing, since they will record only well-established trends and are based predominantly on written language.

Since diversity is regularly underestimated, one thing we have to be careful about is that politically and socially dominant cultures in some countries attempt to project the view that these countries are monolingual and monocultural, where this is a grossly oversimplified view or just out of date. Britain, for example, does superficially appear to be a monolingual country. Almost everybody speaks English, and there is no need to speak any other language in order to live there. But this view ignores both the indigenous Celtic languages (Welsh, Irish and Scottish Gaelic) and also the enormous linguistic diversity due to recent immigration, especially since the 1950s.

Scottish Gaelic, for example, has always been ignored, to all intents and purposes, by politicians. It has around 80,000 speakers, all bilingual with English, with main concentrations in north-west Scotland, but it has no official status in Scotland. Even the Scottish Nationalist Party only formulated a policy on Gaelic in 1974. And given the failure in 1979 to bring about Scottish devolution, and the reduction of SNP numbers in parliament at Westminster in the 1979 election, there is little hope of future official support for Gaelic. (See chapter 11.)

However, the main source of linguistic diversity in Britain is the immigration into London and the big conurbations in the Midlands, such as Birmingham, Nottingham and Leicester. It is not very surprising that the politicians have not yet caught up with this diversity, since the whole linguistic configuration of many areas of Britain has changed drastically in just twenty years. We do not even have statistics on the languages spoken by immigrants, since census figures refer only to country of origin: and this can give only a very rough indication of language for someone coming from multilingual countries such as India or in West Africa. The first major report on the teaching of English in England was the Newbolt Report, published in 1921 (HMSO 1921): it just makes no reference to any language other than English. The most recent is the Bullock Report (DES 1975): it does discuss the problem, although it refers rather coyly to 'children of families of overseas origin' and is very sparse on statistics.

An estimate (Campbell-Platt 1976) of the most widely spoken immigrant languages in Britain, in descending order is: Punjabi, Bengali, Gujerati (northern Indian languages), German, Polish, Italian, Greek, Spanish, Cantonese, Hakka. Many other languages could be added. It is common now for teachers in some English cities to have classes where native English-speaking children are in the minority.

A large number of children in Britain's ethnic minorities in fact attend evening or weekend classes in their mother tongue outside the normal school system, although little is known about the extent of such provision (Saifullah Khan 1976). There are many motivations for such classes: parents who are not fluent in English, although their children are; parental pride in the mother tongue; a hope that the children will return home to marry; a fear of compulsory repatriation at some time; or religious reasons. One estimate for Australia (Grassby 1977) is that 100,000 children attend such ethnic schools in twenty-five languages.

The mixture of languages in British cities is leading to the creation of new varieties. For example, recognizably London varieties of English creoles from the Caribbean have developed. London Black English might be learnt by Black teenagers who were born in Britain, and who choose to learn the variety in their teens as an act of ethnic identity, or by Black Africans. We now even have the phenomenon of white youths learning to 'talk Black'.

In Australia, the dominant cultural view is again of a monolingual country. This view crops up in unexpected places. For example, the *Encyclopaedia Britannica* article (Potter 1974) on English language claims that 'Australia has no European language other than English within its borders'. This is quite simply false. Admittedly Australia has a very homogenous population, due to immigration controls. But altogether migrants have come from about sixty countries: 45 per cent from Britain, 40 per cent from Europe, and 15 per cent from other countries (Jones 1974: 31). Figures on school children whose native language is not English appear to differ. The Australian Department of

Education (1977: 18) figures based on the 1971 Census is 300,000 children (11 per cent) in Australian schools 'with at least one parent whose native language is not English'. But Grassby (1977: 4) cites a figure well over twice as high.

Summary and some implications

Let me now try to sum up some of the things that I have been saying, before I go on to make some proposals for a syllabus which studies contemporary English language. I have suggested that English has to be defined according to its use in the world. In international terms, English is extremely important. This is a truism: but even a truism may be true. English now has an unprecedented number of speakers, and is in contact with an unprecedented number of other languages. There are new pressures on English, which mean changes in the relation between English and other languages, changes in what we mean by literacy in English, and changes in the methods that have to be used to study English. A traditional historical view is inadequate on its own; so also is an approach which sees English primarily as a vehicle for imaginative literature; and so also is a narrowly linguistic view. All such views, on their own, will simply miss major facts about the uses of contemporary English.

The importance of English is due, of course, to social and historical accidents. It is not due to any linguistic superiority: that concept makes no sense. But in discussing the place of English in the world we are dealing with powerful political, social, attitudinal and technological pressures. The study of contemporary English therefore rests on a substantial body of knowledge, is socially important, relates to the everyday experience of pupils, and involves interesting intellectual and conceptual problems.

The teaching of language is a social and political act. This can and should be explicit, and such discussion can form part of the content of a syllabus. We are talking, for example, about the historical and social forces on world languages and minority languages, the relationship between languages and cultural groups, the dissipation of migrant and Aboriginal languages, and the tolerance of linguistic diversity. Given the decline of foreign language teaching in Australia, English teachers have all the more responsibility to promote understanding of such issues. We are not just talking of yet another content area which English teachers might cover, but of changing students' attitudes. If we *understand* the extraordinary complexity of anyone's use of language, it becomes impossible to be intolerant of language diversity.

The teaching of contemporary English language

Finally, then, I want to propose one type of syllabus for the study of modern English language, which can be based on the view of English I have discussed. The whole chapter so far has, of course, been concerned with the kinds of things teachers ought to know about English, and which are often rather different from the traditional, historical, literary or narrowly linguistic approach to English. In the next section, I will put forward a few suggestions at the level of lesson plans, and in the appendix I will set out an outline syllabus more systematically.

One comment first about the academic level for which such a syllabus might be appropriate. I have in mind mainly secondary-school pupils. A discussion of contemporary English requires an understanding, for example, of the enormous geographical and social spread of English, and young children just do not have this grasp of geographical and social space. There is no problem in extending the syllabus upwards into college and university education to make a conceptually exciting course for students. It may therefore be felt, however, that the syllabus is too abstract and academic for all but the most academic and highly motivated school pupils.

I would answer this objection as follows. First, many of the things I have discussed have had to do with the real everyday experience of language diversity and language contact in contemporary societies: this is not abstract, but real and socially important. Second, I think children are often more sophisticated about such language diversity than their teachers give them credit for: teachers regularly underestimate the range of pupils' language abilities. Third, I am not proposing that all I have said should be taught to pupils in the form I have presented it here. In this chapter, I am discussing primarily the powerful ideas about English which should inform the teacher's approach: things teachers ought to know. Sometimes, it may be appropriate to teach such ideas abstractly and explicitly. Sometimes they may provide a framework for practical activities: a principled base for the teacher to refer to. A real objection to such a syllabus is that it requires a great deal of time and commitment from teachers to learn about new ways of analysing variation in English.

Some practical suggestions

The syllabus could cover content areas such as the following: written versus spoken language; literary versus non-literary language; standard versus non-standard language; child versus adult language (i.e. native language acquisition); English as a native versus a foreign language; regional accents and dialects; pidgins and creoles; dictionary making; attitudes to language; ways in which English is currently changing. Each topic could then be treated in three ways: through the study and comparison of real texts, and the development of analytic skills for describing language in use; through factual work on types of variation which languages display, and the concepts necessary to describe this; through studies of policy-making and the kinds of practical social decisions that such linguistic diversity requires. (Cf. chapter 1.)

Consider as one example the topic of the differences between spoken and written language (cf. Stubbs 1980, and chapters 5 and 11, for much more detailed discussion of this topic). The textual study could involve the comparison of samples of language: formally printed, literary, non-literary, informally written, audio-recorded and transcribed. It could involve also samples of pupils' own creative writing, discussed and analysed. The study of language variation could involve a study of different kinds of writing system, and what it means to be able to read and write. The study of policy-making could look at the problems of the acquisition of literacy in particular countries or world-wide. All I can now do in the space available is mention a few topics which might figure on such a syllabus: just a list of practical suggestions, at the level of lesson plans, within the topic of the relation of spoken to written language.

One interesting way of investigating what English *is* is to study marginal varieties or limiting cases of English. Some restricted varieties of English are only possible in written form: the language of technical manuals (e.g. car repair); computer languages; crossword clues; newspaper headlines; telegrams; recipes; knitting patterns; forms and questionnaires; legal language (e.g. guarantees). Others are essentially spoken: baby talk; the language of air traffic controllers; shipping forecasts on radio; glossolalia - pseudo-language used by Pentecostalists; and some varieties of English mixed almost inextricably with other languages, such as Yinglish, Yiddish-influenced English. There are many sources of such limiting cases of English in literature of all kinds from Lewis Carroll to Goon Show scripts to Tom Stoppard's plays.

Such samples raise very difficult problems, such as: how far can English be distorted and still remain intelligible? Very important work on this topic has been done by Professor Stanley Unwin (Unwin and Dewar 1961). He has studied Angloid in detail right down to the smallest, however transmitted: written down by the scribbly scribe, and, of course, viva voce, when air is expelled from the mouse. The most importaload and fundermold principle to come out of Professor Unwin's work, is that all languishing have a very high redundaload faction, so that even though the world of mouth is twisty and false, with many a slip twixt club and limp, neverthelesson is that this does not needly preventilate us from grasping at a crow and following hard on the wheels of what someone is trying to . . . Rightly is Professor Unwin's work fully fame the worm over, and read with leisure by people in their manifolds, from Great Brixton to the antipoles.

Another possibility is to use literary sources to study representations of dialects, or accounts of language teaching or language snobbery. Famous examples include Mrs Malaprop, Dickens's character Sam Weller, or *Pygmalion*. (Quirk 1974 gives a large number of observations of Dickens along these lines.) More recent examples include humorous books by Leo Rosten about the character Hyman Kaplan, or by George Mikes, or serious literature by authors such as Richard Wright. All such writing can lead into a discussion of people's attitudes to language variation.

Another example: it might be thought that spoken language is relatively simple compared with written language. One way to question this is to point out the complexity of the grammatical competence often involved in understanding jokes, spoken or written. Consider a superficially simple example. A lodger is complaining to his landlord:

Lodger   And another thing – I don't like all these mice in my room.
Landlord Well, pick out the ones you like and throw the rest out.

Now this joke can be understood instantly by any native speaker of English. But it hinges on the ambiguity of the scope of the quantifier *all*, which can only be fully explained with recourse to predicate logic. We might propose as paraphrases, that the lodger intended to say: 'For all x, if x is a mouse in my room, then I don't like it'. Whereas the landlord interpreted his utterance as: 'There is an x, such that x is a mouse in your room, and you don't like it'. Jokes can provide a neat way of demonstrating the impressive complexity of grammatical knowledge.

One could go on listing such ideas ad infinitum. Students could: make language maps, showing the distribution of different writing systems in the world; collect samples of spoken and written English from all over the world; find new words, used in print or speech, but not yet recorded in dictionaries; study types of concrete poetry which exploit characteristics of written language; make translations between varieties of English which are conventionally only written or spoken.

It is important, however, that such activities are related, in ways appropriate to the age of the pupil, to general principles, and not left as isolated facts: just something else to be learned. Taking just the first example in the last paragraph, note that the geographical spread of the major writing systems in the world corresponds very closely to major political, economic and religious power blocs: Roman, Cyrillic, Arabic, Chinese. (Cf. Stubbs 1980: 82-95, for a more detailed discussion of the relation between writing systems and political and religious movements.)

Many of these ideas doubtless correspond to activities which readers are already using in classrooms. And many other ideas have doubtless also occurred to readers. As often happens, the careful study of language in use provides a large number of ideas for use in the classroom. And, just as important, it provides a principled basis for such work, by providing a way of relating such activities to a coherent overall framework for describing language. This is what should be meant by 'applied linguistics': theory which suggests and illuminates interesting practice.

I think the kind of English syllabus I have proposed has considerable attractions. First, it can be based on samples of real language in use in the world. Second, it is therefore 'relevant': English language in the world is important. Third, it emphasizes throughout the diversity of English in use. This should not only extend students' own stylistic competence, but should also increase their understanding of diversity, and therefore their tolerance of diversity. Fourth, since it is based throughout on comparing and contrasting varieties of English, it provides a meaningful way of teaching grammar: analytic methods are introduced because they are needed to solve problems, not for their own sake. Fifth, all the things I have suggested can be taught at widely different degrees of sophistication. Sixth, a lot of the work can be fun: serious but not solemn. Seventh, the syllabus has a coherent theoretical basis in current linguistic work in language variation.

Types of English curriculum

Lawton (1983: 5-13), following Skilbeck, distinguishes clearly between three types of curriculum, contrasting ideologies which may rarely exist in pure forms, but which can be identified for the sake of analysis, and which can be seen in essence in recent versions of English teaching: classical humanist, progressivist and reconstructionist.

A classical humanist curriculum is based on the idea of a cultural heritage, a body of productions and knowledge about them, which are the intellectual and cultural property of an elite group and which are passed on to selected students. Some forms of teaching English literature would take this form: passing on what is considered to be the best out of hundreds of years of writings to a small group of students who are thought able to appreciate them. Such an ideology is essentially anti-democratic and counter to the principle of equality of educational access for all.

A progressivist curriculum is essentially child-centred. Thus in much recent English teaching the emphasis has been on the child's own personal experience and creative writing, on what the child can discover for him or herself, rather than on a received and transitted body of knowledge about a body of 'great' writing. A danger here is that such a curriculum is based on an extremely optimistic view of human nature, expecting children to rediscover for themselves what it has taken others hundreds or thousands of years to discover collectively. More fundamentally, being essentially personal in orientation, it fails to relate educational knowledge to society and culture.

A reconstructionist curriculum sees education as a way of understanding and improving society. No utopian assumptions are necessarily made: it need not be assumed that there is one ideal kind of society, or that perfection will be attained. But students are given the ability to analyse, criticize and possibly reconstruct social norms and practices. The curriculum is essentially democratic in that all children have the right of access to such means of cultural analysis. An example of a reconstructionist syllabus for English would therefore be the type of course in language awareness which I have proposed in this chapter (and in chapter 5).

A reconstructionist ideology rejects extreme versions of the other two types, but this does not mean that all aspects of the other two types are rejected. For example, a reconstructionist ideology does not reject the study of literature. However, neither would it simply accept a body of 'great' literature as given, as something to be taken for granted: it would raise the question of how some literature comes to be considered as uniquely of value and what social forces lead to its being transmitted from generation to generation. Such values are socially constructed. Similarly, a reconstructionist ideology is child-centred to the extent that teachers have to start from where the child is: there is, logically, nowhere else to start. Also, it would attempt to make children active in doing-their own analyses of their culture, guided but not dominated by teachers.

In their ideal typical forms, then, these ideologies have the following characteristics. A classical humanist curriculum has a narrow view of culture in the sense of minority taste and high culture. It is centred on a body of knowledge and on the concept of specialized disciplines. A progressivist curriculum runs the danger of ignoring the culture altogether, as it concentrates on personal and individual experiences and is child-centred. A reconstructionist curriculum analyses culture in the sense of the whole complex of beliefs and values of a society. It aims to move beyond particular subject disciplines and is therefore society-centred.

These three curriculum ideologies can be seen clearly in various forms of English teaching, although they often exist in mixed forms. They are helpful in making clear the possibilities which exist in principle and the implications of each, even if what we want to teach cannot be entirely contained by any one of them.

What is English?

Well, this chapter is already long enough, and I suppose you may have noticed that I haven't yet said what English *is*.

There is the story of an eminent scholar of English who devoted his life to trying to define the essence of English. He wrote many books, trying always to pare away the inessential and the peripheral, and get down to the essential core. English was clearly not homogeneous: but not entirely heterogeneous – structured heterogeneity. It was sometimes categorial: but also gradient. A relatively stable core: but with indeterminate boundaries. How to define fuzziness with precision? His writings became shorter and shorter, and clearer and clearer. He began by writing long textbooks, but soon was writing brief prolegomena, succinct articles, gradually discarding the inessentials. At his death he was known to be working on his ultimate project. He was trying to distil the essence of English into a single word. When he died his disciples were going through his academic papers, sorting out a lifetime's notes. Eventually they came upon the piece of paper with the *word* on it! The culmination of a lifetime's study.

Unfortunately, no one could read his writing.

APPENDIX A SAMPLE OUTLINE SYLLABUS

I suggest below the broad outlines of a course on modern English language. Most of the topics could be taught at widely different levels of sophistication, between secondary school and university.

Course objectives

Given any text, students ought to be able to comment systematically on its interesting features.

Text means any piece of spoken discourse or written text which has actually occurred in a real social situation. Texts could therefore include: children's speech; samples of regional and social dialects; literary texts; casual conversation between adults; samples of pidgins, creoles and code switching; etc. This implies *contrastive stylistic analysis of real language*, and not the development of some descriptive linguistic framework for its own sake. (See also appendix B.)

Students ought to be aware of the types of language variation which occur in society, and of concepts required to describe such variation.

Types of variation include: social multilingualism of different kinds; dialectal variation, regional and social; and stylistic variation.

Given the first aim, students ought to be able to comment precisely on the relevant linguistic characteristics of the variation.

Students ought to be aware of work on practical language planning, i.e. policy making.

This involves work at all institutional levels from national governments down to institutions such as publishing houses and schools. Such linguistic policy-making includes choosing and modernizing national languages, literacy programmes, language teaching policies at national and school level, 'Language across the curriculum', etc.

Sample content areas could be divided into blocks, each treated from these three points of view as follows.

Course outline

TX Textual analysis
LV Language variation
LP Language planning

Block 1. Styles of language

TX Samples of different styles, registers, functional varieties, for contrastive analysis.
LV Grammatical versus communicative and stylistic competence. Concept that language is not correct in any absolute way, but is appropriate or inappropriate to different purposes.
LP Attitudes to language. Institutionalized styles of language, e.g. legal.

Block 2. Native language learning

TX Samples of children's versus adults' language.
LV How children acquire language. Language and cognitive development, language and intelligence.
LP Teaching the native language in schools. Language policies in schools.

Block 3. Dialects and codes

TX Samples of regional and social dialects and accents. Most extreme dialect variation in creoles.
LV Language and social class.
LP Attitudes to accents and dialects.

Block 4. Multilingualism

TX Samples of code switching: stylistic, bilingual, bidialectal.
LV Language and ethnic groups. Societal multilingualism: case studies of different countries. Relations between English and other languages. Individual bilingualism.
LP Foreign language teaching in schools; English as a second language and as a foreign language. Roles of English as an international language.

Block 5. Written language and literacy

TX Samples of written versus spoken language.
LV Nature of written language and writing systems. Literacy in different countries, world literacy rates.
LP What it means to be able to read and write. Teaching literacy. The standardization of English by dictionary makers, printers and publishers.

Block 6. Literary language

TX Samples of literary versus non-literary language.
LV Literary and linguistic stylistics. Nature of literary criticism.
LP Teaching literature in schools, aims and objectives.

APPENDIX B DESCRIPTION OF CONTEMPORARY ENGLISH

I have discussed in the body of this chapter the possibility of describing samples of real language in use and of contrastive text analysis. This clearly needs some framework for describing texts, but I have not discussed this at all. This is partly because it does not really matter which framework is used, as long as it obeys various criteria. It must be non-prescriptive and fairly comprehensive: able to describe what actually occurs. If teachers are familiar with, for example, tagmemic grammar, systemic grammar or various other descriptive frameworks, then these could serve.

If I had to recommend one particular framework, however, I would recommend *A Grammar of Contemporary English* by Randolph Quirk and his colleagues. I would recommend this for various reasons.

1 It is fairly traditional in many ways. It is based on some of the best of contemporary descriptive linguistics, but many of the concepts are compatible with more traditional notions of English grammar, and will therefore be accessible to many teachers.

2 It is based on a survey of contemporary English usage, spoken and written.

3 It is published in various forms: a substantial, basic reference volume (Quirk et al. 1972), and also two more condensed versions by Leech and Svartvik (1975) and by Quirk and Greenbaum (1975). The second of these also has an associated workbook. Quirk et al. (1985) is a revised version.

FURTHER READING

Hawkins, E. W. (1984) *Awareness of Language: an Introduction*. London: Cambridge University Press.

ACKNOWLEDGEMENTS

This chapter is a revised version of an article first published in *English in Australia*, 51: 3-20, 1980. It is also reprinted in R. Carter (ed.), *Linguistics and the Teacher*, London: Routledge and Kegan Paul, 1982, pp. 137-55.

I am grateful to Margaret Berry, Oscar Collinge and Anne Gunter for providing data and ideas for this article; and to the audience at my address in Perth, Western Australia, for formulating over fifty questions on the lecture and for giving me the opportunity to respond to some of them.

5

What is Standard English?

Introduction

In Britain, Standard English is a central issue of language in education, since Standard English is a variety of language which can be defined only by reference to its role in the education system. It is also an example of a topic which requires careful conceptual analysis, since there is enormous confusion about terms such as 'standard', 'correct', 'proper', 'good', 'grammatical', 'academic', etc. English, and such terms, are at the centre of much debate over English in education. A major role for linguistics is the steady unpicking of unreflecting beliefs and myths about language, especially where such beliefs affect the lives of all children in schools.

This chapter provides a case study of my proposal in chapter 1 that topics in language in education must be approached from four directions. We need a technical linguistic description of the forms of Standard English: for example, its syntax. We need a sociolinguistic theory to explain its functions: how and when it is used. We need an applied analysis of planning and policy: for example, how it should be taught. And we require an ideological analysis of Standard English as a major factor in the ways in which people experience power and control in their lives. Standard English has to do with passing exams, getting on in the world, respectability, prestige and success. Anyone who expresses such perceptions is also expressing an awareness of the ways in which Standard English reflects the historical and social forces which created and maintain it. Children who have difficulty in using Standard English when the education system demands it, do not talk and write as they do for perverse idiosyncratic reasons of their own, but because their families, friends and communities talk in that way, and because of the historical forces which have created a multidialectal English.

Together such forms of analysis (although they are of course by no means complete in this chapter) can contribute to a cultural analysis of the social world we live in (cf. chapters 1 and 4), and to the critical and cultural role which English teachers in particular can play in schools.

In this chapter, I will use *Standard English* as a technical term. The term *standard*, as I discuss below, is extremely ambiguous in English, and it is important to be clear that the term *Standard English* has technical meanings which are not derivable directly from the everyday uses of the word.

I will also use the following abbreviations:

SE   Standard English
NS   Non-standard
NSE Non-standard English
RP   Received Pronunciation

SE in education

Schools are probably the single most important place of contact in our society between speakers of different language varieties: in particular, between speakers of standard and non-standard varieties of English. There are other institutional settings in which there is increasing contact between people who do not share the same norms of language or of language use, but they all tend to be narrow contexts which are crucial for people's life chances: medical, legal, bureaucratic – and educational. Outside such settings, contacts between people are likely to be less formal, and to be between people who share the same language varieties.

An extremely important question therefore, which requires detailed consideration by all educationalists in all English-speaking countries, is what is Standard English?

SE has a central place in the education system, and is in fact partly defined by the place it occupies there. In practice, every time a teacher corrects a pupil's spelling or a grammatical form, some process of standardization is taking place. Teachers need to be very clear about the nature of such corrections: about whether they are correcting spelling, where the issue of standardization is relatively simple and uncontroversial; or whether they are altering a non-standard grammatical form, and effectively trying (probably unsuccessfully and confusingly) to change the pupil's native dialect. In order to avoid confusing such very different types of 'correction', teachers therefore need to be very clear about what SE is. The extent of the confusion possible in this area can be seen when one native speaker of English tells another native speaker that something they have said 'is not English'. Yet how could a native speaker of English be speaking anything but English? This can happen even between two apparently highly educated users of SE, as, for example, when a letter appears in the quality press complaining about some linguistic usage from a BBC newscaster.

Questions of standardization arise essentially because of linguistic variation. There are variants within English, people choose between them, and recommend one variant in preference to another. The issue becomes critical in education when there is a mismatch between the language of the school and the language of the pupil, bearing in mind that the large majority of the population of Britain speak NSE.

The major problem in defining SE precisely is that a very wide range of facts has to be taken into consideration. It requires to be defined in a technical linguistic descriptive way, in terms of its phonetics, phonology, morphology, lexis and syntax. But it also requires to be defined sociolinguistically, in terms of the functions it serves in the community and of people's attitudes towards it. It requires to be defined historically, in terms of where it came from, who created it, who is still maintaining it, and how it has changed and is still changing. And it requires to be discussed from a political and ideological point of view, in terms of its position as a prestige and dominant language variety that helps to maintain hegemonic relations between social classes. It is related, in particular, to the power and wealth of the educated middle classes and, conversely, is used to exclude others from certain roles and professions. It is quite clear, for example, that success in public examinations, such as O and A-levels, depends heavily on a mastery of written SE. One may or may not agree that it should: but it does, and teachers must therefore know what such a mastery implies. SE is neither merely a dialect of English, nor a style: it is an intersection of dialectal and functional variation, and this makes it particularly difficult to define.

The power of SE is not, of course, absolute. Most people after all do not speak SE themselves, certainly not all the time. Written SE is marginal in many people's lives. British schools and the wider society are full of many counter-language varieties of resistance. Moreover, working-class varieties of English can have their own prestige as 'tough', 'virile' and the like.

From the point of view of providing teachers with useful information about NS dialects of English, it is unfortunate that we do not have for English in Britain what is available, for example, for German teachers in Germany: contrastive grammars of standard High German and dialects such as Swabian. Ammon and Loewer (1977) simply take it for granted that a high proportion of the population of Germany speak NS dialects, that these dialects may have a long tradition of being highly valued, that pupils nevertheless need to learn the standard language in school, that there will be interference problems in such learning, and that teachers need succinct and accurate statements of the points of contrast where such interference is likely to occur. As such, this is an extremely useful model to be followed for teachers' aids. My main criticism of their particular book is that it appears to assume a rather simple view of contrastive analysis: that just identifying the points of contrast between language varieties will automatically predict points of difficulty for learners; this has been found not always to be the case with learners of foreign languages. In addition, the authors assume that learning a standard language as a second dialect is the same as learning a foreign language, whereas there are some rather obvious differences. Nevertheless, the contrastive information provided is extremely useful in allowing teachers to distinguish between errors in pupils' work which are genuine mistakes and errors which are due to interference from the native dialect.

It is clear, then, that any serious cultural analysis must include a substantial analysis of SE: what it is in formal linguistic terms, what it does, what its roles in society are, and what are the dominant meanings and values which it carries.

Terms and an initial definition

There are several terms in everyday use which mean approximately what linguists mean by SE. In the USA, the term *Network English* is used, and this is close in intent to the British term *BBC English*. Other British terms are the *Queen's English* and *Oxford English*. Such everyday terms are not very precise, and the last two are rather out of date in their assumptions about sources of prestige in British society. In addition, the last term often refers to an accent (pronunciation), rather than a dialect (vocabulary plus grammar). However, such terms identify a social reality for most people and do no harm, if they are not taken too literally.

There is, however, another term, *Received Pronunciation*, which causes confusion and does not mean at all the same as SE. RP refers to an accent which is socially prestigious, mainly in England. There are certainly other prestige accents, for example in Scotland, where RP may be regarded as slightly odd and affected. Even in England, RP does not have the prestige which it once had. (See Wells 1982 and Gimson 1984 for detailed discussion.) However, the main point here is that RP refers to pronunciation only, whereas SE refers mainly to grammar and vocabulary, and only secondarily to pronunciation. Part of the confusion here arises because of the peculiar relation between RP and SE. All users of RP speak SE: this is not logically necessary, but is an important fact about language and social class in Britain. On the other hand, only a minority of speakers of SE (even in England) use RP. For example, I speak SE with a regional west of Scotland accent. It has been claimed that there is no standard accent of English at all, and that SE is spoken with many different accents across the whole English-speaking world, but I will question extreme statements of this view below.

A natural preliminary definition of SE can be provided simply by listing some of its main uses. This would provide an *ostensive definition*: SE is defined by pointing to clear instances of it. It would also be a *functional definition*, which is a natural type of definition in many everyday cases: try, for example, to define *knife* or *bed* without making any reference to what these objects are used for. SE, then, is the variety of English which is normally used in print, and more generally in the public media, and which is used by most educated speakers most of the time. It is the variety used in the education system, and therefore the variety taught to learners of English as a foreign language. These examples tell any native speaker roughly what is meant by SE. On the other hand, they leave unclear whether SE is a predominantly written variety, and whether it is a prescriptive norm imposed by the education system, or a description of the language which some people actually use as their native language.

The terms *Network English* and *BBC English* are particularly socially revealing. The control of the public media is in the hands of a small social elite. This points to a relationship between the public media, a social-class group and SE. It is impossible to separate the prestige of the media, of the media personalities and of the language they use. SE is therefore a prestige dialect. It is also the variety that is used in formally printed books, and these have their own prestige.

There is one simple, but widespread confusion, which is easily disposed of. In so far as SE is the native language of a social group (the educated middle classes), SE is a dialect, and like any other dialect it has internal stylistic variation. That is, SE may be either formal or casual and colloquial. Thus the following sentences are all SE:

1 I have not seen any of those children.
2 I haven't seen any of those kids.
3 I haven't seen any of those bloody kids.

(The use of the word *bloody* is British rather than American: we will come to that in a moment.) Speakers of SE can be as casual, polite or rude as anyone else, and can use slang, swear and say things in bad taste or in bad style. But this all has to do with questions of stylistic variation or social etiquette, and not with dialect. The following sentence is not SE, however:

4 I ain't seen none of them kids.

It is not incorrect SE: it is simply not SE at all. The double negative, the use of *them* as a demonstrative adjective and the use of *ain't* are all perfectly regular grammatical features of many NS dialects of English. Vocabulary can also be NS. For example, *bairns* for "children" is regionally restricted to dialects in the north of Britain.

Note, then, that we have to avoid formulations that imply that NS dialects are a deviation from SE. This would be both logically and historically inaccurate. NS dialects are linguistic systems in their own right. Note also that I am not assuming the existence of 'pure' or 'genuine' dialects, spoken (in the stereotypes of many people) by old rural inhabitants. There are urban and rural, standard and non-standard dialects: everyone speaks some dialect.

Different aspects of standardization

I have pointed out briefly so far that there is stylistic variation within SE, but otherwise I have discussed SE as though it was equally standardized throughout. This is, however, obviously not the case: certain levels of SE are much more standardized than others, and it has been argued (although I will question this below) that some levels are not standardized at all.

The most obviously and uncontroversially standardized level of SE is spelling. Standard spellings are simply listed in the major dictionaries. There are of course two major forms of standardization, British and American, but these two norms cannot themselves be mixed with each other. Otherwise, with very few exceptions (for example, *judgement, judgment*), there is just one way to spell each word, there are no variants in normal usage, and the standard spellings just have to be learned. It is easier to standardize written than spoken English, since it is easier to bring it under conscious control. In addition, spellings have no direct analogue in the spoken language (not even in phonology: see chapter 12), and can therefore remain relatively unaffected by unconscious spoken behaviour.

Conversely, for accent or pronunciation there is no single standard, and SE can be spoken with a range of accents. In a series of influential statements on SE, Trudgill (e.g. 1974, 1975; Hughes and Trudgill 1979; Trudgill and Hannah 1982) has defined SE as a dialect, involving lexis and grammar, but not pronunciation. For example, Trudgill (1984a: 32) writes:

> SE . . . is a set of grammatical and lexical forms which is typically used in speech and writing by educated native speakers. It follows, therefore, that SE is a term that does not involve phonetics or phonology, although, of course, accents do differ considerably in social status.

Trudgill's definitions always place primary emphasis on SE as a social dialect, and, although they usually mention accent and diatypic function, I do not think they give sufficient weight to these aspects of language, nor to people's own perceptions of SE. For example, he goes on to admit (1984a: 32) that in fact SE occurs normally only with 'milder' regional accents. But this already seems to undermine the claim that phonetics and phonology are not involved in people's ideas of SE. Apart from anything else, the very fact that there are such things as elocution lessons, which focus on accent, means that people have an idea of what is and what is not standard in pronunciation. Elocution lessons are one way in which people try to change other people's accents (although they are not as prevalent as they once were) and are therefore one mechanism, however insignificant in practice for the language as a whole, of linguistic standardization.

Coates (1982) has argued in detail, however, that even if we admit that there is no standard accent for English, there are nevertheless standard pronunciation features: that is, the range of permissible accents which Trudgill seems to have in mind all share invariant features. Two examples of NS pronunciation features are: a *t*-sound pronounced as a glottal stop between vowels in words such as *butter*; and *h*-deletion word-initially on lexical words such as *house*. These features are themselves variable, such that a low percentage of glottal stops might not even be noticed at all, but above a perceptual threshold the accent will be perceived as NS. Similarly, all speakers delete word-initial *h* on unstressed grammatical words (e.g. *has, his*) in informal conversation, but deletion on stressed lexical words is perceived as NS. (Deletion of word-initial *h* is extremely complex historically in English: see Stubbs 1980: 35–40.)

Given that there is a very large area of common ground between SE and NS dialects, it might be better even in the area of syntax to talk of NS syntactic features, rather than of NS English per se. Such terminology would also reflect the fact that speakers may not consistently use either standard or non-standard forms: they will typically occur variably. Having said that, it is then possible to characterize SE negatively, at the syntactic level, by simply listing NS syntactic forms. The following all occur widely throughout NS British dialects and are not restricted to any one particular geographical region. This list is based on fuller lists in Trudgill (1984a) and Edwards, Trudgill and Weltens (1984).

1 Multiple negation.
  I didn't do nothing.
2 *Ain't* as a negative form of *be* or auxiliary verb *have*.
  I ain't doing it. I ain't got one.
3 *Never* used to refer to a single occasion in the past.
  I never done it. (SE: I didn't do it.)
4 Extension of third-person *-s* to first and second-person verb forms.
  I wants, you wants, he wants.
5 Regularization of *be*.
  We was, you was, they was.
6 Regularization of some irregular verbs.
  I draw, I drawed, I have drawed.
  I go, I went, I have went.
  I come, I come, I have come.
7 Optional *-ly* on adverbs.
  He writes really quick.
8 Unmarked plurality on nouns of measurement after numerals.
  twenty year, ten pound.
9 Different forms of the relative pronoun.
  The man as/what lives here.
10 Regularization of reflexive pronouns.
  myself, yourself, hisself, herself; ourselves, yourselves, theirselves.
11 Distinction between main and auxiliary verb *do*.
  You done it, did you? (SE: You did it, did you?)

Note that the last case shows very clearly that we are dealing with a different rule-governed NS system, and not with 'sloppy' or 'incorrect' usage. First, the NS dialect shows a distinction which is not marked in SE. Second, in neither SE nor NS dialects can one say *You done it, done you?*

The above list is an over-simplified list of features, which are geographically widespread. There are of course many other such features, some regionally restricted. Also, some of the features listed occur higher up the social-class scale than others. The list is also over-simplified in that it implies the existence of an extreme or idealized NS dialect, whereas individuals vary in the extent to which they use dialect features and use such features variably in different contexts.

SE as a social dialect

Although the NS features listed above are widespread within Britain, they are nevertheless British, rather than American. One of the most important defining characteristics of SE is that it is not regionally restricted. There is slight regional variation between the SE used in Scotland, Wales, Ireland and England, but very much less than in NS varieties. In fact, there is a remarkably uniform international SE. Again, there are small differences among the standard varieties used in Britain, North America, South Africa, Australia and New Zealand. The differences in vocabulary and grammar, however, are surprisingly minor, given its very large number of speakers, its very wide geographical spread, and the large common core shared by all these standard languages. One might, for example, read a newspaper article without knowing whether it was printed in New York, London or Sydney: the only clue might be occasional words for local places or artefacts (barring spelling differences). Trudgill and Hannah (1982) provide a summary of such differences between all the varieties of SE in the world.

It follows that SE is not a regional dialect. It is a *social dialect*: that dialect which is used by all educated speakers, at least for some purposes, and some people have it as their native language. It is intuitively obvious that there is much more variation in the English used by working-class people than by middle-class people. (This is much less marked for other languages, for example, German, especially if Austrian and Swiss speakers are included.) Thus business people or teachers from London, Glasgow, Sydney and San Francisco would have little, if any difficulty in understanding each other, and the most noticeable differences in their language would be in accent, not in dialect. But farm labourers from south-west England, north-east Scotland and the Appalachians would speak very differently and might have considerable difficulty in understanding each other: although they might shift towards SE to facilitate communication. Trudgill (1975 and elsewhere) illustrates the relation between social and regional diversity as a triangle without its apex (see figure 5). That is, as we move up the social-class scale, there is less regional variation in dialect, although even at the very top there is still a little.

SE and diatypic functions

However, SE is not just a dialect: it is used for particular diatypic functions (cf. chapter 2). There is a particular relationship between SE and its uses in written language. This, in turn, relates to the relatively small amount of variation within SE. Spoken English is more variable than written English, due to

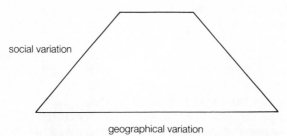

social variation

geographical variation

Figure 5   Relation between social and regional diversity in English

a convention that written English is formal. A simple example of this convention is the restriction against forms such as *don't, doesn't* and *isn't* in printed books. It is not an absolute constraint, but a strong tendency. In chapter 11, I have discussed in detail some aspects of the relation between SE, written English and formal language.

Here is a slightly different way of discussing the relationships. There is a strong tendency, in many areas, to talk in terms of dichotomies, such as *standard* versus *non-standard*, or *written* versus *spoken*. However, both of these pairs of terms label large classes, and collapse together several different dimensions, which typically co-occur, but which are logically independent and can vary independently. The main dimensions are as follows:

written	spoken
formal	casual
public	private
planned	spontaneous
non-interactive	participatory
not co-present	face-to-face
standard	non-standard

Most written language is formal: this is a strong social convention, and certainly the most formal written language is more formal than any spoken language. But there are, of course, informal personal letters: we are talking about typical correlations of features, not deterministic relations. Again, most written language is public (i.e. published) and most spoken language is private, although there are private letters and public debates. Most written, certainly almost all published, language is planned, edited and redrafted, whereas most spoken language is composed spontaneously as it is spoken. However, there are mixed modes, such as lectures, which may be based on previously written language, even if they are not just written language read aloud. Most written language is non-interactive: it is a monologue in so far as the reader cannot break in and interrupt or give feedback, whereas most spoken language is participatory dialogue. However, written communication between individuals sitting at separate computer terminals may be interactive, spoken language on television or radio cannot be interrupted, and many lectures are only marginally participatory. In typical spoken communication, the participants are face-to-face and visible to each other, whereas in written communication writer and reader are not co-present: but children can pass written notes to each other in class, and speakers on the telephone are not face-to-face. Similarly, speakers are usually co-present at the same moment in time: although new technology in the form of telephone answering machines has altered the possibilities even here.

It is also frequently claimed that written language is typically more explicit than other language, and there is clearly some plausibility in this observation. This is of particular interest to teachers, since the aim of making things explicit is central to education. However, the claim is not at all straightforward, since explicitness is not a function of a particular piece of language in the abstract: it is not an intrinsic property of texts, but of texts in context. A text that is perfectly clear and explicit to one reader may be unclear and obscure to another, since explicitness depends on the purpose of a text, and on assumptions about what the audience knows about the subject matter. One can never say everything about anything. Explicitness therefore depends on a balance between what can be assumed and what needs to be said. A related formulation is the claim that written language is context-free, whereas spoken language is context-dependent. But, of course, even formal, written journal articles and the like make many assumptions about what their readers already know. The confusion here is often that written texts do not depend on their context of production (it does not matter to the reader that I am writing this particular text in the south of Germany - I am as it happens): but what is crucial is the context of reception. (Nystrand 1983b discusses this common confusion in detail.)

Finally, SE will be seen to be associated with the written-formal-public ends of the various dimensions. Again, these are correlations which represent a particular socio-cultural view of the functions of SE, rather than a deterministic view of language. (Similar dimensions to those above are discussed by Brazil 1969; Rubin 1980.)

The very strong social conventions that all printed English is standard means that only occasional examples of dialect poetry or some kinds of community writing in NSE (see Gregory 1984), get into print. Examples of dialect poetry by writers such as Robert Burns or William Neill for Scots or by James Berry or Linton Kwesi Johnson for Caribbean creole are as striking as they are rare. If a language is highly standardized, this implies in fact that it has a written form. This is because standardization implies deliberate codification and planning of the language by dictionary makers, grammar-book writers and the like. This brings us again to the special relation between SE and the education system, for it is the education system which is a powerful instrument for promoting such codified norms of language.

People, including dictionary makers and schoolteachers, observe what they think is good usage. This may well be a mixture of local prejudice about what is a 'good' accent, sometimes outdated norms of educated usage, and notions of written or even literary usage, which may be inappropriate to spoken language. On this basis, they may formulate rules which can become quite rigid. Once established, such rules can become self-perpetuating. SE is used by prestigious people for prestigious purposes. The prestige of the people rubs off on the language, and the circle continues. SE, the social elite who use it, and the public functions which it serves become inseparable.

For many people, the social practices which have created SE, in particular over the past 250 years, have been lost to sight. For example, the actual means of production of dictionaries is a total mystery to most people. They are treated as given, not constructed. Dictionaries just exist and are treated as sources of impersonal authority: words can be looked up in the dictionary to settle disputes, although people have really no idea where dictionaries come from or who makes them. (Despite a certain amount of publicity which has been given recently to Robert Burchfield as editor of the *Oxford English Dictionary*, the source of his authority remains implicit.) This is part of the hegemonic power of SE. It is accepted as normal, taken-for-granted reality by many of those who are dominated by it. Children, of course, often have their own sources of resistance against it, in their own forms of counter-language; it may be teachers, however, who do not themselves ever question the source of the system they perpetuate.

If one then asks who standardizes English, the answer can be: almost anyone. Sometimes it is individuals such as Samuel Johnson or Noah Webster; but it is also groups such as secretaries, proof readers, editors, people who write to newspapers to complain about usage on the radio, and ultimately people arguing amongst themselves about the 'correct' pronunciation or meaning of a word. If individual people did not follow the prescriptions of dictionary makers and the like, then dictionaries and grammar books would have no effect.

Probably the major social group ultimately involved in standardizing English is schoolteachers. It has frequently been pointed out that lower-middle-class women are over-represented in the teaching profession. And it is known from sociolinguistic work that lower-middle-class speakers, and women as opposed to men, are often particularly sensitive to prestige norms in language. (See Fasold 1984: ch. 9, for a very clear general discussion of language standardization.)

Dialects and diatypes

In summary, then, what is SE? In chapter 2, I distinguished between dialects and diatypes. I further distinguished between regional, social and temporal dialects; and distinguished between diatypic or functional varieties of language according to the field, tenor or mode of discourse. I can now therefore define SE, in relation to these definitions, as an intersection of dialectal and diatypic varieties.

SE is closely related to regional dialects spoken in the south-east of England. This looks like a regional definition, but in fact SE is no longer regionally restricted. This is actually a disguised historical definition: SE developed historically out of a dialect used in London, especially in the court. This already implies that SE is a social dialect. Historically, because of the power and prestige of its speakers, SE spread geographically, and is now the social dialect used by the educated middle classes all over Britain, and with only minor variation in other countries. It is also the variety used in education (field of discourse), in formal settings (tenor of discourse), and in print (mode of discourse).

These definitions are not in themselves prescriptive: they describe certain social facts which govern how SE is used. These facts are socially, politically and economically loaded, but I have not passed any judgement in the last paragraph on whether they are desirable or not. However, it is easy to see how the borderline between a prescriptive and a descriptive definition breaks down. The reason for one further confusion should now be clear. SE is prestigious and, because of its speakers and users, it is highly visible. The very fact that it is used in print makes it visible, whereas NS varieties are generally restricted to spoken language. People therefore come to think of SE as *the* language. They confuse one socially prestigious variety with the whole language.

The linguistic view of SE is often misrepresented. It is often said, for example, that linguists argue that SE is just a dialect of English, like any other, with no privileged position. This is not so. It is quite evident that SE holds a special position. What linguists emphasize, however, is that this special position is not due to any inherent linguistic superiority of SE: it is due to a complex of historical, geographical, social, political and functional factors. Linguists do not therefore argue, as they are often held to, that 'all languages are equal', but they argue that the reasons for inequality between language varieties are not inherently linguistic.

The term *standard*

In an extremely useful essay, Williams (1976: 248ff) has analysed the ambiguities in the different everyday uses of the term *standard*. In uses such as *royal standard* or *standard bearer*, the word means a distinctive flag or symbol of authority. In *gold standard*, it means a basic unit of comparison. In *standard foot*, it means an authorized unit of measurement. In *standard size*, it means usual or accepted. A *standard work* (for example, on the French Revolution) is an accepted authority. In *standard of living*, the word refers to a level which has been attained in some hierarchy, although here no precise measurement is possible. Similarly, if we talk of *maintaining standards* in education, we talk of assessment or grading, levels of achievement or competence, although again such things are here not objectively measurable. Note also that *standards* is laudatory, although *standardization* can often be pejorative. So it is not necessarily contradictory to talk of the need 'to maintain standards without standardizing education'. Williams's historical analysis of the shifts in the term also shows that several of its senses are involved in people's complex perceptions of the concept of Standard English, and in the different aspects of standardization discussed in this chapter.

SE in schools

The following pedagogic principles seem to follow from the arguments of this chapter. First, all children must have access to SE, and therefore must be taught it in school, if necessary. If they are not competent in SE, at least for some purposes, then areas of the dominant culture are closed to them. In particular, they need to be competent in written SE. If they are not, then they are not competent in written English itself, and they must also have competence in written language to have access to aspects of the dominant culture. This view is quite compatible with the view that school should be more understanding and tolerant of NS dialects and should be free of dialect prejudice. SE is basically the language of wider, non-regional, public communication, and a basic principle must be that children should be able to communicate along all the lines of communication that are important to them: family, community, education and public life. It follows from this, in turn, that SE must be taught in ways that do not denigrate the native home dialect: this is, of course, one of the most difficult tasks. However, it is crucial to realize that the view that children must learn SE is not at all the same as the view that children should be anglicized (if they are from an ethnic minority group) or that they should assimilate to the dominant, mainstream, middle-class culture (if they are from a working-class group).

All of this, however, still leaves open how such teaching of SE should be done. Two principles which can guide such teaching are as follows. First, teachers clearly have a responsibility to teach children that some forms of language are expected within the examination system, and that other forms will be penalized. If they do not make this explicit to children, then they are not teaching their pupils about one of the major gate-keeping functions of SE. Second, it may be soon enough to begin such teaching a few years before such formal examinations, and explicitly in relation to them. It is debatable how soon is soon enough, but the underlying principle is that early writing is bound to be based on the children's spoken language and is therefore bound to show more variation than is conventional in formal written language. Furthermore, if the conventions of written SE are insisted on too early, then there is the danger that the child has to learn all at the same time: mechanical handwriting skills, spelling, other conventions of written English, and a second dialect. It therefore seems pedagogically correct to allow children to write in language that is closer to their native spoken dialect than is conventional, until they are confident in writing as such. (Richmond 1982 discusses such issues.)

It is very much more doubtful whether children should be explicitly taught spoken SE. They must be able to understand it, of course; but it is doubtful if schools should try to teach or insist on production in spoken SE. First, such an insistence is unlikely to be successful. Children know that not everyone speaks SE, and an insistence that they should speak it is likely to alienate them from the school or their family or both. In any case, the habits of the spoken language are usually so deeply ingrained that they are impervious to conscious teaching for a few hours a week in school. People need to be very highly motivated in order to change their native dialect. Normally they need to be motivated to join another social group that uses the target language. If children are on good social terms with their teachers, they will shift naturally towards SE when the occasion demands it. Much sociolinguistic work has now shown that children of primary-school age can already adapt their language to different audiences. (See Milroy 1980, for a detailed converse demonstration that it is the most non-standard speakers who have the closest ties with their local community.) Writing depends much more on conscious language behaviour, and is therefore open to explicit teaching in a way in which spoken language is not.

However, it is extremely important that teachers should have enough knowledge of their pupils' native spoken language varieties to allow them to distinguish between genuine mistakes (for example, in spelling) and interference from NS dialects. If both kinds of linguistic feature are merely 'corrected' in the same way, this will at best be confusing for pupils, and at worst will be tantamount to criticizing the native language, which symbolizes their home and community. (Richmond 1982 gives helpful examples.)

Finally, there is a very basic question to which the answer is not yet at all clear. Are the differences between standard and non-standard varieties of English merely surface differences that have purely symbolic value? Or are the differences ever large enough to cause serious comprehension problems? It is clear that some differences are purely of surface form: they annoy many people who take a prescriptive view of language, but would never cause any genuine communication problems (for example, forms such as *we was* are widely condemned as 'wrong', but are understood by everyone). There are other cases, however, where communication problems may arise.

The argument that dialect differences do not cause communication problems is as follows. We can all obviously understand many speakers of different dialects. Many people are bidialectal and can themselves switch between a NS dialect and SE. Most people can recognize speakers from different parts of the country and can even imitate other dialects to some extent. It is clear that our linguistic competence is not narrowly restricted to one dialect.

The converse argument is that dialect changes are rarely entirely successful, and that even after years of living in a new area, people still cannot imitate the local dialect with complete accuracy. Although we can obviously understand speakers of other dialects, our understanding is irregular and ad hoc, and depends on the contexts as well as on the language alone. By their very nature, failures of communication are likely to go undetected, and there are therefore likely to be many more such failures than we notice. We think we have understood, but we haven't.

As linguists carry out a more detailed analysis on a wider range of dialects, they are starting to question to just what extent speakers of different dialects do share the same linguistic system. It has been argued, for example (Milroy 1984), that there are quite profound differences between the systems of tense and aspect in Irish English and in SE, and that these differences can cause serious, but often unnoticed communication failures. It has also been argued (for example, by Edwards 1979) that there are similar problems with Caribbean creoles, due to different tense and aspect marking and also to features such as the lack of overt distinctions between active and passive sentences, and that therefore Caribbean children in Britain may have some comprehension problems with written SE in schools.

Not enough detailed description has yet been done on British dialects to be sure how important or widespread such problems are. However, something which is certain is that modern towns and cities are not speech communities in the classic sense. People who do not share the same dialect are brought together increasingly frequently. Modern industrial urban society is increasingly diverse, with increasing contact between speakers of different social, cultural and ethnic backgrounds. Gumperz (1982a, 1982b) provides case studies. Misunderstandings do obviously occur in speech events such as meetings, interviews, debates and trials: precisely the kinds of speech events that are crucial for people's life chances. It seems very likely that social life is increasingly full of semiotic mismatches. As the main arena for the contact between standard and non-standard varieties of English, schools therefore have a special responsibility to understand the nature of these differences.

FURTHER READING

Milroy, L. and Milroy, J. (1985) *Authority in Language: Investigating Language Prescription and Standardization*. London: Routledge and Kegan Paul.

ACKNOWLEDGEMENTS

This chapter is published here for the first time. I am grateful to Gabi Keck for comments on a previous draft.

6

Language development, lexical competence and nuclear vocabulary

Introduction

This chapter provides a detailed example of part of the model of linguistic description proposed in chapter 2, by studying the relation between vocabulary and diatypic variation in English: that is, the relation between words and the field, tenor and mode of discourse. It shows in detail that an understanding of the vocabulary of English must be based on a theory of language variation, dialectal and diatypic. However, it shows that the structural internal relations between words themselves must also be studied. Words must be related both to their social contexts of use and also to each other. Systematic analysis of language requires both purely linguistic and also sociolinguistic description.

A major part of the descriptive problem is that, for historical reasons, the vocabulary of English is extremely large and rich in synonyms. How therefore can we describe synonyms in ways which explain how they are both similar to and different from each other in meaning? This chapter also provides a partial answer to the question posed in chapter 4: what is English? I argued there that English has fuzzy boundaries. For hundreds of years it has borrowed extensively from many sources, giving enormous diversity within the language. Much of this book is about language variants and the problems they cause (see especially chapter 5). But the logical concomitant of a study of language variation is a theory of what does not change across the many different uses of English. Given all the dialectal and diatypic variation in English, there is nevertheless a common core. This chapter tries to define this common core with reference to lexis.

The chapter also illustrates in detail a general type of argument used by linguists. It starts from intuitions which native speakers have about English. A linguistic method does not reject intuitions: on the contrary, they are essential in a study of linguistic competence. The aim, however, is to explain such intuitions. The chapter therefore sets up a series of tests which make these intuitions more precise. Subjective impressions are not rejected, but are used as data for a more (but never completely) objective discussion.

When people think of a language, they think almost inevitably of words: vocabulary. When they think of language development, they also tend to think of vocabulary enlargement. There are obviously many other aspects of language development, and there is the danger that an attempt to 'increase someone's word power' leads to a quiz mentality. Nevertheless, the notion of extending someone's vocabulary is a perfectly plausible one in itself. It rests on a powerful, though sometimes hazy, intuition that some words are simpler, more important or more basic than others. It underlies the common-sense fury against much bureaucratic gobbledegook; and the often-repeated observation that children's everyday vocabulary does not prepare them for reading the unfamiliar academic vocabulary in school textbooks (Perera 1980).

This chapter sets out in detail several criteria for defining basic or nuclear vocabulary, and discusses some of the implications of the concept: for theoretical linguistic studies of lexis, for psycholinguistic studies of children's language development, and for practical educational concerns.

In some form, the idea of basic vocabulary must underlie all vocabulary teaching. It certainly underlies vocabulary lists of various kinds including Ogden's (1930) *Basic English*; Thorndike's (1921) and Thorndike and Lorge's (1944) *Teacher's Wordbook*; West's (1953) *General Service List*; Kučera and Francis's (1967) *Computational Analysis of Present-day American English*; Carroll, Davies and Richman's (1971) *American Heritage Word Frequency Book;* Hornby's (1974) *Oxford Advanced Learner's Dictionary*; Hindmarsh's (1980) *Cambridge English Lexicon*; the Keyword scheme in Ladybird readers; and, in fact, lists of vocabulary in any language textbook. Historically, the distinction between basic and non-basic expressions can be traced back to seventeenth-century speculations on the possibility of a logical universal language. This work exerted a powerful influence on Roget's (1852) attempt at a Thesaurus, which logically classifies the whole vocabulary of English. It also influenced Ogden's (1930) *Basic English*, intended as an international auxiliary language (Lyons 1981: 64).

Such lists have very different purposes, including teaching English as a foreign language to different groups; facilitating international communication, given the position of English as a world language; and making prescriptions about the educational level expected of native English-speaking schoolchildren of different ages. Underlying some such lists is therefore a concept of the 'usefulness' or 'communicative adequacy' of different words. A clear statement of the fundamental intuitive notion involved is made by Jeffery in the Foreword to West (1953: v):

A language is so complex that selection from it is always one of the first and most difficult problems of anyone who wishes to teach it system-atically . . . To find the minimum number of words that could operate together in constructions capable of entering into the greatest variety of contexts has therefore been the chief aim of those trying to simplify English for the learner.

The widespread use of such a large number of lists in teaching of different kinds illustrates how important vocabulary development is felt to be, sometimes as an end in itself, and sometimes as a way of facilitating cognitive development.

There remain problems, however. For example, later lists have generally been constructed on the basis of earlier lists, which have themselves built-in biases in their sampling. The Thorndike list, often used by later scholars, was based on a corpus of 4.5 million words, of which 3 million are from 'the Bible and the English classics', including Boswell's *Life of Johnson* and Gibbon's *Rise and Fall of the Roman Empire*. Earlier work is of course generally reinterpreted, but via a 'teacher's discretion' (Hindmarsh 1980: ix); and some lists (for example, Van Ek and Alexander 1977) are set up with no indication at all of how they were constructed.

Frequency counts are obviously inadequate on their own, although basic frequency data cannot be entirely ignored. Totally inexplicit use of intuition is also inadequate: apart from any other reasons, intuitions about lexical frequency are often wildly inaccurate. This chapter therefore aims to provide a more precise concept of what might be meant by 'basic' versus 'non-basic' vocabulary, by returning to first principles and using published lists only at a later stage. I do not aim to provide a review of empirical research on vocabulary development, although some work is referred to. The aim is rather to discuss the systematic linguistic basis for a distinction which has far-reaching implications for linguists, child language researchers and teachers.

Words are idiosyncratic

It is regularly pointed out that words are idiosyncratic. Every individual word is unique in its etymology, and in its meaning and behaviour, including its collocations. Furthermore any individual speaker's vocabulary is unique: an idiosyncratic network of personal connections, which do not appear to concern linguistic competence as this is usually understood.

Phonological and grammatical competence are essentially different from lexical competence in this respect. Any adult native speaker of any dialect of English (or any other language) has basically the same phonological competence, involving intuitive knowledge of the phonemes of the language, their allophonic variants, their possible phonotactic constraints, and so on. This competence is acquired by about the age of 7 years: after that there is simply no more to learn. The same is true of much of the grammar of the language: in most of its main features this is learned by the age of 5 or 6 years, although some of the more complex syntactic structures may be learned later; and some stylistically formal syntactic structures, largely restricted to written language, may be learned in adulthood, if at all. Lexical competence simply never approaches this kind of completeness. The learning of new vocabulary is clearly very rapid in early childhood, and then slows down. Nevertheless a person's vocabulary may continue to grow throughout their whole life. New meanings can be learned for old words, and new relations between words can be formed.

Relational lexical semantics

Despite this apparent inherently idiosyncratic aspect of lexical competence, there are, of course, systematic ways of studying vocabulary. One set of approaches could be called relational lexical semantics, and comprises semantic field theory (especially Roget 1852 and Trier 1931; but also other work by Humboldt in the 1800s, and by Meyer and Weisgerber between 1900 and 1930); structural semantics (Lyons 1963, 1968); and componential analysis (Lehrer 1974; Nida 1975). The basic concept is that meaning is a relational property of language systems: words have no absolute value or meaning, but are defined in relation to other words. The sense relations involved include synonymy, antonymy and hyponymy, and these can be given formal definitions in terms of logical entailment and contradiction (cf. test 6 below). Such approaches are well known and well reviewed in many standard textbooks (see especially Lyons 1977, vol. 1). I will therefore not discuss them here, except in so far as they can help to support a rather different way of discussing relations between words: a distinction between nuclear and non-nuclear vocabulary. Nor will I explicitly discuss the question of how children acquire such semantic relations. There are detailed analyses of children's acquisition of the hierarchical organization of vocabulary, their initial overextensions and later narrowing of word meaning, and the structure of their concepts, by Clark (1973), Livingston (1982), Nelson (1982), Palermo (1982) and Rosch (1973).

The common core

An important part of native speakers' linguistic competence is the ability to recognize that some words are 'ordinary' English words, in some sense, whereas others are rare, exotic, foreign, specialist, regional and so on. Such intuitions are by no means always accurate: for example, regional words are often not recognized as such. As a speaker of Standard Scottish English, I realized only recently that *skelf* ("splinter of wood stuck in a finger") is regionally restricted to Scotland and some other northern areas of Britain.

This intuitive notion that part of the vocabulary is more basic than the rest underlies the definition of the vocabulary of a language which is discussed in detail in the Introduction to the *Oxford English Dictionary*. It is argued there that the vocabulary of English is 'not a fixed quantity circumscribed by definite limits', but rather a nebulous mass with 'a clear and unmistakeable nucleus [which] shades off on all sides . . . to a marginal film that seems to end nowhere'. The Introduction also provides a helpful diagram which neatly sums up this concept (see figure 6).

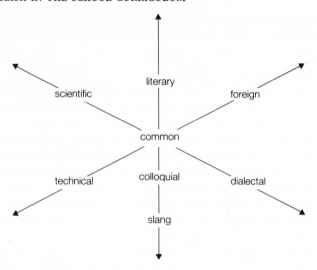

Figure 6   The organization of English vocabulary

Dialectal and diatypic variation

The concept of 'core' evident in the position adopted by the *OED* is, however, not quite the concept that we require here. Comprehensive dictionaries and grammars wish to define the whole of what is 'unquestionably' English. What we require is a considerably more restricted subset of this core. In addition, the 'core' in the sense already discussed occurs naturally as the intersection of many different varieties. We require also to build in the concept of a deliberate and planned selection within this core. Quirk (1981) and Stein (1978) call such a reduced and planned English *nuclear English*, with reference to the lexical and syntactic characteristics of a restricted variety of international English. Dixon (1971, 1973) and Hale (1971) also use the term *nuclear* in a relevant sense.

Blum and Levenston (1978) point to a related aspect of lexical competence which is closer to our requirements. An important part of native speakers' linguistic competence is the ability to use less than their full vocabulary when required to do so. Native speakers have an intuitive sense of which words to avoid when, for example, talking to younger or older children or to foreigners (cf. Bohannon and Marquis 1977; Snow and Ferguson 1977); or, conversely, which words ought to be taught first to foreign learners or used in simplified reading books for children, and, in general, which words are of maximum utility (Blewitt 1983; Cruse 1977; Rosch 1975; Shipley, Kuhn and Madden 1983). Native speakers have many strategies for avoiding words, if they need to do so. One strategy is to use a paraphrase or circumlocution: instead of *waddle*, they might talk of a *clumsy walk*, and such paraphrases are constructed in systematic ways (see below). However, such intuitions have limits, hence the debates over which words should be taught in foreign language textbooks, and also the need for criteria that are not purely intuitive.

In order to develop this sense of nuclear vocabulary, I need to develop the concepts in figure 6. It is usual to distinguish between regional or geographical dialects (e.g. Scottish versus Anglo-English); social dialects (e.g. working class versus middle class); temporal dialects (e.g. Old English versus Middle English); and individual dialects (usually called idiolects). There are exceptions, but many individual speakers have full native competence in only one dialect, defined geographically, socially and temporally, and fixed in adolescence. On the other hand, any individual uses many different diatypes, according to the field of discourse (the activity going on at the time), the tenor of discourse (the social relations between the speakers), and the mode of discourse (predominantly speech versus writing). My formulation here is a Hallidayan one (see Halliday 1978; or Gregory and Carroll 1978, for a very simple account; and chapter 2 of this book).

There is no implication that dialects and diatypes are separate. There was obviously regional and social variation within Old English; and there is diatypic variation within all dialects. Moving to a formal social situation may involve dialect switching as well as diatype switching. Standard English is an intersection of dialect and diatype. It is not a geographical dialect, since it is used everywhere: 'normal' dialects are geographically restricted. It is a social dialect, used predominantly by the educated middle classes, which has particular diatypic uses, for example, in education (field), in formal settings (tenor) and in writing (mode). (See chapter 5.)

The essential idea, then, is that English vocabulary has a central area 'whose Anglicity is unquestioned', which contains a smaller, naturally occurring common core. Within this, it is also possible to select, for some communicative or pedagogical purpose, a planned nuclear English. The wider and the more restricted foci have fuzzy boundaries and shade off imperceptibly into marginal and peripheral forms, including obsolete words (restricted to earlier temporal dialects), regional words (restricted to particular geographical dialects), rare, specialist, technical or foreign words (restricted to certain fields of discourse), colloquial or slang words (restricted to particular tenors of discourse) and literary words (restricted to an intersection of field and mode), and so on.

Here is an initial example, before I give a more detailed definition. The word *child* and its plural *children* are both common core and nuclear, not restricted in dialectal or diatypic usage. There are, however, many related words which are restricted, for example: *childe* (archaic, "young man of noble birth"); *childer* (an archaic or regional plural); *kid* or *kiddy* (colloquial); *offspring* and *progeny* (formal or technical); *paedophilia* and *paediatrics* (technical); *babe* (archaic or religious or American colloquial for "young woman"); and so on.

The tests that follow are intended to make explicit our strong, if sometimes hazy, intuitions that some words are more basic than others.

Nuclear vocabulary: definition and tests

First, nuclear vocabulary is pragmatically neutral, in the sense that it conveys no information about the situation of utterance. (By pragmatics, I mean the study of relations between language and its contexts of use.) The nuclear vocabulary can be used by anyone, to anyone, at any time, to speak or write about anything.

A second general observation is that nuclear words are known by all normal, adult native speakers. This is a first requirement, a *sine qua non*. No user of English knows its whole vocabulary. A large unabbreviated general dictionary such as the *OED* contains half a million entries, many of them unknown to most speakers. This gives us, in effect, a rough distinction between everyday and specialist words, and therefore concerns field of discourse. Words are not nuclear because they are known to all speakers. They are known to all speakers because they are nuclear: because, for example, they are pragmatically neutral and occur in a wide range of contexts. More precisely, we have to say that nuclear words are known in a particular sense. For example, speakers may know the word *frog* in its everyday sense of "small reptile", but few will know its specialist sense of "recess in a brick to save weight".

For ease of discussion, I will generally refer below simply to words, but what is really at issue is nuclear lexemes.[1] A more detailed discussion would distinguish systematically between word forms and lexemes; words and lexical items (phrasal verbs are a major complication here); and between different senses of homonyms. Different meanings of word forms will be left almost entirely out of account (except in test 10 below). This last point is a serious lacuna, since it begs the question of what it means to 'know' a word. Probably most words are known by most people in only some of their meanings. Are we, however, talking about active use or passive recognition? These points also have important developmental implications. Nevertheless, they will have to be left for a more detailed discussion elsewhere, and I will assume here that it is possible simply to recognize the central or 'normal' meaning of a word.

Here, then, is a series of tests that elaborate these general points.

Pragmatic neutrality of nuclear vocabulary

1 Nuclear words have a purely conceptual, cognitive, logical or propositional meaning, with no necessary attitudinal, emotional or evaluative connotations. For example, to call someone *thin* could be good or bad. Consider:

  a She is lovely and thin. She is horribly thin.

On the other hand, part of the meaning of *svelte* is "elegant", and the word implies a positive value judgement. This test is also an indication that nuclear words are less specialized in meaning and that they can occur in a wider range of contexts and collocations (cf. test 9). This does not deny that words may have idiosyncratic connotations for individual speakers, and that they may be used with such connotations in context. However, they may be used without such connotations, and therefore be pragmatically neutral: they need not convey any information about the speaker's attitude to the referent.

2   Nuclear words are culture-free. This criterion is a development of points made above about the geographical neutrality of nuclear vocabulary. In any language variety, it is lexis which reflects culture, whereas phonology and grammar do not. For obvious reasons, languages have specialized vocabularies for local flora and fauna, and the like. Again, for obvious reasons, when words are borrowed from one language into another, it is very often words that relate to new cultural artefacts, trading products, religious, cultural and artistic customs: consider the French words in English which are connected with cuisine, and the Italian musical terms. On the other hand, it is rare, but not unknown, to borrow words for the universals of human experience, including basic bodily and biological functions, natural physical phenomena, dimensions of size and shape, words for pronouns.

Arguably, words such as *sleep, eat, sun, earth, big, round* are culture-free in the sense intended. However, an attempt to set up a variety of a language which is 'as culture-free as calculus, with no literary, aesthetic or emotional aspirations' (Quirk 1981: 43) may be exaggerated, if carried too far. The criterion probably has to be relaxed to admit words that are culture-free relative to some geographical or cultural area (such as Western Europe or the UK and North America). This would admit such words as *aeroplane, upstairs, shop, school,* even though there are obviously many areas of the world that have no need of such words in everyday life.

Dixon (1973) points out that nuclear verbs such as *give* have no cultural associations, and are typically easy to translate between languages. Non-nuclear *donate* and *award* have complex selectional restrictions, which depend on cultural institutions. For example, one can donate only to a deserving cause and with no expectation of anything in return. Such non-nuclear verbs are typically difficult or impossible to translate directly.

3   Nuclear words are also pragmatically neutral in that they give no indication of the field of discourse from which a text is taken. For example, if we come across the words *port* and *starboard*, we know that the general context has something to do with ships or aircraft: the words *left* and *right* have almost the same logical meaning, but are not restricted in this way at all. The most obvious distinction here is between specialist and everyday terms. Thus for parts of the body, we find pairs such as:

b   brain, cerebellum; shin bone, tibia; skin, epidermis; stomach, abdomen; teeth, dentition.

Admitting that the technical term is often more precise in meaning, and that there are rarely, if ever, true total synonyms, both members of each pair convey the same logical meaning: they differ in the additional meaning they convey about the social setting of the language used.

4 Nuclear words are also neutral with respect to tenor of discourse: they are not restricted either to formal, or to casual or slang usage. This implies that nuclear words are also neutral with respect to mode of discourse, since written language is, on average, more formal than spoken. For example, alongside nuclear *help*, we have colloquial *give a hand*, and more formal *come to the aid of* and *render assistance*. Alongside *drunk*, we have formal *intoxicated* and *inebriated*, and a very large number of colloquial words, including *pissed*, *smashed*, *sozzled*. The last is also non-nuclear on the grounds that it is out of date: that is, it belongs to an earlier temporal dialect. Taboo subjects such as death and insanity attract a very large number of approximate synonyms. Thus alongside nuclear *mad*, we have formal *insane*, and many colloquial words: *crackers*, *nuts*, *loony*, and so on. *Mad* also has much wider meanings (cf. also test 10).

5 Nuclear words are used in preference to non-nuclear words in summarizing original texts. This is a statement about the use of vocabulary for different purposes. For example, I performed the following experiment (reported fully in chapter 7). I gave copies of Hemingway's short story 'Cat in the Rain' to a hundred people, and asked them to summarize the story in their own words. A cat is an important character in the story and different words for "cat" appear with the following frequencies: *cat*, 13; *kitty*, 6; *tortoise-shell*, 1; *gatto*, 1 (Italian for "cat": the story takes place in Italy). Despite the fact that *kitty* is common in the original story, and that the story lays considerable stress on the fact that it is a small cat, which a woman wants to hold and stroke, informants overwhelmingly preferred the word *cat* in their summaries. Nor did they introduce other non-nuclear words such as *kitten*, *pussy*, *moggy*, *feline*. This characteristic of nuclear words presumably reflects the fact that speakers intend summaries to represent propositional content, but not the style and attitudes of the original author (cf. test 1).

Syntactic and semantic relations between nuclear words

Tests 1–5 are concerned with the relation between words and social context. The next series of tests, 6–11, involve syntactic and semantic relations between words: the essential notion underlying them is that nuclear words are generic rather than specific. Note therefore that these two series of tests point to two rather different senses in which vocabulary may be 'basic' or 'simple'. The pragmatic neutrality tests above concern, roughly, the notion of everyday, non-technical words. The tests that follow concern the notion that words may be 'basic' in the sense that they could be used to define a greater proportion of the vocabulary, and could therefore be useful in constructing an elegant and systematic semantic description of a language (Lyons 1981: 65). There is no logical reason why such generic terms should be everyday words: in fact, many are clearly not (for example, *mammal*, *substance*, *state*, *event*). However, the extent to which the same words are defined by both series of tests is an empirical question (cf. further below). Bearing in mind these points, I will now outline the next six tests.

6 Nuclear words tend to be superordinate rather than hyponyms. More accurately, they are not the most specific hyponyms. Hyponymy or class inclusion is a basic sense relation. A rose is a kind of flower: if something is a rose, then this logically entails that it is a flower; but not all flowers are roses: the reverse entailment does not hold. The concept seems most obviously applicable to nouns that denote classes of objects, but it applies also to adjectives (*scarlet* is a hyponym of *red*), and to verbs. Consider the words *kill, execute, murder, assassinate*. If A assassinates B, then this entails that A murders B, and this in turn entails that A kills B. But the reverse entailments do not hold. A might kill B by accident, and this does not count as murder. *Execute* is similarly more restricted in meaning than *kill*. This test is discussed by Mackey and Savard (1967).

7 Since nuclear words are generic, it follows that nuclear words can substitute for non-nuclear, but not vice versa. The examples with *kill* above may be reconsidered from this point of view. Similarly, *give* can be substituted for any of the italicized verbs in the following examples:

c I *donated* money to the hospital.
d I *awarded* him the medal. (Cf. gave him it for services rendered.)
e I *lent* him the car. (Cf. gave him it for a short period.)

Conversely, the non-nuclear *donate, award, lend* cannot occur in sentences such as:

f I gave him a book for Christmas.
g I gave him a lift.

The above examples are adapted from Dixon (1973), who argues further that nuclear verbs have all the syntactic and semantic properties of non-nuclear verbs, but not vice versa. Consider:

h I gave it to him. I gave it him. I gave him it.
   I donated it to him. *I donated it him.
   *I donated him it.

Mackey and Savard (1967) propose that it is possible to calculate the replacement value of a word by using a dictionary of synonyms or a thesaurus. We would find, for example, that *seat* can replace more words than *chair*.

8 It follows from test 7 that nuclear words (which are known to everyone) are used to define non-nuclear words, but the reverse is difficult or impossible. The following types of definition are typical:

non-nuclear verb = nuclear verb + adverb
chuckle = laugh softly

non-nuclear noun = adjective + nuclear noun
drudgery = tedious work

non-nuclear adjective = adverb + nuclear adjective
svelte = elegantly thin

This is yet another way of saying that the meaning of nuclear words is more general and less specialized than non-nuclear words. Versions of this test are discussed by Dixon (1971), Hale (1971) and Carter (1982a). Mackey and Savard (1967) propose further that the defining power of a word can be measured by calculating how often it is used in the definitions in a chosen dictionary. For example, *young* would be useful in defining *calf, lamb, puppy* and many other words. Ogden's (1930) dictionary of *Basic English* is constructed in just such a way, by using a self-imposed restricted vocabulary of 850 words to define, and therefore replace, other words. Less radically, the definitions in the *Longman's Dictionary of Contemporary English* are written in a 'controlled vocabulary of approximately 2,000 words'. A study such as Mackey and Savard propose could to some extent be circular, since the Longman editors selected their controlled vocabulary from published frequency and pedagogical lists. Nevertheless, even a study of the Longman dictionary would show which words it is possible to use for such a purpose: some selections would not have worked.

9   Words vary enormously with respect to the freedom with which they can combine syntagmatically with other words, and this provides another test. Nuclear words have a wide collocational range. Collocation refers to the relation between a word and its co-text. For example, *good* can collocate with almost almost any noun. In some contexts, it is a near synonym for *mild* (*good/mild weather*). *Mild* and *lukewarm* are almost exact conceptual synonyms, but they have very narrow and very different collocational possibilities:

i   mild weather; *mild liquid; ?mild reception; *lukewarm weather; lukewarm liquid; lukewarm reception.

In the following examples, based on Carter (1982a), a plus indicates a possible collocation, and a blank indicates an impossible collocation and therefore an ill-formed string:

	man	baby	belly	animal	lie	paycheque
fat	+	+	+	+	+	+
stout	+		+			
obese	+		?			

Fat is shown to be nuclear on the basis of its wider collocations. Rudzka, Channell and Putseys (1981) give a large number of observations on such collocations for English.

This test is a consequence of the pragmatic neutrality criterion (no restriction on diatypic occurrence), and of the generic criterion (wide uses). It leads directly to the next test.

10 Since nuclear words are generic, it follows that they have the property of extension: the power to create new meanings (Mackey and Savard 1967). It is commonly observed that everyday words have wide general meanings, and are consequently often more difficult to define than specialist words. A simple measure of extension is the number of dictionary entries which a word (lexeme) has for related, but different senses. This obviously depends on the unexplicated intuition of the lexicographer, but the figures are usually striking enough. The following figures are from the *Collins English Dictionary* (Hanks, ed. 1979), which groups together related senses of a lexeme, irrespective of part of speech:

run 83, sprint 3;
walk 24, saunter 3, stroll 3;
strong 20, potent 5, powerful 4;
give 29, award 4, donate 1;
fat 19, stout 5, obese 1;
kill 19, murder 8, execute 8, assassinate 2;
thin 9, slim 3, svelte 2, emaciated 1;
house 28, mansion 5, villa 3, bungalow 2;
father 14, paternal 3;
child 9, kid 5, paediatrics 1.

The following words all have relatively high figures and are therefore candidates for the nuclear vocabulary:

blind 31, block 39, key 31, pair 14, raise 34, stop 39, time 60.

11 A final measure of the nuclearity of a word is the number of compound lexical items it can help form. Again (as proposed by Mackey and Savard 1967), this can be studied in published dictionaries. For example, *Collins* lists about 150 combinations starting with *well*, and 32 for *run* (e.g. *runabout*, *runner*, *run-of-the-mill* and phrasal verbs such as *run up* (*debts*)).

The structure of the nuclear vocabulary

A third and final characteristic of nuclear vocabulary is that it is not simply an unstructured list of words, but a unified whole. This can probably best be tested by experimental methods. In general, the structure of semantic relations between words can be studied by word-association tests. It is well known that, especially for common, unemotive words (cf. test 1), people's responses to stimulus words are not original, but follow predictable paths. English has particularly high levels of associational stereotypy. (Meara 1980 discusses such data in the context of foreign language vocabulary acquisition.) The following test is one reflex of this general claim.

12   Nuclear words have obvious antonyms. For example, in elicitation experiments, *good* will predictably elicit the antonym *bad*; similarly, *fat, thin*; *clean, dirty*; etc. On the other hand, responses will be much less predictable with *excellent, obese, spotless*. This criterion amounts to the claim that nuclear words are more tightly integrated into the structural organization of the vocabulary.

Tests 7-12 above show that the nuclear vocabulary is self-contained and communicatively adequate for some purposes, in so far as nuclear words can substitute in different ways for non-nuclear words. These tests also show that the general structuralist notion of the vocabulary of a language as a single, integrated, coherent system is not entirely adequate. The nuclear vocabulary is more tightly integrated than the rest. This is perhaps the main theoretical point of the argument of this chapter. Lyons's (1968, 1977) concept of sense relations has been criticized as applying only to the type of carefully chosen examples that he discusses, and not to the language as a whole. (Sense relations are purely internal linguistic relations between words, such as synonymy, antonymy and hyponymy.) But this criticism can be turned on its head: taken together, sense relations define nuclear vocabulary. This point also has important psycholinguistic implications for the mental organization of the lexicon, and this could provide an interesting topic for research.

Nuclear words: other tests

There are other tests for nuclearity which I will mention much more briefly. For example, there is a broad split in English vocabulary between words of Germanic and Romance origin: this has many reflexes in field, tenor and mode of discourse. For well-known historical reasons, much of the vocabulary of the law, religion and government is Romance. But the split is much more widespread than that, as is seen in pairs such as the following, with the nuclear Germanic word first in each case:

j   strong, potent; mother, maternal; teach, instruct; sheep, mutton.

There is a related tendency for nuclear words to be simple rather than compound. Consider:

k   thin, undersized; strong, powerful; work, drudgery.

Finally, for a well-defined semantic field, Berlin and Kay (1969) have given a careful set of definitions for what they call basic colour terms; these definitions are intended to be universal, although I will illustrate them here only from English. A basic colour term: (a) must be monolexemic (*blue* not *bluish*); (b) must not be a hyponym (*red* not *scarlet*); (c) must not be restricted to one class of objects (not *blond*); (d) must be psychologically salient and stable in meaning in all idiolects; (e) must have the same distribution as other basic terms (*reddish, greenish, *chartreusish*); (f) is suspect if it is also the name of an object (not *gold, rose, claret*); (g) is suspect if it is a recent loan (not *beige*). Several of these specific tests are obviously related to the more general tests I have given above.

Frequency, range and evenness of distribution

It may seem odd that I have not used frequency at all as a criterion of nuclearity. This is because raw frequency will clearly not do on its own, and it is best to discuss other criteria and then to interpret frequency in relation to these. First, frequency and related statistics are an empirical consequence of nuclearity, not a test for it, as such, although some frequency statistics can be used to identify nuclear words. Second, as Mackey and Savard (1967) have shown, indices of usefulness correlate only weakly with frequency. By usefulness, they have in mind such indices as use in definitions (cf. test 8), genericness (cf. test 6), extension (cf. test 10), and combination (cf. test 11). Third, frequency counts go out of date rather quickly (some words are prone to fashion); and they can differ significantly for British and American English, and for adults' and children's language.

The best known word lists for pedagogic purposes are 'general' in the sense that they are not designed for any particular subject, topic, purpose or diatype. This reveals a serious limitation on such lists: for any purpose, students must know all of the first few hundred items on a general frequency list; but after that there seems little to choose between the next item and an item a few hundred or a thousand ranks down. The dilemma appears in a sharp form, if one considers text coverage. The word *the* accounts for about 7 per cent of an average English text. The 100 most frequent words in the language account for about 50 per cent of an average text. The 1,000 most frequent words account for about 70-75 per cent. The curve of text coverage is clearly flattening off quickly, and the next 1,000 and the 1,000 after that give little extra in terms of text coverage: around 7 and 3 per cent respectively. It is clear what is happening in general. A few words are very frequent; most words are relatively infrequent; and some words are vanishingly rare, and are unlikely to occur more than once or twice in a corpus of millions of words. Many basic lexical statistics have been calculated for corpora such as the London-Lund corpus of about half a million words of spoken British English, and the Brown University and Lancaster-Oslo-Bergen (LOB) corpora of about one million words of written English, American and British respectively.

Of the 100 most frequent words in English (as calculated, for example, for the Lund, Brown and LOB corpora: see Svartvik et al. 1982), most are grammatical words.[2] The lexical words in the first 100 of the Lund corpus are: *know, got, see, now, just, mean, right, get, really, people, time, say, thing*. Presumably one would want to include all such words in a list of nuclear words. This provides in any case a way of including grammatical words, many of which do not get identified on the tests above. And presumably there would be little disagreement on the next 300 or 400 words. After that, however, raw frequency of occurrence is of limited direct interest.

There are, however, two related statistics which are very easy to calculate, especially with computational techniques. The first is *range*: the number of different texts in which a word occurs, if only once. The second is *evenness of distribution*: that is, the fact that a word occurs with significant and relatively even frequency in a wide range of texts. In combination, these two calculations provide statistical measures of pragmatic neutrality, since they show whether a word is restricted to particular diatypic uses.

It should be clear that I am not claiming that the set of nuclear words is entirely clear-cut. A typical situation in linguistics is that a class of words (for example, nouns or grammatical words) is defined by a series of tests: some words pass all or most of the tests and are the clear, central or focal members of the class. Other words are more or less central. (See Comrie 1981: 100, for a sensible discussion of such multi-factor definitions which are stated in terms of prototypes, rather than in terms of necessary and sufficient conditions; and Rosch 1975 for psycholinguistic discussion of the concept of lexical and conceptual prototypes.)

Some educational implications

This chapter has been concerned with some of the principles underlying the organization of the vocabulary. I have mentioned only in passing data on children's language development and pedagogical issues of how vocabulary should be taught. I have, however, discussed an issue which appears to give considerable problems to educationalists. It is obvious that the vocabulary of English is very large, and that selections have to be made from it for many educational purposes. It is generally accepted that the vocabulary known by individual speakers is related to their educational skills: it is widely agreed (Jenkins and Dixon 1983) that there is a significant correlation between vocabulary size and both reading comprehension and overall verbal intelligence (although there is no real agreement at all on whether vocabulary influences IQ and reading comprehension, or vice versa, or whether the relation is indirect). There are, however, major uncertainties about how or whether to try and teach vocabulary, and one major problem is: where to start? This chapter has attempted to provide some principles that are directly relevant to this question.

I have discussed the question: how can we talk systematically about the dimensions of diversity along which lexical competence can develop, with or without instruction? Many ideas for teaching materials do, however, follow in fairly obvious ways from the criteria for nuclear vocabulary: the tests specify, in effect, dimensions along which vocabulary can be extended. As Meara (1980) points out, the type of argument I have put forward is concerned with the management of learning, not with learning itself. In this chapter, I define a set of words which will in normal circumstances be known already by native speakers, and suggest ways of structuring learning and teaching so that this vocabulary can be extended in principled ways.

In addition, these definitions can also be used to help assess the linguistic difficulty of texts for use in schools, or to help simplify existing texts for various purposes (for example, language teaching, making bureaucratic documents more readable). There are many so-called readability formulae for calculating the difficulty of texts, and they generally operate on word and/or sentence length, variously calculated. Such formulae have their place, but they are open to well-known problems (cf. Harrison 1980; Perera 1980), since ease of comprehension depends also on features of syntactic structure, discourse organization and subject matter (Perera 1984). Familiarity of the vocabulary is also a major factor. It has been widely recognized since the nineteenth century that vocabulary is the single best predictor of text difficulty. The relationship is not a direct causal one. However, word length and frequency correlate: long words tend to be less frequent and also tend to be technical or abstract. Although there are legitimate purposes for simplifying texts by controlling their vocabulary, I am not, of course, recommending that textbooks ought to be written in nuclear English: it seems best to state that explicitly.

Directions for research on language development

Despite hundreds of years of interest in basic vocabulary and many relevant studies of child language in recent years, there is still very little research concerned directly with the developmental and educational implications of nuclear vocabulary. In particular, there is a lack of research that is based directly on speakers' actual usage of lexical items in conversations with children. I will therefore conclude with some specific suggestions for textual and observational research.

First, the definitions of nuclear vocabulary that I have proposed require to be developed. The following steps define, in themselves, a substantial research project. A candidate list of nuclear words (lexemes) can be provisionally established by including (a) the 500 or so most frequent words in English, and (b) words in a chosen dictionary with a large number of distinct listed senses, say six or more (cf. test 10 above), and/or a large number of listed combinations (cf. test 11). Check all the words on this candidate list against all the tests above. This in itself will doubtless lead to a more precise formulation of some of the tests. Check if there are any words which are, on intuitive grounds, nuclear, but which have not been captured: for example, check the next 5,000 words on frequency counts for English; check published lists of 'basic' vocabulary. It is intuitively plausible that there will be a correlation between the results of the various tests. Check if this is so. Rank order the words on the list according to how many tests they pass: i.e. from most to least nuclear. Collect experimental data on those tests where this is appropriate: for example, on the antonymy test. Investigate more generally the word associations between words on the list. Check the list against a corpus which contains as wide a diatypic range as possible: for example, there is a prediction that the nuclear words occur in a wide range of texts at least once, and in addition are evenly distributed across different samples. This can be checked easily by computational methods. Take texts that are intended to be written in a reduced vocabulary: for example, texts for beginning readers or for English as a foreign language. Calculate measures of richness of vocabulary. For example, in a type : token ratio of the form $1 : n$, one would expect n to be relatively high.[3] Similarly, one would expect the number of hapaxes (words which occur only once) to be low. Assuming that such texts do, as predicted, have relatively 'poor' vocabulary, check whether they have correspondingly high percentages of nuclear vocabulary. Take published lists of 'basic' vocabulary: test their adequacy against the now considerably revised definitions of nuclear vocabulary.

A research programme along these lines and the resulting list and associated detailed specifications of the words would have many applications in studies of children's language development, in teaching English as a mother tongue and as a foreign language, in studies of readability, and in the design of dictionaries.

Given a well-tested list of nuclear vocabulary of this kind, many developmental questions, such as the following, are then also open to investigation. It is plausible that children acquire nuclear words first and most rapidly: is this the case? Do adults use mainly nuclear words in talking to children? This would require a study of the spontaneous speech of parents and teachers to children of different ages in different situations. How and when do children acquire non-nuclear vocabulary? How much is acquired through reading? Is the acquisition of non-nuclear vocabulary related to other developmental variables? Is it, for example, a predictor of any other measures of educational success?

Finally, it is intuitively highly plausible that nuclear vocabulary is a universal: that is, for any language, native speakers will always feel that some words are more important and basic than others. Most of the tests proposed above are applicable to any language, and comparative research is therefore a possibility.

NOTES

1 The ambiguity of the term *word* is evident in the following uses. Suppose I say 'This short story contains a thousand *words*', then I am referring to *word forms*: in this case orthographic word forms, that is, strings of letters between spaces. A speech might similarly contain a thousand phonological word forms. For some purposes we might want to say that *I'll* or *don't* are one word form each, although they consist of two words each in another sense. Suppose I say 'This dictionary contains fifty thousand *words*', then I am clearly not referring to word forms. Word forms in a text might include: *am, is, are, was, being*, etc. These are forms of the *lexeme* BE. We would not expect to find the separate word forms listed in a dictionary, but only the lexeme. Similarly, a dictionary would not list the forms *boy* and *boys* separately,

but only the lexeme BOY. It follows that lexemes are abstract underlying categories.

I might also wish to say that although an idiom such as *paint the town red* contains four words, it is nevertheless a unit. The term *lexical item* can be used in a neutral way to cover both such units and also single words.

2 Lexical words are nouns, main verbs, adjectives and adverbs. Grammatical words are anything else: pronouns, conjunctions, articles, prepositions, auxiliary and modal verbs. There are many tests to distinguish these two classes, but very briefly it can be stated that lexical words comprise large open sets with hundreds or thousands of members in common use, whereas grammatical words comprise small closed classes with only a few (less than around 20) items in common use.

3 In a story of 1,000 words, it is highly unlikely that there would be 1,000 different words. Words such as *a* and *the* would be likely to occur frequently. That is, there might be 50 tokens of the type *the*.

FURTHER READING

Harrison, C. (1980) *Readability in the Classroom*. London: Cambridge University Press.

ACKNOWLEDGEMENTS

This chapter is a revised version of an article first published in Kevin Durkin (ed.), *Language Development in the School Years*, London: Croom Helm, in press.

I am grateful to: Ron Carter, for getting me interested in the topic of this article, and for several points on defining nuclear vocabulary (see Carter, 1982a); Kevin Durkin, for detailed comments on previous drafts and several references; Joanna Channell, Walter Grauberg and Gabi Keck for helpful discussion and comments on previous drafts.

7

Stir until the plot thickens

Introduction

This chapter gives detailed suggestions for studying literary texts in class-rooms in ways that could fit into the English syllabus proposed in chapter 4. The chapter is theoretical in so far as it draws on recent work in linguistics. However, the aim is to show that practice and theory must be closely related. The chapter proposes entirely practical ideas for the classroom, but they are nevertheless firmly rooted in theory. I try to show that it is possible to study a literary text via activities, by giving children things they can actually *do* with the text. This means that criticism and creativity are not separated. Such a separation is apparent in much of the anti-intellectual and anti-analytic tradition in literary criticism. The chapter also provides ways of talking about the formal organization of texts. For historical and social reasons (to do with the history of linguistics, early and abortive attempts of linguistics to influence literary criticism and school teaching, and the separation of 'language' and 'literature' in many school and university courses), the formalist argument is often badly misunderstood. Briefly, pupils must learn to analyse forms, if they are to understand not just the overt content of texts (literary and non-literary), but also how messages are produced and conveyed. Forms also convey meanings.

The following book review appeared in the American magazine *Field and Stream*:[1]

> Although written many years ago, *Lady Chatterley's Lover* has just been reissued . . . and this fictionalized account of the day-to-day life of an English gamekeeper is still of considerable interest to outdoor-minded readers. Unfortunately one is obliged to wade through many pages of extraneous material in order to discover and savour these sidelights on the management of a Midlands shooting estate, and in this reviewer's opinion the book cannot take the place of J. R. Miller's *Practical Gamekeeper*.

Many comments spring to mind: not least the basic principle that the meaning of a text does not just sit 'in' the text waiting to be taken out by readers; but that readers actively construct the meaning in the light of their background interests and expectations. Nevertheless, there are limits on readers' freedom to do this, and the humour of the review (whether intended or not) is of course that it does not provide a satisfactory account of the content of Lawrence's book. It does not provide anything like a fair summary of the plot.

A method for investigating narrative structure

This chapter is about ways of studying the organization of stories or narratives; that is, ways of investigating the narrative structure of short stories, novels and so on, especially ways of investigating the concept of the *plot* of a story.

There are no well-developed methods for analysing narrative structure. I do not mean that no work at all has been done on analysing narratives, but that there is little consensus on how one might go about the analysis: no firm agreement even on what the *units* of a narrative might be. This chapter is primarily concerned with developing a *method* for doing such analyses and for working out the organization or plot of narratives. The chapter is therefore primarily methodological or procedural: hence the title – stir until the plot thickens. We require recipes for making good plot summaries. And we also want to be able to specify ways to spoil the broth: that is, we want to be able to predict what will be regarded as deviant or poor plot summaries.

The argument should be of interest at several different levels. At the most obvious level, it provides a close analysis of a particular literary text, a short story by Hemingway, and an interpretation of this text. It should also be of more general interest to literary critics, since it provides a way of discussing certain kinds of ambiguity in texts, and a way of discussing what is and is not crucial to the interpretation of narratives.

The argument should also be of interest to linguists, since ways of describing the semantic structure of texts are poorly understood, although they are of great importance to our understanding of how language is used.

It should also be of interest to teachers, since a common activity in much teaching or examining requires students to make summaries of different kinds of material. I will make some apparently abstruse points about semantics and the propositional structure of texts. But, if you stay with me, I will then try to show that these points are, after all, not as abstruse as they seem, and can illuminate some very common features of everyday story-telling - not to mention telling lies! Finally, I will provide a list of practical suggestions for English-language work in classrooms, which follow directly from the main argument. And I will show briefly how such activities can fit within a syllabus for teaching modern English language (see chapter 4).

Literary competence

The basic argument is as follows. Competent readers of stories are able to identify the plot, distinguish the plot from background information, summarize the story, discuss the adequacy of such summaries, decide whether two summaries are equivalent, identify borderline cases, and so on. This ability is part of our literary competence, and the organization of plots or narrative structure must therefore, in principle, be analysable. (This argument is put forward by Culler 1975: 205.)

What we require therefore is a way of collecting evidence about this competence. The procedure which I adopted was as follows. I gave readers copies of a short story by Hemingway (1925b) of around 1,000 words, 'Cat in the Rain', with instructions to make two summaries of the plot of the story. The informants were schoolteachers and university students and lecturers, that is, readers who could be expected to have the kind of competence which I wished to investigate. There would have been little point, at least initially, in giving the task, for example, to school pupils or foreign learners, who might simply not have had the literary ability which I wanted to investigate. The exact instructions were:

Read the story and summarize the plot. The summaries must be accurate - that is, other people should be willing to accept your summary as a fair summary. Make two summaries, one of less than 60 words and one of less than 25 words.

Note the following points about these instructions. First, the instructions are vague, but deliberately so, since the aim is to investigate informants' understanding of plots. More precise instructions, including, for example, some definition of *plot*, could have imposed my preconceived ideas on informants. Despite this vagueness, however, almost no one questions the instructions: they appear to be entirely meaningful and precise to informants. They also appear to be interpreted in an almost identical fashion by informants, since the summaries which are produced are all very similar.

What appears to happen is therefore as follows. People respond to the ill-defined instructions in well-defined ways, and produce summaries. These summaries are people's models of the original story: simplified representations, idealizations which pick out certain essential points and ignore others. They are the products of interpretations of the story. Clearly there is no way of observing the process of interpretation itself: you cannot look inside people's heads. But at least the products can give data for making inferences about the interpretation: especially if informants' summaries are all very similar, and therefore presumably the products of similar interpretative processes.

One reason for eliciting summaries was simply that it generates ideas. The summaries can be compared with the original to see which points are retained and essential in some way, and which points are regularly omitted. The shorter and longer summaries can be compared with each other in the same way. It can be seen whether any points are included in all or most summaries. And on this basis, it might be possible to construct an ideal, or at least a consensus summary: a model of the main features of informants' models. Comparative analysis is always a good way of producing ideas.

The complete text of 'Cat in the Rain' is easily accessible and published in several places. (See Hemingway, 1925b.) It tells a superficially straightforward story of an American couple staying at a hotel in Italy. They are introduced in the first sentence of the story:

There were only two Americans stopping at the hotel.

The wife looks out of the window of their hotel room, and sees a cat sheltering from the rain under a table. She goes down to get the cat: the 'poor kitty' as she keeps referring to it throughout the rest of the story. On her way out, she passes the hotel-keeper, a dignified old man, for whom she feels a great liking. The maid accompanies her outside with an umbrella. They look for the cat, but it has gone. Back in the hotel room, the wife complains to her husband:

'I wanted it so much,' she said. 'I don't know why I wanted it so much. I wanted that poor kitty.'

She goes on to complain that she is tired of the way she looks, of her clothes, and of her way of life in general. The story ends as follows:

George was not listening. He was reading his book. His wife looked out of the window where the light had come on in the square.
Someone knocked at the door.
'Avanti,' George said. He looked up from his book.
In the doorway stood the maid. She held a big tortoise-shell cat pressed tight against her and swung down against her body.
'Excuse me,' she said, 'the padrone asked me to bring this for the Signora.'[2]

Here are four samples of shorter and longer summaries collected from informants.

a A woman sees a cat in the rain and tries unsuccessfully to bring it indoors. But the owner of her hotel later sends her one.
b A woman, ignored by her husband, goes to search for someone to love. Her need is sensed, but not fully understood, by a foreign admirer.
c An American and his wife are in a hotel and it is raining hard. Outside there is a cat crouched under a table. The wife sees it and goes to rescue it, but it disappears. She returns to the room. She says she wants a cat.

The maid knocks on the door holding one, a present from the hotel-keeper.

d An American couple are staying at a hotel in Italy. The wife observes a cat outside, in the rain. She wants the cat. The hotel-keeper is interested and offers a maid and an umbrella. But the cat has gone. On her return she becomes distressed and longs for the cat. The maid then brings the cat.

Propositions in stories

Consider the following example. Many of the summaries were committed to the truth of one or both of the following propositions. (Propositions will be enclosed in double quotes, to distinguish them from sentences.)

1 "The couple are American."
2 "The hotel is in Italy."

The term *proposition* will be defined more carefully below. But for the moment we can say that a summary is committed to the truth of (1) if it includes phrases such as

3 The American couple.
4 An American and his wife.

Similarly a summary is committed to (2) if it includes phrases such as

5 An Italian hotel.
6 The couple are in Italy . . . in a hotel.

Consider first just two possibilities: that propositions (1) and/or (2) are conveyed; or that (1) and/or (2) are omitted, and that no position is therefore taken on their truth-value. The distribution of the two propositions was found in a hundred summaries of 60 and 25 words (see table 2).

Table 2 Distribution of two propositions

	60 words		25 words	
	Included	*Omitted*	*Included*	*Omitted*
1 "The couple are American."	95	5	48	52
2 "The hotel is in Italy."	80	20	13	87

According to these figures, the fact that the couple are American appears to be seen as more important than the fact that the hotel is in Italy. Proposition

(2) is frequently conveyed by the longer summaries, but it is one of the propositions to be regularly dropped in the shorter summaries. Proposition (1), however, is conveyed by almost all the longer summaries, and still by around half of the shorter summaries.

On reflection, the fact that the couple are American might not seem essential to the plot. It might be seen as central to the *theme* of the story (for example, the theme of marital discontent), to the atmosphere of a typical Hemingway story, and so on. But the fact makes no difference at all to the development of the narrative, in the sense that nothing in the action hinges on it. A proposition such as

7 "The woman sees a cat."

is, however, central to the plot: without it, there would be no story at all. However, the point is that the informants *did* systematically include proposition (1), and we are concerned with collecting data on what *they* regarded as being essential or peripheral.

Note one complicating factor here. The summaries were constructed according to a word-count limit. But it takes just as many words to say, for example, *a man and his wife* as to say *an American and his wife*. And several informants reported this as a factor in their choice of information to be included: if it is possible to include more information in the same number of words, then do so. Note that phrases such as *a couple* or *two Americans* are shorter than *an American and his wife*, but they are also ambiguous: the fact that they are husband and wife is crucial to the story - at least, as we have noted, to the theme, if not strictly to the plot.

So the ingenuity involved in having to produce short summaries may distort their value as evidence of informants' literary competence. But the proposition about the couple being American is arguably more important than simply being an artefact of the artificial word-limit. It is, for example, stated in the opening sentence of the story. In addition, this opening sentence has a particular grammatical form which will be fully discussed below.

The concepts of plot and summary

Consider a few general points about the concepts of a summary and of a plot. First, a summary of a literary work of fiction (such as a novel, short story, play or poem) is not the same kind of object as a summary of a non-literary work (such as a textbook, academic article or factual newspaper article). The relationship between the summary and the original is different in each case. A summary of a poem is no longer a poem, and a summary of *Hamlet* is no longer *Hamlet*. The difference between a play and a summary of it probably accounts for the vaguely humorous quality of Lamb's *Tales from Shakespeare* (Lamb and Lamb 1822), in which Lamb tells the story of the plays. Or consider Tom Stoppard's play *Dogg's Hamlet* (1980), which presents two versions of *Hamlet*, as performed by a cast of schoolboys: a 'fifteen-minute *Hamlet*', followed by an Encore where the original is reduced to a hilarious two pages of text performed at breakneck speed. These versions are not intended to be either summaries or performances of *Hamlet*. However, a summary of the main points of an argument in a textbook *is* still an argument. Or an abstract at the beginning of an article in an academic journal *is* the same kind of object as the original article.

Second, therefore, a summary of the plot of a work of imaginative literature may well have a surface or trivial character. It is intuitively clear that Hemingway's story is not 'about' a woman fetching a cat out of the rain, although this is what the summaries report. This point is made by Lodge (1978):

> although *Cat in the Rain* is a narrative, and perfectly coherent and intelligible as such, the narrative structure itself does not satisfy the reader's quest for meaning. This can be demonstrated by trying to make shorter and shorter summaries of the story. By the time you pare it down to, say twenty-five words, you will find that in trying to preserve what is essential to the narrative – the quest for the cat, the disappointment, the reversal – you have had to discard what seems most essential to the meaning of the text as a whole. . . . The action of *Cat in the Rain*, trivial in itself, brings into focus a rift or disorder in the relationship between husband and wife.

This is not to say that some works of imaginative fiction do not comprise something approaching pure plot. Certain kinds of folk tale and certain kinds of detective story may approach this. And this may be one reason why certain kinds of folk tale and myth have seemed particularly amenable to structuralist analysis. But the point shows immediately that the kind of analysis proposed in this chapter does not exhaust the literary possibilities of the text. This is rather obvious, but it is worth stating explicitly, since it is sometimes thought that linguists claim to provide complete or exhaustive analyses of the meaning of bits of language. This is, if anything, a rather crude misunderstanding, since, if a detailed linguistic analysis shows anything, it is that language is so amazingly complex that new levels of meaning can always be found in it. The whole linguistic approach, in fact, is to look for different levels of organization and meaning in language.

Third, *summary* or *plot* must be semantic concepts. This is so, because two plot summaries could be equivalent, and yet contain no sentences in common. A plot cannot therefore comprise syntactic units which consist of clauses or sentences. As I have already begun to indicate, it is probably best to regard plots as consisting of semantic units such as propositions. It is in principle conceivable that two summaries might be equivalent and yet have no words in common. Such summaries would clearly be difficult, if not impossible, to construct in practice, but equivalent propositions could in principle be constructed using synonyms for major lexical items. Thus the following two sentences have identical truth-conditions in the context of the story:

8   The American lady goes to get the cat.
9   The wife sets off to fetch the kitty.

The possibility of two summaries not sharing vocabulary becomes remote for the following interesting reason, however. Almost none of the summaries collected contained the word *kitty*, although it is common in the original story: they all preferred the word *cat*. Arguably, languages have a core vocabulary and a vocabulary of more peripheral items. Thus *cat* is a core word, whereas *kitty, pussy, feline* are non-core. Studying words used in summaries can provide one way of identifying this core vocabulary. I would predict that summaries will contain very low frequencies of non-core items, even if these occur in the original. Core vocabulary would, of course, have to be identified independently, in a different way, or the procedure would be circular. (See chapter 6 for detailed discussion.)

Note here one practical point for teachers. In making summaries, pupils are often required to make summaries 'in their own words'. But this instruction will be much easier to follow in some cases than in others.

There is one complication which I will mention here, but not discuss in detail. The ability to summarize certainly has linguistic aspects, including those I have mentioned: the ability to find lexical synonyms, and to use propositions which are logically compatible with propositions in the original text. However, it is also possible to summarize non-linguistic sequences, such as a silent film or a road accident. And formulating a summary also depends on non-linguistic understanding. For example, you cannot summarize what happened in a game of American football, unless you understood the game. Making a summary therefore involves not purely semantic knowledge, but also pragmatic knowledge.

The semantic analysis of plots

As far as this chapter is concerned, then, in discussing plots, we are dealing with semantic relationships between words, sentences and propositions. It might be easier to state some of the important relationships between two summaries, or between a summary and the original text, than to state the semantic structure of a text.

These relationships include synonymy, contradiction, presupposition and entailment. For example, suppose that two summaries convey the propositions:

10   "The hotel is in Italy."
11   "The hotel is in Greece."

Then these two summaries would be *contradictory*. That is, one cannot assert the truth of both (10) and (11). To assert the truth of one involves the denial of the other. Alternatively, a summary might simply not mention where the hotel is: such a summary would therefore be compatible with both of the first two summaries, since it has no commitment one way or another to the truth-value of (10) or (11).

Or consider another example. A proposition such as

12 "It is raining hard."

entails the proposition

13 "It is raining."

That is, we cannot assert that (12) is true, without being committed to the truth of (13). But the entailment does not hold in the opposite direction: (13) does not entail (12).

Propositions: entailments and presuppositions

We are now at a point in the argument where we require a more systematic statement of what is meant by *proposition* and by various semantic relations which might hold between sentences and propositions.[3] A proposition is part of the meaning of a sentence. More accurately, the meaning of a sentence may be represented as a set of propositions, and this set may be quite large. Each of the propositions has a truth-value: it may be true or false. Another informal way of defining a proposition is to say that it is what is expressed by a declarative sentence. But propositions are not the same as declarative sentences, since different sentences may express the same proposition. For example, in the context of the story, the two sentences

14 She goes back to the room.
15 The wife goes back to the bedroom.

both commit us to the truth of the proposition which could be expressed informally as

16 "The American woman returns to her hotel room."

That is, propositions are abstract representations of meaning, which ignore grammatical and lexical form.

Propositions may be related by entailment. Proposition A entails proposition B, if B follows logically from A. That is, if one asserts A, one is committed also to claiming the truth of B. A sentence will typically entail a large set of propositions, and some of these propositions will themselves be related by entailment. For example, the sentence

17 An American woman tries unsuccessfully to bring a cat indoors.

entails

18 "A woman tries to bring a cat indoors."

and (18) in turn entails

19 "A woman tries to bring something indoors."

There are different kinds of proposition. The *presuppositions* of the sentence are necessary preconditions for the sentence being true or false. The test for presuppositions is that they remain the same whether a sentence is positive or negative. For example, both sentences

20 The American woman found the cat.
21 The American woman did not find the cat.

presuppose

22 "The woman is American."

Presuppositions can be questioned. One might say:

23 She's not American: her husband is.

But (20) and (21) presuppose her being American. Presuppositions also remain constant if a sentence is made interrogative. So (22) is also presupposed by

24 Did the American woman find the cat?

Existential presuppositions: or how to tell jokes

One type of presupposition is an *existential presupposition*. For example, (20), (21) and (24) all presuppose:

25 "There is an American woman."
26 "There is a cat."

If an existential presupposition is not fulfilled, then the original proposition has no truth-value: the question of its being true or false does not arise. One might wish to interpret the story (although I would not) by arguing that the cat is a delusion of the wife: but the propositions of the story presuppose its existence. For example, it is semantically very odd to say

27   The American woman found (did not find) the cat, but there was no cat.

Such points may seem unnecessarily abstruse. But in fact the assertion of an existential proposition is a common and recognizable way of beginning a story or joke in everyday conversation. Consider examples such as:

28   There was a Scotsman, an Englishman and an Irishman . . .
29   There were these two literary critics and they were stranded on a desert island . . .

The opening sentence of Hemingway's story also uses this form:

30   There were only two Americans stopping at the hotel.

These facts may account for so many informants conveying the proposition "the couple are American" in their summaries, when this proposition is apparently not required for the development of events in the plot.

Coreference: one cat or two?

Finally, there is a type of proposition which concerns identity of reference at different points in a text. I am not familiar with any standard term for this, but will use the term *coreferential propositions*. For example, suppose one has two sentences in a text:

31   An American and his wife are in a hotel. The wife sees a cat.

Then one is committed to the proposition

32   "It is the American's wife who sees the cat."

That is, we are dealing with matters of coreference: it is the same wife that was mentioned before. (In order to analyse such questions fully, we would need to study the various kinds of cohesion which a connected text may display, especially relationships of anaphora. See Halliday and Hasan 1976 for a full discussion.)

Again, such points are not mere logic-chopping, for a matter of coreference is crucial to the whole point of Hemingway's story. The summaries I have collected are fairly evenly divided between three different propositions:

33   "The maid brings the same cat that the woman has seen."
34   "The maid brings a different cat."
35   "The maid brings a cat which may or may not be the same."

If we look at Hemingway's story, then the third option appears to accord with the original: although this proposition (35) is not asserted. On the other hand, the second option accords with my understanding of the story: the 'big tortoise-shell cat' which the maid brings, does not sound like the 'kitty' which the woman has gone to look for. This provides a fairly precise way of stating the ambiguity at the crux of the story: (35) is, strictly speaking accurate, but (34) seems most likely.

Entailments and implicatures: and how to tell lies

We now have another puzzle, however – and this puzzle is of central importance to the interpretation of literature – concerned with this non-literal use of language. How is it that we can understand a proposition such as (34), which is neither asserted, nor presupposed, nor entailed by what is said? There are, of course, many meanings which are conveyed by almost any use of language, but which are neither stated in so many words, nor which follow logically from what is said. So, it is quite unusual to say things such as: John implied X, but he didn't actually say as much. How is it, then, that we can convey messages which are not directly related to the linguistic content of sentences?

Note, first, a further ambiguity at the end of the story. When the maid knocks, the wife is looking out of the window, as she is also the first time that she is mentioned in the story. It is George who calls 'Avanti' and who sees the cat. It may be that we are intended to understand the description of a 'big tortoise-shell cat' as being solely his perception, and differing from his wife's perception. In any case, we do not know at the end of the story whether the wife has yet seen the cat or not, and we do not have her reaction.

Suppose, then, that we imagine questioning the wife some time later. We might say:

36 Question   Did you get the cat?
     Wife   I got a big tortoise-shell cat.

I think we would normally interpret such an answer as: "No, I didn't get the cat you are referring to", although this is not asserted in so many words. Similarly, suppose we ask:

37 Question   Did you get the little kitty?
     Wife   I got a cat.

Again, I think the normal interpretation would be: "No, I got a different cat".

Before I propose a solution to how such utterances get interpreted in this way, consider the following genuine conversational interchange:

38 A   How many chocolate biscuits have you eaten?   a
    B   Three.   b

A You've eaten the whole packet!   c
B Well, then I must have eaten three.   d

Assuming that the packet contained more than three biscuits, is (b) a lie? One definition of a lie is that it is an utterance intended to deceive. And there are many ways of using language to deceive, apart from making utterances which are literally false. The literal truth of a sentence is not sufficient for honesty, since, as we have seen, any sentence characteristically commits the speaker to a whole set of presupposed and entailed propositions. And, in addition, speakers may deceive by leaving things unsaid. Now, the proposition

39 "I have eaten a whole packet of biscuits."

clearly entails

40 "I have eaten three biscuits."

If (39) is true, then (40) is true. The reverse entailment clearly does not hold. So, (38b) is literally true. But one does not normally answer questions by stating only an entailment of the expected answer. And this begins to provide an explanation of why (38b) is misleading. We might say informally that (38b) implies

41 "B has eaten *only* three biscuits."

But (38b) does not entail (41). The implication could be cancelled, for example, if B says

42 I've eaten three biscuits - in fact, I've eaten more than three.

However, presuppositions and entailments cannot be cancelled in this way, hence the oddity of sentences such as

43 I've eaten three biscuits, but there were no biscuits.
44 I've eaten three biscuits, but I've not eaten anything.

where (43) attempts to cancel an existential presupposition ("there were some biscuits"), and (44) attempts to cancel an entailment ("I've eaten something"). These tests therefore distinguish presuppositions and entailments, on the one hand, from other kinds of propositions which may be conveyed by sentences. This distinction is drawn in a famous paper by Grice (1975). He uses the term *implicature* to refer to the type of proposition that may be cancelled, and I will use this term here to distinguish this notion from the term 'implication' which is used loosely in many different ways in everyday English.

A comparable example was provided by a recent quiz programme in the radio series *Top of the Form*. One question asked was

45 Henry VIII had two wives. True or false?

The question-master accepted the answer 'False', saying 'Correct – he had six wives'. Now, of course,

46 "Henry VIII had six wives."

entails

47 "Henry VIII had two wives."

but (47) would normally be taken to implicate

48 "Henry VIII had *only* two wives."

No confusion was caused by the question: the schoolboy answering it got the answer right, having interpreted the question in the way it was obviously intended.

Maxims of quantity

We are not yet quite there in explaining why (38b) is a lie: that is, intentionally misleading, although it is literally true. To do this we need to invoke the Maxims of Quantity which are formulated by Grice (1975: 45):

> Make your contribution as informative as is required (for the current purposes of the exchange). Do not make your contribution more informative than is required.

On any reasonable interpretation, (38a) is demanding to know the total number of biscuits eaten, and (38b) therefore deliberately violates a Maxim of Quantity. What we are concerned with here, then, is the difference between what is said and what is implicated (but not entailed); and with rather general conventions that govern the normal conduct of conversation. For example, we expect speakers to tell us what we want to know and not deliberately to mislead us.

I therefore have little sympathy with the argument put forward by the Professor of English, that he was not lying when he was stopped by a flag-seller, and said

49 I've been stopped already.

This was true, but nevertheless misleading and deliberately so; since, in context, (49) implicates "and I have already contributed to your charity". That is also a genuine example, by the way!

Implicatures

Back then to the cat, or cats. What is at issue is giving readers just the amount of information they require, no more and no less. We have already seen that Hemingway fails to assert either that it is the same cat, or a different one, and this already weakens his commitment to the truth of both these propositions. My interpretation is therefore that Hemingway implicates that it is not the same cat. He does this by inserting information which is otherwise irrelevant: that the maid brings 'a big tortoise-shell cat'. Informally, we might say that there is no reason to mention what kind of cat it is, unless this is significant, and unless we are expected to draw our own conclusions. But being an implicature, it would be cancelled, by saying, for example:

50 The big tortoise-shell cat didn't look like the kitty the wife had seen
   - but it was.

We are dealing therefore with a kind of deception. Hemingway's story is deliberately ambiguous: he intends, as we might say, to keep his readers guessing. Such Maxims of Quantity are, notice, particularly relevant in literature, where every detail may be expected to have potential significance for the interpretation. This has nothing to do with the language used, but with the expectations with which readers approach literary texts.

This is another reason, incidentally, why the kind of analysis I am discussing could never be expected to provide a complete analysis of a literary text. It is also a reason why the analysis could not be automatic or 'objective' in any simplistic way. The kind of analysis we do always has to be carried out against a background of knowledge which will include the conventions of various literary genres.

However, there is no point in being over-modest, since we have made some progress. We now have a yet more precise way of talking about the ambiguity at the end of the story. A characteristic of implicatures is that they can be cancelled: they may be denied without logical contradiction. (They are a relatively safe way to tell lies, since they *can* be denied!) They are therefore essentially ambiguous. So we might represent the end of the story as follows, to show the relation between asserted and implicated propositions.

a "The wife says she wants a cat, and the padrone sends her one."
b "But it doesn't look like the cat she saw."

Where (a) implicates that her wish is fulfilled, but (b) cancels this implicature.

b "It doesn't look like the cat she saw."
c "But it is – she was deluded about what she thought she saw through the window."

Where (b) implicates that it was a different cat, but (c) cancels this implicature, and allows a different interpretation of the story. We can continue with this game more or less indefinitely:

c "She was deluded about what she thought she saw through the window."
d "But she is delighted about the cat anyway – it suggests that the padrone understands something of her longings."
e "But he is just catering for the whim of a guest."
f "But the woman is a special guest and has a special rapport with the padrone."
g "But not all that special."

Summary

I have argued that literary competence involves the ability to understand several different kinds of semantic relationship: between a text and a summary of it; between different summaries; between sentences and different kinds of propositions conveyed by them; and between what is said and what is implied. These distinctions give more precise insight into some aspects of literary fiction, since a traditional concern of literary criticism is the ambiguity and multiple meanings of literary texts, and how meanings may be conveyed without having to be stated in so many words. It therefore also gives some insight into the conventions involved in interpreting fictional texts, and how they differ from factual reports.

My discussion of 'Cat in the Rain' has been deliberately overbuilt. It may be felt that we do not need to go to such lengths to explain what is, after all, a very short and simple story, although I hope I have shown that the complexity involved even here is considerable, and is easy to underestimate. However, the pay-off would come if the concepts are more widely applicable. I have shown already how the analysis can be of general interest to literary critics and linguists, since it touches on questions of the ambiguity and semantic organization of texts. I now have to show more explicitly its interest to teachers in the classroom.

Some general educational implications

Consider, then, the direct relevance of such apparently abstruse ideas about the semantic organization of texts for teachers.

First, some general educational points. It is very common for teachers to get students to do summaries. This is common enough in English classrooms; but it is also a skill required in other subjects, where it is necessary to be able to give accurate paraphrases of factual material. Any increase in our understanding of what is involved in such an ability is therefore of interest to teachers. The ability is one which even university students have often not fully acquired, when it comes to producing fair, succinct and accurate summaries of books or complex arguments and theories.

Second, there is the question of how such exercises are assessed. Paraphrasing exercises are often set in public examinations in English language. As we have seen, however, the question of what constitutes a correct or acceptable summary is difficult, and the question therefore arises of how such exercises should be assessed in a principled way.

Third, as all teachers know, students often produce summaries of original material, when this is *not* what is required! That is, they often produce summaries when what is required is a critical account; or they retell the plot of a poem or story, when what is required is a statement of the theme.

Fourth, on a topic of general educational interest, concepts of summaries, paraphrases and so on are of central interest to librarians. Indexing systems are traditionally organized to cater for searches for key words and expressions that summarize the content of documents. More recently, the literature on indexing and classification has begun to discuss alternative methods of indexing, based on the concept of the semantic structure of texts (see, for example, Hutchins 1978).

English language in the syllabus

I have made detailed proposals elsewhere (chapters 1 and 4) about how English language can form the basis of an English syllabus at senior school, college or university level. The basic proposal was that studies of English language should comprise (a) the detailed study of literary and non-literary texts, (b) the study of the general principles of language variation (stylistic, regional and social), and (c) the study of practical language planning problems concerned with teaching literacy, teaching foreign languages, dealing with language conflicts in different countries, and so on.

What I am concerned with here is providing detailed ideas and activities for (a) textual study. The general aim of this part of the syllabus could be stated as follows. Given any text, students ought to be able to comment systematically on its interesting features. Text means any piece of spoken discourse or written text that has actually occurred in a real social situation. Texts could therefore include both literary texts, and also non-literary examples, such as children's speech, regional dialect, casual conversation between adults, or written legal or religious language. In general, such work implies contrastive stylistic analysis of real language, and not the development of some descriptive linguistic framework for its own sake.

I will make suggestions here under three headings: guided reading; guided writing; and the logical status of fictional discourse (cf. Searle 1975, from whom I take this phrase). My basic questions here are: how can an analytic approach to language help in teaching students to appreciate literature? and, more generally, how can linguistic and literary study be integrated?

Guided reading

One problem for teachers is that students may read a literary text and find that it simply has no effect on them. They do not know what to look for, and therefore they do not know how to interpret it. A teaching problem is how to focus students' attention on significant features of the text - to force them to notice important characteristics, without simply telling them what to look for in one particular text. Widdowson (1975a) develops this argument that linguistic clues can lead to literary interpretation, and that stylistic analysis can provide a general strategy for the close reading of literature - a 'way in' to understanding the text. Depending on the age and level of the students, analysis can be more or less explicit. But an analytic approach to text implies a concern with how the text is constructed. And there are many ways in which students can be made to manipulate and think about the organization of texts.

First, there are many games that can be played with short stories. Pupils can be asked to read a story, and then to retell it some time later: this can lead to discussion of which items are remembered and why; and therefore which items are essential to the development of the plot, or the point of the story. Or a version of the familiar chain-story can be set up: A reads a story and tells it in his own words to B, who tells it to C, and so on. The last version is then compared to the original. Stories or summaries can be manipulated in other ways. For example, a summary can be divided into sentences which are written separately on pieces of card, and mixed to form a jigsaw puzzle. Students then do the puzzle, and discuss how, if at all, they are able to reconstruct the story. Or the whole original story can be made into a jigsaw in a similar way: to draw students' attention to features of the cohesion or narrative sequence. (Exton 1984 and Moy and Raleigh 1984 provide other comparable teaching suggestions.)

When I have done such work with teachers, they have sometimes objected that literary texts are 'too precious' to be artificially manipulated in these ways. This is a version of the argument that, by analysing or dissecting, somehow the literary text is destroyed. Needless to say, I reject such an argument. I have no space to answer it fully here, and can only make a couple of points. First, analysis does not 'destroy' a text in any literal sense: the text is still there afterwards. Second, *all* reading involves interpretation and analysis of some kind. More explicit and systematic analysis can therefore lead to a more interesting interpretation and deeper understanding.

However, there are practical problems in the artificial preparation of texts, by cutting them up or scrambling them in various ways: it involves considerable amounts of teacher preparation time. And some kinds of manipulation may force students to read texts in ways clearly not intended by the author: for example, in the wrong sequence. Some teachers may feel, as I do, that this may be justified for teaching purposes. But others may prefer methods that do not involve the artificial preparation of texts, and there are many such teaching strategies.

One is to select naturally-occurring texts which are particularly appropriate to the point being taught. One of my main topics in this article has been the relation between original texts and summaries of various kinds. This approach is particularly relevant to short stories, although it could also be applied to novels, plays and narrative poems. A useful collection of source material is Asimov's collection of *short* short stories (Asimov, Greenberg and Olander 1978). This contains one hundred short short stories: the longest is about four or five pages, the shortest is six words (plus a four-word title!). In his introduction, Asimov argues that in a long story, the 'point' may be hidden by many sub-points and developments. In a short story, the point looms larger. Whereas 'in the short short story, everything is eliminated *but* the point.' This is not strictly true, of course: Asimov is clearly exaggerating in order to make a point. . . . But this general argument is valuable. Each story in the collection is, in addition, introduced by a 'one-line blurb' by Asimov: students could study the relation between the blurb and the story. Does it always accurately identify the point of the story?

Other source material is provided by other short stories by Hemingway: for example, 'A Very Short Story' (Hemingway 1925c) is suitable for older pupils or students.

In other words, such reading exercises all provide different ways of forcing students to search out the significant features of the text, by giving them a precise task to do.

Guided writing

Similar problems can arise with students' writing: they are given a topic, but have 'nothing to say'. Therefore teachers often require ways of giving students guidelines, by making them write to a directive: this can include summarizing, correcting, rewriting, or completing what someone else has written (Nash 1980 provides a large number of ideas along these lines.)

Another artificial way of manipulating texts of short stories is to give students only part of the story, say the first paragraph, and ask them to continue. The effect of doing this with 'Cat in the Rain' is quite striking. On the basis of only the first paragraph, readers have no way of predicting how the story will continue, and often suggest that the waiter is likely to be a central character in the story. They can be given the rest of the story one paragraph at a time, and asked to construct the continuation of the story each time, and to study how their predictions change at each stage. With a story like 'Cat in the Rain', they could be given the whole story, told it is incomplete, and asked to complete it in a paragraph! The semantic competence involved in such writing exercises could remain largely implicit with younger pupils, or be discussed quite explicitly with older pupils or students.

Such writing exercises can lead also to students' understanding a fundamental characteristic of all language in use: that in listening to or reading any language, we are constantly making predictions about what will come next.

We make such predictions, guesses, hypotheses at every level of language. Given the first half of a sentence, we automatically try to predict the rest. The same holds for a whole story or just given the name 'Hemingway', a sophisticated reader will already start making predictions about the expected style and topic of the story. Our expectations may turn out to be wrong, of course. But whatever does occur will be interpreted in the light of what was anticipated. This general view of understanding language is psychologically very plausible. We sample what we hear or read, make predictions on this basis, and then test what follows to see if it matches our predictions. (Cf. chapter 3.)

At this level, then, practical classroom activities can lead to discussion of a general and powerful model of language and understanding. Such a model has been developed, for example, by Goodman and Smith, who see reading as a 'psycholinguistic guessing game' (e.g. Smith 1973). Learning to appreciate literature and learning a language are both cases of learning to have the right expectations.

Other activities can also lead to more advanced discussion, as advanced as the teacher wishes. Students can be asked to produce shorter and longer summaries, to compare their summaries, to discuss their equivalence or lack of equivalence, to construct 'ideal' summaries based on different students' attempts, and so on. They can be asked to construct the shortest possible summary: what is the limit here? why does such a limit occur? what seems to happen to the main point of the story as the plot summary gets, say, below ten or fifteen words? One summary provided by one of my informants was: 'Beware of machismo door-keeper.' Related tasks could ask students to propose alternative titles which reflect their interpretation of a story. (With Hemingway's 'A Very Short Story', this is not an artificial exercise!) Or they could be asked to find a proverb which fits the point of the story. All such exercises force students to formulate as succinctly as possible the 'point' of a story, and to consider the equivalence of different formulations.

Another strategy is to ask students to rewrite stories in a different style, such that they still have the same plot and are committed to all or many of the same propositions as the original. This would draw their attention to the distinction between logical or propositional content and the grammatical and lexical expression of this content: a distinction which is, of course, central to an understanding of literature. One summary I received of 'Cat in the Rain' began:

A princess, held captive by her possessor, is stirred by sensations, originating from her own psyche . . .

Or they could study accounts of the 'same' incident in different newspapers to investigate whether the accounts are logically equivalent or mere stylistic variants with the same underlying propositions.

A comparable example to this idea is provided by a version of *Alice in Wonderland* in Pitjantjatjara, an Australian Aboriginal language (Sheppard 1975). It began as follows:

Alitji was getting very tired of sitting on the creek bed. She and her sister had been playing milpatjunangi, a story telling game. . . . Alitji had become very bored as her sister's voice went on and on, and her eyelids began to droop. . . . Suddenly a kangaroo hopped past her, saying, 'Oh dear, oh deary me, I'm late,' And the extraordinary thing was that he was white. . . . He hurried on anxiously, clutching a dilly-bag and a digging stick, and disappeared from view down a hole in the ground.

The version is referred to in the Introduction as the forty-fourth translation of *Alice* into another language. But this clearly begs the question of the level of language at which translation is claimed to be faithful. The version is clearly not equivalent at the level of individual propositions, although it might be claimed to have some general overall cultural equivalence: that the overall effect produced by the two versions is roughly the same. Semantics has hardly even attempted to answer questions of this kind. As I have emphasized above, the linguistic analysis of literary texts poses interesting problems for linguists as well as literary critics.

Another writing exercise can involve expanding summaries back into stories. Here is an example:

Write a story based on the following plot, provided by an 8-year old child.

Once upon a time there was a cat and there was another cat and he ate mice. They got so fat they exploded. Their cat baskets caught on fire and the whole house burned down. But the fireman forgot about the budgies in their cage.

(Carol, aged 8)

This particular exercise would lead to discussion of the problems involved: does the summary present a well-defined plot? does it have a clear ending?

Another idea is to ask students to provide summaries of stories which are 'odd' in some way, for example, stories from a culture which has different story-telling conventions. This may turn out to be difficult or impossible, if it becomes clear that the conventions are so different as to render characters' motivations and actions unintelligible to us. This would inevitably lead to discussion of literary conventions - which often remain invisible to students accustomed to 'realist' writing.

The logical status of fictional discourse

Finally, the general way I have approached the semantic organization of texts can provide a way of beginning discussion of a topic of central literary concern: what is meant by 'realistic' writing?

I have talked above about author and reader being committed to the truth or denial of propositions. But, of course, no reader of any sophistication would think that the story is true in any literal sense. This is despite the fact that

Hemingway's style is often described impressionistically as simple, matter-of-fact, journalistic, reportage and so on. If the propositions have a truth-value, it is only within the universe of discourse constructed by the author. The term *plot* itself implies fictional discourse, since one talks of the plot of a novel or play, but not normally of a biography or documentary report.

Students could begin to consider the differences between fiction and factual reporting by studying documentary reports of some event (possibly compared with a clearly fictional account of a comparable event), and to consider questions such as: what is said in the reports and what is implied? in what sense do reports 'report' what happened? and in what sense are they highly interpretive and selective accounts, which involve the use of story-telling conventions even if they are 'factual'? In what ways, in other words, are events turned into stories? An obvious source of comparative material is Hemingway's fiction versus his news-reporting (now usefully collected in Hemingway 1968).

And so on

Many of these ideas doubtless correspond to activities that readers are already using in classrooms. And many other ideas have doubtless occurred to readers. As often happens, the careful and precise study of language in use provides a large number of ideas for use in the classroom. And, just as important, it provides a principled basis for the work that is done, by providing a way of relating such activities to a coherent overall framework for describing language.

This is what should be meant by 'applied linguistics': theory which suggests and illuminates interesting practice. For literary critics, it means ways of making clearer statements about how literary texts are interpreted. For classroom practice, it means ways of developing pupils' understanding of how language is used.

Intuition, activity and analysis

Several of my suggestions for teaching activities above are based on the idea of children being made to make intuitive predictions beyond the information they are given, and then to analyse how they have done this. Bruner (1974: 111) points out that such ideas of structure are often held to apply more accurately to science and mathematics than to literature, but that this embodies a misunderstanding of what is meant by structure. He proposes essentially one of the same classroom ideas as I have discussed above:

> Consider the nature of a play. Can the third act drift off independently of the first two? Likely not. A student who has pondered the first two acts should be able to write a reasonably appropriate third act - though it may differ from the original. In comparing his version with the

playwright's, the student should become aware of subtle constraints that he did and did not take into account.

Bruner also shows that the idea of prediction and going beyond the information given is readily transferable to other spheres of intellectual activity. He gives an example of a maths lesson based on a game of 'hidden numbers':

> Before the pupils enter the classroom, the teacher writes a set of numbers on the board and covers them up. He gives the students a few clues about the set - for example, that it sums to less than twenty. It is up to the class to ask further questions about the numbers in order to infer what they are. . . . the children come to recognize the constraints of the information they have already received in guiding their guesses as to the nature of the numbers.

Teaching students to make use of available clues in forming inferences from partial information can lead to greater confidence in intellectual activity. But having reached conclusions on the basis of insufficient evidence, they must then also know how to enquire after new evidence. Bruner is arguing for the place of both intuition and analysis in education: intuition buttressed by more rigorous follow-ups.

With specific examples from the study of a literary text, I have tried in this chapter to relate intuition, practical activities and analysis.

NOTES

1 Quoted in the *Sunday Times*, 6 December 1981, from John Julius Norwich's collection *A Christmas Cracker*.

2 The ending is reprinted here as it appears in Hemingway (1925b) and subsequent editions. However, the penultimate sentence reads oddly, and this may be a misprint for: 'She held a big tortoise-shell cat pressed tight against her and *its tail* swung down against her body.' (Emphasis added.)

3 I did not wish to introduce any formalism into this chapter, and throughout I represent propositions informally as sentences, distinguishing propositions only by double quotes. My definition of the terms *proposition, entailment*, and *presupposition* is necessarily brief, but precise enough for the present argument. Fuller discussions can be found in many introductory textbooks (e.g. Smith and Wilson 1979: chs 7-8). I also simply take it for granted that presuppositions should be distinguished from entailments, although this has been questioned, for example by Kempson (1977), who provides another fuller discussion of such concepts (cf. chapter 14). Similarly, my definition of *implicatures* is inevitably sparse and ignores various further distinctions which Grice (1975) draws. The problem of how ideas can and should be simplified for practical classroom use is an important one, but, as far as I am aware, has received little attention from linguists.

FURTHER READING

Miller, J. (ed.) (1984) *Eccentric Propositions: Essays on Literature and the Curriculum.* London: Routledge and Kegan Paul. Especially chapters 5, 11, 12, 14.

ACKNOWLEDGEMENTS
This chapter is a revised version of an article first published in R. Carter and D. Burton (eds), *Literary Text and Language Study*, London: Edward Arnold, 1982, pp. 56-85. A version is also published as chapter 10 of M. Stubbs, *Discourse Analysis*, Oxford: Blackwell, 1983.

The chapter owes much to other people, and the acknowledgements themselves verge on a narrative. The story begins with John Sinclair, who pulled copies of 'Cat in the Rain' out of a cupboard before a staff seminar at the University of Birmingham, and provoked a shower of articles on the story. Deirdre Burton provided the title to this article, as well as the theme and the plot, leaving me only to fill in the characters and develop the sub-plots. Florence Davies invited me to prepare an early version for a seminar. Margaret Berry discussed many aspects of the article with me and suggested several ingredients. David Lodge and Henry Widdowson made useful comments on previous drafts; so did Ron Carter, who also provided some additional material. Lecture and seminar audiences in Australia, Britain and China provided data and summaries, some of which are quoted in the article. Despite the cast of thousands, I did actually write the article, and am therefore responsible for the propositions which it asserts, as well as for the propositions which it presupposes and entails. If challenged, I could, however, without logical contradiction, deny its implicatures.

Spoken Language

8

Oracy: the quality (of the theory) of listening

Introduction

One of my main themes in this book is that educational theory and practice are often based on inadequate models of language. Language is felt intuitively to be important, but it is not systematically analysed. This chapter studies a particular case where an educational linguistic concept has been developed in influential work, and where corresponding teaching and testing materials have been proposed, but where both the underlying concept and also the practical materials have been underanalysed, and where important aspects of children's linguistic competence have therefore been ignored.

The term *oracy* is used to mean ability in spoken language: it refers both to the production of spoken language and to listening comprehension. If we are thinking of teaching or assessing oral production, then this could involve, for example, getting pupils to tell narratives, give explanations or mini-lectures, challenge views put forward by other speakers, take part in discussions, and so on. Their language would be judged according to its appropriateness to the situation, whether this involved talking to a group of other pupils or to a single adult, whether teacher or examiner.

The term *oracy* is particularly associated with the work of Andrew Wilkinson, which began to appear in 1965 with an influential book entitled *Spoken English* (Wilkinson, Davies and Atkinson 1965). But the concern with assessing spoken English is, of course, much wider than this. CSE boards are obliged to offer an oral element in their examinations, although some boards award only a low percentage of marks to this component, presumably as a reflection of how the component is valued by the board. The range of marks allotted is between 10 and 35 per cent. (Few O-level boards have any such compulsory component.) CSE examinations characteristically attempt to assess such abilities as: fluency, clarity, audibility, liveliness, intelligibility, developing an argument, or sustaining an interesting discussion. Such abilities might be assessed in situations such as: formal prepared talks, discussion alone with an examiner, or informal group discussion (Marks 1980).

I am not concerned here with whether such aims are attainable, but cite them merely to give some approximate indication of the extent of the concern with assessing oracy.

The quality (of the theory) of listening

My aim in this chapter is much narrower. I will discuss the model of language and communication which underlies the concept of oracy in the various publications by Wilkinson and his colleagues. As my main source, I will take one of the more substantial statements, the book *The Quality of Listening* by Wilkinson, Stratta and Dudley (1974), henceforth *QL*. Other sources include several articles by Wilkinson listed in the references. Although *QL* was published several years ago, in 1974, the approach does not seem to have developed significantly in the meantime, and there are few, if any, other comparable books on listening comprehension. (However, Brown and Yule 1983a, and Brown et al. 1984 provide discussions of oracy that are much more systematically based in an understanding of the relationship between spoken and written language.) More recently, much of Wilkinson's work has been concerned with assessing children's written language, and although I will not discuss this directly, many of the points I make would apply to this work too.

This article is therefore an extended, if rather belated, review of *QL*. I will argue that the model of language underlying the book's concept of oracy is not sophisticated or explicit enough to support the teaching practices or testing techniques which are based on it. In particular, it seems that the concepts of *meaning* and of *discourse* require to be developed and made much more explicit. If this is not done, then pupils will be tested on their ability to make distinctions (for example, between the literal and underlying meanings of utterances) which are not made clear by the theory. Similarly, teachers will be left with an inexplicit and intuitive model of what they are to teach, when they try to develop their pupils' command of spoken language.

Many of the ideas underlying the concept of oracy derive from recent, particularly Hallidayan, linguistics. But I will suggest that many lessons which could have been learned from linguistics have been ignored.

Educational linguistics and models of language

There are various kinds of models of language: linguists' (theoretical) models, teachers' (pedagogical) models, and users' (in the present case, pupils') models. (These distinctions are developed in greater detail in chapter 14 of the present book.) One task for educational linguists is to interpret for teachers the bewildering variety of theoretical models. Many theoretical ideas are relevant to classroom practice, but they may not be expressed in the appropriate form. Many other ideas are not relevant at all, and have to be selected out. This reformulation and selection is not easy, since it involves, for example, trying to distinguish ideas of lasting value from the latest shift in fashion. More generally, applied linguistics can be seen precisely as this kind of analysis of those aspects of language which are basic to different practical activities. Widdowson (1979a: especially chs 17-18), usefully develops these views with reference to foreign language teaching; but many of his points are applicable to mother tongue teaching.

QL's model of language

In *QL*, there is an attempt to provide precisely this kind of mediation between theory and practice, and almost half the book is taken up with setting out models of language and communication. The question is whether these models are adequate for the teaching and testing of oracy.

The communications model (e.g. *QL*: 20) comprises essentially addressor, addressee, topic and context, and these categories are further elaborated. This model is comparable to Firth's model of context of situation, and to models of the speech situation put forward by scholars such as Jakobson, Hymes and many others.

The model of language is separate from, and not explicitly related to, the communications model. It is based loosely on early work by Halliday (as interpreted, via Davies (1965), in the first main publication on oracy by Wilkinson et al. in 1965, but it is not the same as Davies's model). Language is said (*QL*: 14) to have three levels: lexis, grammar and phonology. This model is only very roughly articulated, and I will make only two points about it. First, there is no reference to the place of semantics in the model: meaning is discussed throughout *QL*, but has no clear place in the overall framework. Second, there is no discussion at all of discourse as a level, although there is constant reference in the tests to sequences of utterances. These two points mean that aspects of language that are central to the whole concept of oracy, meanings in sequences of discourse, are discussed only in a scattered fashion, and not given a clearly defined place in the model at all. In addition, if the view of language as discourse and of 'doing things with words' was developed, then this would provide a coherent way of relating the models of language and communication.

A related model of written language is also put forward. It is said (*QL*: 26) that: 'Written language effectively relies on only two levels - the grammatical and the lexical . . . [The] third level of language is missing, and therefore the primary means of symbolisation is absent.'

This is a very confused account of the relation between spoken and written language. Graphology provides a level analogous to phonology and it is not adequate to regard letters merely as symbols of phonemes (the symbols-of-symbols view of written language). The English writing system has its own, partly autonomous, internal organization, and relates to syntax and semantics as well as to phonology. (This is discussed in detail in chapter 12 of the present book.)

The relationship between spoken and written language is discussed in *QL* (pp. 21-7), but no systematic account is given of this relationship, although it would be central to any teaching of oracy. People are generally very confused about this relationship, and their users' models therefore require to be supplemented with a more consistent account.

The personal growth model

In addition to the models which are partly explicit in *QL*, one might also wonder whether the authors also hold other models which are alluded to, but hardly made explicit at all: for example, models of the relations between language, personality and cognition.

A set of background assumptions which underlies the view of oracy in *QL* is a 'personal growth' model of mother tongue teaching (Dixon 1967). *QL* (p. 65) places oracy 'in the context of . . . general development'. Growth models come in various forms, from, for example, notions of the therapeutic value of English studies (as in Holbrook's work) to work emphasizing the socio-cultural functions of language in use (as in the work of Barnes, Britton and Rosen 1969). *QL* clearly emphasizes the socio-cultural functions of language, but it also lays great stress on the cognitive functions, and talks of 'testing thinking in language' (p. 41). And it is claimed explicitly in earlier work by Wilkinson (1965a: 5) that 'to develop oracy is to develop personality in a more direct sense than by other educational means.

However, although various tests proposed in *QL* aim to get pupils to distinguish between the cognitive, social and affective meanings conveyed by language, again no explicit account is given of these characteristics.

It is no defence, of course, to say (*QL*: xiii) that the documentation, references and discussion have been kept to a minimum to make the book readable to teachers and others. Teachers deserve the best ideas available. And pupils deserve tests which are as explicit and principled as possible.

A relevant model of language

An important question is, therefore, what kind of definition or model of language is most relevant to teaching and testing oracy. Some of the definitions which linguists give are clearly not of immediate interest: for example, a view of language as the defining characteristic of human beings, or as the *sine qua non* of human societies, or as a complex of formal features and structural mechanisms. A relevant model (Halliday 1969; and see chapters 1 and 3 above), on the other hand, is one which is semantically based, and which attempts to unravel the multiple meanings in any utterance; and which is also pragmatically based, and which sees utterances as actions which are performed with language. A central concern of linguistics is the observation of the distance between surface forms and underlying meanings, and of the depth of indirection involved when speakers make requests and perform other speech acts. What I now have to show is that a model of this kind can give precise insights into the kinds of tests of listening comprehension proposed in *QL*.

Tests of content

One type of test is called a test of content (*QL*: 38ff). For example, pupils hear a passage about police setting up a road-block:

> road-blocks aren't blocks . . . in the middle of the road . . . a policeman will stop you . . .

They then have to choose between different definitions of how the road-block was made:

A By putting blocks of stone in the road
B By having police stop cars
C By putting a barrier across the road

The question asks for details of 'this particular road-block', although in the passage the discussion is of several road-blocks (*QL*: 38). This, of course, affects the meaning of the passage. This exercise involves recognizing propositions which are asserted or denied in the surface structure of the text. But the semantic relations involved are not analysed at all. A is denied. B is asserted. But there are also relations between the candidate answers: A entails C, but the reverse entailment does not hold. (By *entails*, I mean *logically entails*. If A entails C, the truth of C follows logically from A.) And C is not actually denied by the text, and is quite compatible with B. Answer B is said to be 'correct', but is A more wrong than C?

Similar problems, due to underanalysis of the task involved, are apparent in the following test of content (*OL*: 39), which uses a text about Sir Gawain and the Green Knight:

> . . . he (the Green Knight) proposed a most strange party game . . . one of the knights there should cut his head off . . . in return a year hence he the Green Knight should cut that knight's head off . . .

Pupils have to decide which sentence 'best describes' what he suggests.

A Gawain should cut the Green Knight's head off
B They should cut each other's heads off
C The Green Knight should cut Gawain's head off

There is ambiguity, first of all, in that the passage does not say that Gawain is the knight who is involved, although the test items assume this: let us also assume it. Again, there are relationships between multiple-choice answers: B entails both A and C. The text, under our assumptions about who is involved, entails A, B *and* C. But the crucial point, I suppose, is whether normal relationships of logical entailment hold in a world in which people have their heads cut off and then return a year later! The candidate is left guessing what is meant by 'best describes'. (The authors do not say in this case which answer they expect.) Such examples throw general doubt on the value of multiple-choice tests of comprehension. A considerable amount of work has been done by scholars such as Van Dijk, in attempting to represent the *content* of texts as networks of propositions. Such theories are still in their early stages, but would nevertheless contain many ideas relevant to constructing such tests of content. Kintsch et al. (1975) developed such ideas for looking at readers' comprehension of written language, and the same ideas are applicable to spoken language.

Tests of contextual constraint

Another type of test is described as follows (*QL*: 33):

> the basic principle (is) to omit a sentence from a conversation and require it to be supplied from alternatives offered.

First, it is not evident that *sentences* are the relevant units involved. Sentences are units of written language. But let us assume that sequences of discourse can be represented as sequences of sentences. It is also claimed (*QL*: 33) that 'any sentence can be an answer to any other'. This is simply untrue. Consider the following two sentences:

John hit Bill.
Bill was hit by John.

In isolation, they are both perfectly grammatical, and they are synonymous. But they cannot occur in the same question–answer sequences.

Q What did John do?
A John hit Bill. *But not:* Bill was hit by John.

A general criticism of the model of language presented in *QL* is its failure to distinguish between sentences, propositions and conversational moves. Yet the ability to make such distinctions is exactly what is being tested.

In *QL* (p. 33) the following invented exchange is cited:

A Where did you go for your holiday?
B Grandfather clocks are quite expensive.

The authors comment that B may be giving 'a perfectly adequate answer' to the question, if, for example, A knows that B has bought an expensive clock, cannot afford a holiday, and therefore went nowhere. But a proposition such as "I spent a lot of money on a clock and couldn't afford a holiday" is not derivable from what is said. It is only derivable via the illocutionary force of B's utterance as an answer, and via an assumption that what B says is relevant as an answer. (I use the term *illocutionary force* to refer to the function of utterances such as: statement, question, answer, promise, threat, and so on). Such a proposition is not entailed, but only implicated by what is said, and could be denied without logical contradiction, for example:

> Grandfather clocks are quite expensive – but I went to Monte Carlo anyway.

Again, this kind of example shows the need for a clear distinction between what is said, what is entailed by what is said, the illocutionary force of what is said, and what can be inferred from the illocutionary force under general assumptions of conversational relevance. And again, the ability to make such distinctions is what is being tested and should therefore be explicit. In using the terms 'implicate' and 'conversational relevance', I am drawing on the famous work by Grice (1975), discussed in more detail in chapter 7.

Note here one way in which my argument might be misunderstood. I am not arguing that any exhaustive account of meaning is possible. On the contrary, it is clear that there will often, if not always, be an idiosyncratic residue of meaning which will escape analysis in any given case. For example, I am informed that Andrew Wilkinson collects clocks as a hobby: for people who know this fact, it affects their interpretation of the example. Such idiosyncratic facts are clearly not part of semantic theory. Nevertheless, there *are* many generalizations to be made about how language conveys meanings.

Tests of relationship

A third type of test is said to be mainly about 'covert information' conveyed about interpersonal relations between individuals (*QL*: 58). The tests cited concern the expression of a variety of things, which are not obviously related: customer–client relationships; conveying sympathy; the amount of agreement between speakers. This looks suspiciously like a rag-bag category.

One way of systematizing it would be to study different types of indirection which are used to convey politeness, conceal disagreement, and so on. For example, one way to make a polite request is to state a pre-condition for fulfilling the request, and to embed the proposition requested in the pre-condition (*QL*: 59, 61):

> If you'd like to withdraw to the waiting-room.
> If you would like to go into the dining-room, sir, they are serving breakfast there now.

Note also, in the second example, that *if* is not being used as a logical connective. No causal relation between the clauses is claimed. A central concern of *QL* is the relation between language and thinking. But there is no discussion at all of how language and logic are related. It is quite clear, for example, that logical operators such as &, →, V are not at all equivalent to natural language connectives *and, if, or*. This is just one example of the kind of logic–language relationship which requires to be made more explicit before 'the thinking involved in response to spoken material' (*QL*: 38) can be properly assessed. For example, the 'non-logical' use of conjunctions is much more common in spoken than written English. Such examples are also another case where a clear distinction is required between propositional content and speech act. One use of *if* is to justify making a speech act. Compare:

There's some cake here if you're hungry.

where the *if*-clause does not indicate a causal relationship, but might be loosely paraphrased as: "this is why I'm telling you X". Or consider the comparable use of the conjunctions, *and, or* and *because* in the following sentences, where it should be intuitively clear that they do not have their 'logical' meanings:

I asked him, *and* he did invent the term oracy.
Here's a book on oracy, *or* aren't you interested?
He did invent the term, *because* I asked him.

Such examples show two things quite clearly, both of which are central to the concerns of *QL*. First, such examples show again the need to distinguish sentences from functional units such as speech acts. The connectives in such cases do not connect syntactic units such as clauses, but have a structure which might be labelled: *assertion*, plus *justification* for making the assertion. Second, much more careful and explicit attention must be paid to how language works, before inferences can be drawn about relations between language and thought. I hope it is clear, therefore, that I have not introduced a whole set of distinctions just for the sake of it. The ability to make such distinctions is precisely what is being assessed by the tests in *QL*.

Summary

There are several other types of test discussed in *QL*. But I think I have demonstrated the main point that the tasks involved in doing the tests are often underanalysed, and that they could be analysed within a model of language which distinguishes clearly between language as structure or form (lexico-syntax), as meaning (semantics) and as action (speech acts or illocutionary force). Also required is a model of how utterances follow each other in discourse.

The tests all involve distinguishing between overt and covert meanings. They must therefore be based on a model which can explicitly represent different degrees of indirection in what is expressed. This requires making distinctions between *utterances* (what is said), and different kinds of *propositions*. These propositions may be logically *entailed* by what is said or *implicated* via the *speech acts* which the utterances perform. There requires to be a much clearer distinction, in 'tests of thinking in language', between logical relationships and natural language relationships. There is also considerable inconsistency in *QL* in the use of the term *sentence*: confusion both between *sentence* and *utterance*, and confusion over whether sentences are units of coversational English.

There is no way to avoid making such distinctions, or their equivalent, since the ability to make them is precisely what is being tested.

It is not enough to emphasize 'the richness and variety of language' (*QL*: 65). An attempt must be made to be explicit about the levels of meaning which language routinely conveys. These meanings are sometimes idiosyncratic and context-dependent. But it is possible to state many generalizations about the kinds of meanings that are conveyed. If teachers understand some of these general principles, they are not restricted to superficial copying of the techniques illustrated in *QL*, and can use them to construct coherent teaching materials and tests.

This chapter has been critical of the model of language and meaning put forward in *QL*. But it has tried to indicate how the complexity of explicit and implicit meanings can be treated more systematically; and to suggest positive ways of making clearer just *what* is being tested.

My criticisms have therefore been internal to the model. I have started from the assumption that tests of oracy are being used, and I have discussed ways of understanding better what it is they assess. I have therefore not discussed problems in the external validity of the concept of oracy. These problems include: doubts about the implied parallelism between oracy and literacy; the difficulty of separating oracy from confidence in the test situation; the danger of testing the examiner rather than the pupil – for example, testing the examiner's ability to elicit effective language from pupils; the logical contradiction involved in trying to test informal language in a formal test; the lack of consensus about what constitutes effective language – since linguistic style may define social group membership; our lack of knowledge about language development after the age of about 5 years, and therefore our lack of knowledge about what to expect from, say, 11- or 15-year-olds. Readers may infer for themselves the implicatures of these final comments.

FURTHER READING

Brown, G., Anderson, A., Shillcock, R. and Yule, G. (1984) *Teaching Talk: Strategies for Production and Assessment*. London: Cambridge University Press.

ACKNOWLEDGEMENTS

This chapter is a revised version of an article first published as 'Oracy and educational linguistics: the quality (of the theory) of listening', *First Language*, 2: 21-30, 1981. It was originally presented to the Assessment of Performance Unit Seminar on Oracy, held in Cambridge, 27-29 March 1980.

For useful comments on a previous draft I am grateful to Margaret Berry, Ron Carter, Walter Grauberg and Jeff Wilkinson. Several contributions at the seminar, from Tony Adams, Douglas Barnes, Gill Brown and Gordon Wells, also contributed to this version.

9

On speaking terms

Introduction

In chapter 3, I argued that a relevant model of language for educationalists must be based on an understanding of language in use in connected discourse, and in chapter 5, I discussed some of the complex relations between spoken and written language. In this chapter, I discuss some characteristics of casual, conversational, spoken discourse. There has been a great deal of discussion recently about the role of talk in schools. But an understanding of the potential roles of talk in the classroom must depend on a description of how talk actually works. This is particularly so since our intuitions are unreliable: casual spoken language is a highly automatic aspect of our social behaviour, and is not open to direct observation. In addition, our perceptions are distorted by our views of written language, which is visible and easier to observe, and which is consciously learned in prescriptive ways. A detailed study of the spoken language that children actually use is also of central educational relevance, because of the extensive differences (for example, in syntax) between speech and writing. These are often underestimated for the reasons noted above, but are essential knowledge for teachers, if they are to understand some of the problems that children have in learning to handle formal written language, in reading or in their own writing.

The main aim of this chapter is to study some of the features of real spoken discourse that are often ignored in linguistic studies of sentence structure or syntax. It is easy to get the impression that discourse analysis is at least a foolhardy, if not a quite impossible undertaking, and that expanding the narrow range of phenomena that linguists study to include natural language in use causes all hell to break loose. Certainly the task is daunting. However, the chaos can be contained in various ways, and, in fact, only some hell breaks loose.

One way of preventing panic and mental paralysis in the face of problems which have so far defeated linguists, sociologists and philosophers, is to study in detail a particular transcript of conversational data. After a few introductory points, I will do so in this chapter. This will provide an opportunity for a detailed informal introduction to the kinds of phenomena that discourse analysis has to explain, and the kinds of discourse phenomena that recent linguistics has typically ignored. It will provide some initial arguments that such conversational data are, after all, manageable and amenable in principle to systematic analysis. Alongside some commentary on data, there will also be, however, brief glimpses into the theoretical chasms over which we are precariously suspended.

Discourse organization

It has sometimes been maintained that there is no linguistic organization above sentence level. However, I suspect that some people believe this because they have never looked for such organization. To maintain this would be to maintain the odd position that conversation or written text consists of unordered strings of utterances. Connected discourse is clearly not random. People are quite able to distinguish between a random list of sentences and a coherent text, and it is the principles which underlie this recognition of coherence which are the topic of study for discourse analysts.

There are several other ways of demonstrating informally that discourse is organized. First, conversationalists themselves frequently refer to discourse structure in the course of conversation, by utterances such as: *oh, by the way . . .; anyway, as I was saying . . .; before I answer that . . .;* or *that reminds me . . .* In everyday situations, conversationalists are aware that not anything can follow anything: some utterances require to be prefaced by such an excuse or a claim of relevance. (Cf. Schegloff and Sacks 1973.) This insertion of such metatext, pointing to the organization of the text itself, is particularly common in certain discourse styles, such as lecturing, and it occurs in written as well as spoken discourse. However, it is also perfectly normal in casual conversation. This ability to jump out of the system and comment on it makes discourse organization significantly different from sentence organization. It is possible, of course, to have isolated self-referential sentences. Common examples are provided by sentences which include explicit performative verbs (such as *ask, tell, promise*):

1 I'm *asking* you who you were with last night.

But in the course of conversation, it is quite usual, and passes unnoticed, for an utterance to step outside the conversation, comment on its progress, and propose a re-orientation:

2 Look, let's consider this in another way.

And there is no analogue to this in syntactic organization. More accurately, such utterances are simultaneously conversational acts *in* the linear sequence of discourse and also acts at a higher metalevel, which comment on the lower level. The routine nature of such utterances has been taken as an argument that such comments from conversationalists give interesting access to the way they themselves understand the conversation, and therefore should have privileged status as data (cf. Schegloff and Sacks 1973). (I discuss such metatext at more length in Stubbs 1976.)

Second, there are many jokes which depend on our ability to recognize faulty discourse sequences. The simplest possible type is:

3   A   Yes, I can.
   B   Can you see into the future?

At the risk of being tedious, this joke depends on two things: the recognition that the question–answer sequence has been reversed; and that the grammatical cohesion has been disrupted. *Yes, I can* is elliptic and only interpretable via the following, instead of the preceding, utterance.

On the same model is the joke about the man who goes into a chemist's shop. The exchange goes:

4   Customer   Good morning. Do you have anything to treat complete loss of voice?
   Shopkeeper   Good morning sir. And what can I do for you?

In this case, the shopkeeper's utterance occurs in the wrong structural position. It occurs second, although it is strongly marked as an opening conversational move: by the greeting, the address term, the content and form of the question.

Such examples demonstrate immediately our discourse competence to recognize that utterances can occur in some sequences, but not others. Therefore, discourse should in principle be analysable in terms of syntagmatic constraints on possible sequences of utterances. Such examples therefore provide one quick and informal answer to the often-repeated claim that in conversation 'anything can follow anything'. (For a much more detailed and formal response, see Stubbs 1983b: ch. 5.)

For the present, I simply wish to point out that deviant sequences are recognizable as such. Some discourse sequences are impossible, or at least highly improbable. Consider this example (based on an example by Labov):

5   I approach a stranger in the street.
   *Excuse me. My name's Mike Stubbs. Can you tell me the way to the station?

The sequence of speech acts is ill formed:

6   *apology + identification + request for directions.

There appear to be two ways of explaining why 6 is ill formed. Either the sequence of acts is itself ill formed: there are co-occurrence restrictions on the sequence. Or alternatively the combination of speech acts and social situation is ill formed: speakers do not identify or introduce themselves to strangers in the street. A plausible rule is that *identification* is uttered only if speakers predict further interaction on a later occasion. Thus speakers are likely to introduce themselves to people they meet at a party, but not in a railway carriage. I am not sure how one could distinguish between these two claims: that the constraint is on the sequence of acts, or that it is between an act and a situation. However, the example has already shown: (a) that although the individual sentences in 5 are well formed, the whole sequence is not; (b) that traditional grammatical descriptions are therefore unlikely to have any useful explanation to offer, since they are restricted to within sentence boundaries.

It is more difficult to find comparable deviance across two speakers' utterances, for our ability to contextualize almost anything readily copes with odd sequences. But deviant sequences do occur:

7 A Goodbye!
   B Hi!

The oddity of this particular sequence is explicable via B's participant knowledge that the exchange occurred after A and B had approached each other down a long corridor. The greeting was prepared in advance of the actual encounter, and the split-second timing of the exchange itself meant that A's contribution was interpreted only after B had spoken.

Examples like the following are similarly recognizably odd, but not difficult to contextualize:

8 A What's the time?
   B Oh no!

B's response might be paraphrasable as "Oh no, I've left a cake in the oven" or, in general, "I've just remembered something important enough to supersede your question." The possibilities of interpretation are indefinitely large. What is important is not only finding or constructing impossible or non-contextualizable sequences, but the ease with which such incongruity may be recognized. It is both apt and significant that in the Theatre of the Absurd there are many examples of odd juxtaposition. These occur at the syntactic level (cf. N. F. Simpson's plays *A Resounding Tinkle* or *The One-Way Pendulum*), but also at the level of discourse. Consider this example from Samuel Beckett's *Endgame*:

9 Hamm Why don't you kill me?
   Clov I don't know the combination of the larder.

It is not difficult to find an implicit linking proposition. One possibility is: "If I kill you, I will starve to death." However, it is our awareness of such conversationally odd exchanges, admidst the situational and artistic absurdities, that gives a further clear indication that conversation is not random. So, in everyday situations, for a conversation to be unmarked, there are constraints on possible sequences of utterances.

Not much is known about such constraints on discourse sequences. They are not entirely analogous, for example, to constraints on syntactic ordering. (Some of the differences between the concept of *well-formedness* as it applies to sentences and to discourse, are discussed at length in Stubbs 1983b: chapter 5.) For the present, it is sufficient to note that there are constraints, and therefore discourse is structured. Such constraints are linguistic. They are not simply reducible, for example, to some form of topical organization. They are constraints on the occurrence of certain conversational acts in certain orders, as well as on the sequencing of propositions and of surface lexical and syntactic cohesion.

Inspecting transcribed data

My general purpose in this chapter is simply to convince the reader that spontaneous conversation, although it may look chaotic when closely transcribed, is, in fact, highly ordered. It is not, however, ordered in the same ways as written texts. I will argue that conversation is polysystemic: that is, its coherence depends on several quite different types of mechanisms, such as repetition of words and phrases, structural markers, fine synchronization in time, and an underlying hierarchic structure relating sequences of discourse acts.

We can make almost no progress without data in the form of a close transcript of audio-recorded natural conversation. This is the least we can get away with. As I have to present a printed transcript to the reader, I will restrict my comments to features easily represented in this form, although I am very aware that important cohesive features are to be found in systems of intonation, in paralinguistic features such as tempo, rhythm and voice quality, and in non-verbal kinesic systems. I like to use the spelling *cohearence* as a reminder that many of the linking mechanisms of conversation require to be heard to be appreciated. (Brazil, Coulthard and Johns 1980 and Brown, Currie and Kenworthy 1980 discuss in detail functions of intonation in discourse. Birdwhistell 1970: 237ff, discusses the structuring functions of gestural systems: kinesic juncture.)

We require closely transcribed data for several reasons. First, intuitions (introspective data) are notoriously unreliable in this area. Second, most people are simply unfamiliar with what such material looks like. Third, given these two points, a close transcript of conversation can allow us to see ways in which conversation is ordered which we would never imagine just by thinking about it, as a sentence grammarian might be tempted to do. Formulating this point in another way, we can say that such data characteristically *look* odd in transcript - but the corresponding audio-recording does not *sound* odd. Transcribing conversation into the visual medium is a useful estrangement device, which can show up complex aspects of conversational coherence which pass us by as real-time conversationalists or observers, and 'through which the strangeness of an obstinately familiar world can be detected' (Garfinkel 1967: 38).

People are, in general, unused to studying close transcripts of conversational data. When they do look at such materials, they tend to see them as chaotic or unordered: relative to written texts or to the highly idealized sentences which are data for the grammarian. Conversational data therefore tend to be characterized in terms of their putative defects. At a recent seminar of linguists, staff and postgraduates, which was discussing the data analysed below, the following characterizations of the data were offered:

> There is no beginning; there is a lack of official stages; the turn-taking is disrupted and fairly random; the speakers don't seem to link things up; one of the speakers is excluded and consciously ignored by the others; and so on.

Some of these comments are factually wrong: the turn-taking is not random. Some are unperceptive: the links and boundaries are there, if one knows what to look for. However, any such implicitly prescriptive comments, which characterize language in terms of putative defects instead of searching for the order underlying surface anomalies, run entirely counter to one of the most fundamental principles of linguistics as a scientific discipline. If we cannot discover the inherent organization of linguistic data, then this is a defect in us as analysts, not in the data.

Some observations on the data

The data, an extract from an interview recorded in an Edinburgh school, are presented in the appendix to this chapter, prefaced by a brief contextual note. Utterances (1)–(24) are included to give the reader the immediate conversational context, including the first reference (17) to the haunted house, which becomes a major topic. Most of my comments are restricted to utterances after (24).

The interviewer, MS, was the author, but the interview was not recorded with conversational analysis in mind. This talk was an unplanned interlude after the main business of the interview was over. It will be clear from some comments below that MS was, in any case, in no position to manipulate the talk, as he lacked the conversational competence to do much more than occasionally disrupt the conversational flow by clumsy expressions of attention and interest. The two boys, G and M, being close friends, were on close speaking terms, and MS was only partly competent in their dialect and style of talk.

Here, then, are some observations on the data, intended not to provide an exhaustive analysis, but to give detailed examples of different types of conversational organization which the reader may then observe in other data. My comments will probably make little sense unless the reader has now read through the data appendix.

An initial obvious, but important point is that conversation is a *joint production*. One immediate implication of this is that speakers constantly take account of their audience by designing their talk for their hearers. This implies much more than saying that speakers shift their style of language to suit the context. It means that speakers must understand their audience: they must have some idea what the audience already knows and what they want to know, and therefore of how to select and present information. For example, G corrects himself as follows:

(32)   somebody you told me when I was about five or six . . .

G (re)designs his talk so that M is brought into the story, and M knows immediately what it is that he has told G: see (34). He knows 'what G is talking about' before G has said it. The use of the second person *you*, instead of the potential choice of *he*, marks a sharp change in addressee. G is not only bringing M into the story, which is primarily directed at MS but is switching to M as temporary addressee and presenting him with a conversational role to which M immediately responds (34). Throughout the data, concessions are made to MS as a stranger: e.g. (14-16), (26), (29-30). It is interesting how at (32) G begins his utterance with a lexical choice designed for MS an auditor without 'common understanding' (cf. Garfinkel 1967): that is, *somebody* is a term that anyone can understand as meaning "a person that you don't know but whose identity is unimportant for the point of my story". G then realizes the inappropriateness of this choice for his other hearer, who shares background information with him, and he quickly modifies his utterance. It is a useful exercise simply to consider how the discourse might differ if MS was absent, and M and G were reminiscing to each other about the haunted house.

Further, conversation is a joint production composed in real time. Consider (32-5):

(32)   G   somebody you told me when I was about
(33)   five - ⌐ or six   there was m -
(34)   M   ⌊ there was money there
(35)   G   money hidden there

M knows what G is going to say, what G has in mind as we often put it, even before G has said it. (34) correctly predicts (35). Conversationalists have the technical competence to make such predictions and interpretations, and to analyse the implications of utterances, in a fraction of a second. This is real joint production. M has a completion ready which proves that he has understood G. That is, (34) is a proof of communication, a proof that the speakers are on the same wavelength. Jefferson (1973) discusses the functions of split-second timing in proving understanding between speakers, and speakers' capacity to place talk with precision by, for example, coming in at just the right moment with a sentence-completion.

What we are concerned with here, then, are ways in which speakers can check on whether their hearers are following, ways in which speakers provide feedback to keep the talk going, and ways in which hearers can claim or prove their understanding. (These are Sacks's terms, see Sacks 1970.) Some feedback items display only that the conversationalist is in touch with the rhythm of the talk: for example, *mm* (65, 82), *uhuh* (71). Some prove that at least part of the point of the preceding talk has been understood: for example, *not much good* (42), or more elaborate endorsements of preceding utterances. Thus in

(60)   aye there was only about that much left of the stair

M both acknowledges a valid contribution to the discourse (*aye*) and paraphrases part of (58-9). Compare how (56-8) endorses (53-5) through the formally recognizable criteria of the linker *as well*, and the choice of words, across two utterances, from a well-defined semantic field: *knocking down, ripped away, tore away, smashed in, tugged, fell in*. Such lexical cohesion could be systematically analysed in the way proposed by Halliday and Hasan (1976).

Insertions like *you know* (47, 67, 70, 76, 80, 83), as well as serving a feedback and sympathetic circularity function, are one literal mechanism for taking account of what other conversationalists do know. In casual conversation it is often possible to be cavalier about supplying information which can be filled in by hearers. Thus coverwords like *thingummy* or *what-d'you-call it* can often be used. Brown (1977: 107ff) discusses the use of such items in conversation. In the present data, there is an example at

(66)   only about – that much of a support y'know for – thing

There are more elaborate ways of telling hearers that they have had enough information. I will comment further on these below.

So far, I have given brief examples of several formally recognizable mechanisms of discourse cohesion: shifts in addressee, synchronization in time and lexical repetition. By emphasizing some specific mechanisms by which conversation is sustained as a joint production composed and interpreted in real time, I am emphasizing how discourse analysis can study interaction.

Narrative organization

I turn now to the overall structure of the talk. It is possible to show that long chunks of apparently casual conversation, stretching over several minutes, have overall structural organization. There is a very simple structural claim which is very relevant here: stories have beginnings, middles and ends. For example, jokes and stories told in conversation do not just start. They are often introduced by one of a relatively small number of prefaces such as *guess what?* . . .; *y'know what?* . . .; *that reminds me* . . . When M says *you shoulda seen me once* (9), he is making an offer to tell a story with a preface functionally equivalent to: "Do you want to hear (I'm going to tell you anyway) what happened to me once." (See Sacks's perceptive work, 1970, on the organization of stories in conversation, and on the concept of prefaces which were the original inspiration for some of my remarks here.)

Similarly, stories do not just stop: they are ended. It is clear for the present data that all three speakers recognize a boundary after (85). There is a two-second pause, followed by a sharp change in topic to procedural matters, expressed in two tight exchanges of quite different sequential structure to the previous talk. We can label these two exchanges roughly as:

(86) MS question
(87) G   answer
(88) MS accept
(89) G   question
(90) MS answer

If we accept the claim that stories must be brought to a close, and not just stopped, then we may be able to find utterances which serve this function by looking closely at the talk before this boundary, which is clearly marked by several independent criteria.

One way to signal the end of a story in casual conversation is to use a cliché-cum-proverb with little informational content, of the type: *Still, that's life*; *Well, that's the way it goes*; *But something may turn up - you never know*; *Still, we may as well hope for the best*. G uses a cluster of such expressions between (74) and (81):

it might have been something . . . you know - that might have been something . . . it makes you think

Such utterances with little significant propositional content provide no new information which can serve as a resource for further talk, and can therefore serve as endings. Repetition of whole phrases is also a marker of endings. MS probably misinterprets (76-7) as requiring a show of interest to keep the talk going, and blunders in with a request for further details (78). But G refuses to treat the wh-interrogative (78) as a question: he simply repeats what he has already said (79-81).

(78) MS what you think it coulda been -
(79) G   well s pieces of bone about that size and you c -
(80)   y' know just - wee bits of bone and it makes you think -

Similarly, repetition introduces no new propositional content. The vagueness of G's utterance is probably also intentional: again, his utterances are probably intended as formal markers of the end of the story, and not as resources for further talk. By (86) even MS has realized that the story is over.

The utterances I have glossed, on loose semantic criteria, as cliché-cum-proverbs without much informational content are, however, also formally marked by almost the only complex tenses in the data; *might have been* (74, 76) and *keep thinking* (75); and by a number of simple present tenses, *you know* (76, 80), *makes* (80). (I am taking *keep* to be a catenative which forms complex verbal groups: cf. Palmer 1974.) These contrast with the predominantly simple past tenses of the story from (32) onwards. Significantly, the only other complex tenses in the data occur at other boundary points. I have already identified *you shoulda seen me once* (9) as a recognizable story beginning: we now see that this boundary is formally marked by *should have seen*. Note two further examples of this discourse function of tense-selection. At (32) G begins his predominantly simple past tense narrative about smashing up the house. This has been prefaced at (29-31) by M, who uses the present tense *folk just go up there and muck about there*. Also, G's other use of *might have been* (45) not only co-occurs with *I was too young to understand then* (49), which is at least potentially a generalization-cum-ending. But also, and more significantly, M chooses this point (51) to begin his longest continuous utterance in the data. Thus G seems to have come to a temporary halt and M seems to recognize this. Note that we thus have evidence that the participants themselves recognized and responded to the boundaries we have identified on independent formal criteria. The boundaries are not merely imposed by us as analysts, but take account of the turn-taking within the discourse.

There are two points here, then. One is descriptive: stories in conversation are structured - they have recognizable and describable beginnings and endings. And one is methodological: once we have candidate categories for structural markers, such as story endings, then we may be able to find candidate exponents of such markers in data where none are immediately apparent. That is, rather than dismiss G's utterances as defective, for example, as vague or repetitious, we may be able to discover their positive structural function. Birdwhistell (1970: 107) makes this point in a more general form: '. . . apparent redundancy is often an agent of reinforcement which serves . . . to tie together stretches of discourse . . . behaviour which appears merely repetitive at one level of analysis . . . always seems to be of special social and cultural significance at other levels'. Note briefly, also, the general implications of these comments on the discourse functions of tense selection. Tense has long been an embarrassment within sentence grammars of English. There is a striking lack of correspondence between tense and reference to time; time references are made by many devices other than tense; and there are problems over the distinction between tense and aspect. Within sentence grammars, little more can be done than to point to these complications and to suggest an ad hoc list of functions which tense selection may have: such as marking an utterance for politeness or formality, suggesting

that an event is unlikely or unreal, expressing tentativeness or certainty, or-
expressing the present relevance of past events (e.g. see Palmer 1974: ch. 3;
Sinclair 1972: 182ff). If it can be shown that tense selection has specific
discourse functions, then some of the problems may be solved. Sentence
grammars can concentrate on what they are designed to do best: describing
the formal aspects of tense formation (for example, the recursive generation of
complex tense forms), and discussion of the functions of tense can be 'lifted
out' of sentence grammar to be formally handled at the level of discourse.
Sinclair and Coulthard (1975) make similar comments on the ceiling effect in
grammar and related remarks on the discourse functions of tense.

A slightly different way of summarizing one of my main points is as follows.
In some ways, the transcribed talk may look chaotic. But on closer study, the
boys turn out to be telling a story which is highly constrained, conventionalized
and ritualized in two senses. First, in terms of content, it has many stock ingredients of a traditional mystery story: a haunted house, hidden money, old
paintings, bloodstains and splinters of bone - *I keep thinking in the night . . .
it makes you think* (75, 80). Second, there is its standard story format and
structure: stories do not just emerge from events - they have to be constructed. Incidents have to be made into talk, by being appropriately prefaced, told and ended in conventional, rule-governed ways. Events have to be
translated into speaking terms. Or, as Labov (1972c) puts it, experience has to
be transformed into narratives. (See below.) We can develop this point by
further considering other systems of organization in the data.

The effect of the narrative as an archetypical adventure or mystery story is
achieved mainly by the lexical choices made by the two story-tellers, who
draw on a common store of semantically related terms. For example, the
nouns most frequently used, and therefore made prominent for the listener,
refer first to the physical environment of the story: the *haunted house* (17, 23,
29, 69, 85), anaphoric references to it (29, 30, 32, 34, 35, 52), and references
to its *rafters* (31, 73), *walls* (36, 53, 58, 59, 83), and *stairs* (56, 58, 61, 63).
This thematic emphasis on the strange environment of the house gives
feasibility to the boys' unlikely discoveries. The shift of scene from the
familar and domestic to the strange and remote is a device common to both
adults' and children's adventure or fantasy literature, and is found in
Medieval Romance, classic novels, science fiction, popular adventures and
fairy tales. Note particularly the sharp shift at (29) from discussion of the
boys' school, their real everyday environment. I have already identified (29)
as a stereotypical story-opening of its kind marked by present tense selection.
A second set of nouns refer to the items found by the boys. Again, these present prominent information due to their frequency: *money* (34, 35), *crutches*
(38, 38, 62, 62, 75, 85), *paintings* (41, 44), and *bone* (68, 70, 79, 80). Collectively, these referents are also reminiscent of traditional trove in treasure and
adventure stories. Note also the frequent, conventionalized *it/that there/they*
+ copula, which is common to much narrative description (33, 34, 44, 51, 60,
64, 66, 68, 83). (In chapter 7 I give a much more detailed analysis of the functions of this construction in narrative.)

The two boys are clearly marking their roles as story-tellers and are making appropriate stylistic choices for the task. One final example: an interesting structure is G's (58-9) *I tugged and I tugged and the stairs fell in*. This is conspicuously reminiscent of the story of the wolf and the three little pigs, and of the wolf's repeated threat, *I'll huff and I'll puff and I'll blow your house down*. Whether or not G's choice of utterance is conscious, it seems an explicit indication that he is aware that he is telling a story. Stories do not just happen: they are constructed in rule-governed ways.

We can also study repeated elements on a syntagmatic axis, by noting various features of lexical repetition. First, repetition of lexical items may simply mark cohesion within single utterances of one speaker. See, for example (29-31, 38-9, 83-4). Second, repetition may mark cohesion in an individual speaker's utterances across a dialogue sequence. That is, a speaker repeats his own lexical items, but these are not necessarily taken up by other speakers. For examples in M's talk, note the repetition of *go up, went up* and *came up* in (30, 40, 43, 46, 52). From (29) to (50) M is in competition for the floor, and there is little shared lexis with G. But when conversational harmony is restored, shared lexis is used as a cohesive mechanism in the dialogue. Third, then, repetition may be continued across two or more speakers' utterances. I mentioned briefly above that such repetition may be a formal marker of joint production, which can function to show one speaker endorsing another's utterance. See, for example, the repetition of *wall, stairs* and *found* across (53-63). Fourth, cohesion across sequences of dialogue may be maintained by the frequent use of lexical items from a well-defined semantic field. Cohesion across (29-85) is marked by items from the semantic fields of destructive action and seeking and finding, that is, simple repetition of near synonyms: *smashed* (32, 35, 45, 57), *burst* (36), *knocking down* (52, 52), *burnt out* (29), *ripped* (54), *tugged* (58, 58), *tore* (56); and *find/found* (37, 38, 39, 41, 53, 59), *hid* (35, 85), *looking* (36), *see/saw* (44, 54), *scattered* (69, 84). As well as typifying the action of the story, these items provide the talk with close lexical cohesion.

Consider also the superficially neat lexical patterning between G and MS at (35-8), where there is one of the few question-answer exchanges in the data. We have the following surface lexical repetition and patterns:

(35-6)	G	I	looking	it (=money)
(37)	MS	you	find	it (=money)
(38)	G	I	found	(crutches)

But note that, although the surface form of G's response (38) is a satisfactory lexical and syntactic fit to (37), G is not, in fact, answering MS's question, but using the question as an entry into another related topic. That is, a fully fitting answer to (37) would be *yes (I found it)* or *no (I didn't find it)*.

A general point follows from these observations. Lexical repetition formally marks discourse cohesion and provides a conversational mechanism by which a polite surface consensus may be maintained. Lack of such cohesion probably marks lack of convergence and orientation between speakers (Sinclair and Coulthard 1975). But such surface fit may function merely to maintain solidarity in constructing the discourse itself, whilst speakers express different underlying positions. That is, such cohesive devices provide a marker of ritual equilibrium (Goffman 1955) in conversation. (Cf. chapter 10 for an extended discussion of this in disordered conversation.)

Interactional roles

The observation above about social roles such as story-teller can be developed as follows. It is an empirical finding that some discourse types can be usefully represented as variations on recursive two-part question-answer (QA) exchanges or three-part question-answer-feedback exchanges. I use *exchange* to mean the minimal unit of interactive discourse. For example, Sinclair and Coulthard (1975) propose that teacher-pupil talk is often characterized by an underlying exchange structure:

Teacher	initiation	I
Pupil	response	R
Teacher	feedback	F

A hypothetical dialogue might proceed:

Teacher	what's the capital of France?	I
Pupil	Paris	R
Teacher	right	F
Teacher	and Germany?	I
Pupil	Bonn	I
Teacher	good	F

Similarly, Coulthard and Ashby (1976) propose for doctor-patient talk, a three-part exchange structure of:

Doctor	initiation	e.g. you've only had one attack?
Patient	response	well, as far as I know
Doctor	follow-up	yeah

These are clearly not the only exchange types possible in these situations, but they are characteristic; and they provide a way of formalizing a mechanism by which one speaker, teacher or doctor, retains the conversational initiative.

It is intuitively clear that some types of interview (speech event) might be structured largely by such QA pairs or IFR triplets, with the interviewer filling the first and third slots in each exchange. However, this type of exchange structure does not hold for the present data. The conversational initiative does not return to MS after each of the boys' utterances. On the contrary, MS makes only a few follow-up utterances (42, 65, 71, 82) and two follow-up questions (37, 78) which are closely tied to something G has said. Thus, it would be of no help whatsoever to approach the present data with the notion that it is an interview and that the conversational roles are interviewer and interviewee. Such roles do not exist in the abstract. They have to be realized and sustained through particular discourse strategies. Roles such as *teacher*, *doctor*, *pupil* or *interviewer* cannot be abstracted from the interactional activities which constitute them.

The exchange structure in the present data might usefully be represented as an initiation (I) by one speaker followed up by some kind of supportive item. If we take conversational support to be one kind of feedback (F), we can propose an exchange structure IF. Exponents of F are the types of acknowledgement, endorsement, claims and proofs of understanding discussed above. This structural formulation permits a close study of the general observation that listeners in two-party or multi-party discourse are primarily expected to provide audience appreciation and ritual support to the speaker. Lack of such conversational support on the telephone, for example, quickly leads to a breakdown in communication and to *Hello! Are you still there? I thought you'd hung up.*

Discourse analysis and interaction

One important implication of discourse analysis is as follows. One of the biggest linguistic conundrums of all is: how do we understand what someone is talking about? Traditional linguistics has little directly to say about this. However, I have shown here that conversational analysis can answer an answerable version of this question, namely: how do speakers show that they understand each other? I have suggested several mechanisms by which conversationalists can show that they are in conversational touch. Sacks (1970) proposes the concepts of claiming and proving understanding, which I have used above; Sinclair and Coulthard (1975) talk of speakers' orientation to each other; McIntosh (1963) talks of markers of involvement; Bernstein (1971a) talks of sociocentric sequences. And these concepts are all ways of making more precise Malinowski's concept of phatic communion. Elsewhere (Stubbs 1976), I develop further the metaphor of speakers keeping in touch with each other. It is clear that, whereas linguistics studies language, discourse analysis can study the actual mechanisms by which communication, understanding and interaction are maintained. Language (static structures and systems) and communication (dynamic processes) are by no means parallel concepts.

Expressed more generally, this means that discourse analysis must be concerned with ways in which information is selected, formulated and conveyed between speakers; or alternatively, assumed to be known and shared knowledge, taken for granted, and not selected at all. It is therefore concerned not just with whether statements are true or false, but with states of information, and differential access to information. Part of a speaker's task is to understand his or her hearers, what they know already, and what they expect and want to hear. Such points immediately make clear the importance of concepts such as information focus, and given and new information. (Again, see chapter 10 for a detailed discussion of the importance of these concepts in conversation).

However, if we recognize this view of meanings being negotiated between speakers, we are left with a very general problem which has been called the co-ordination problem (Bennett 1976: 186-7). How is such co-ordination possible? Speaker and hearer always have different problems. And there is no pre-existing fact to which they both have access, and to which they can refer. The speaker wants to convey X, and makes a guess about what the hearer knows already. Hearers want to make sense of this, taking into account what they think the speaker is assuming. And so on. It is not at all obvious what has to be co-ordinated with what. This problem of negotiating mutual understanding, when speaker and hearer inevitably have different perspectives, gives a glimpse of one particular theoretical void over which discourse analysis is suspended.

Narrative structure

My analysis in this chapter has, admittedly, been informal, although it has been quite detailed; and I have indicated how it could easily be made more systematic, for example, by using Halliday and Hasan's (1976) method of analysing textual cohesion. Another way of making some of my observations more systematic is to analyse the narrative in ways proposed by Labov (1972c). His structural analysis of narratives of personal experience allows me to draw together several points I have made in this chapter.

Labov (1972c) defines a minimal narrative as a sequence of two clauses which are temporally ordered: a change in their sequence results in a change in the sequence of the narrative events. For example, the following tell two different stories under a normal interpretation:

10 I hit John and John hit me.
11 John hit me and I hit John.

Although neither temporal sequence nor cause and effect are explicitly mentioned, we would normally assume that a different person started the fight in each case. (Cf. chapter 10 for more detailed discussion of how such conjunctions are interpreted.)

Such *narrative clauses* are also characterized syntactically by (a) simple past tense, and (b) unmarked word order, namely subject-predicate-complement -adjunct (SPCA). The skeleton of the narrative told by G can therefore be identified from such clauses, for example (56-9):

S	P	C	A
I	got	a rope	
	smashed in		at the side of the wall
I	tugged		
I	tugged		
the stairs	fell in		

As I suggested above, clauses with other tense forms and other possibly more complex syntactic structure have functions other than sustaining the narrative action. Thus most stories contain at or near the beginning some identification of the time, place or persons of the story. A syntactic marker of such *orientation clauses* is past progressive tense, for example, at

(2)   I used to go along there when I was much younger.

Orientation clauses are also characterized by the fact that their place in a longer sequence can be altered without necessarily altering their interpretation.

Labov's analysis of the ways in which personal experience is transformed into narrative form is much more complex than I can show here. However, my brief comments should indicate how an overall structural analysis of such data is possible on the basis of formal features of the language. These include the discourse function of different syntactic structures and tense selection; and the function of a shift away from basic simple narrative syntax (cf. Wolfson 1979).

The complete structure which Labov proposes for narratives of personal experience includes the following structural elements:

Abstract	providing a summary or encapsulation of the story.
Orientation	identifying the time, place, persons, activities and situations; usually marked by past progressive tense.
Evaluations	indicating the point or interest of the story.
Narrative clauses	as defined above.
Result	saying what finally happened.
Coda	signalling the end.

The only obligatory element is at least two narrative clauses. Narrative clauses also differ from other elements in that their relative sequence is fixed, although the abstract and orientation will tend to occur near the beginning. I do not have the space here to analyse the whole story in this way, but it should be clear in general terms how my observations could be reorganized in such a way.

In the remainder of this chapter I will make explicit the general interest of such analyses of conversation for an understanding of language.

Natural conversation

An important general notion which I have used several times, without proper definition, is the concept of *natural* conversation. In fact, I have used, without distinction, several roughly synonymous terms, and other terms are found in the literature. For *natural* conversation, one finds terms such as *spontaneous, unplanned* and *casual.* These terms are opposed to terms such as *artificial, contrived, invented, introspective, intuitive* and *hypothetical.* I may even appear to have argued myself into a contradiction, for I have talked of the boys' conversation as being both spontaneous and also as highly organized. This objection is easily answered: behaviour may be automatic, unselfconscious, and in that sense spontaneous, yet nevertheless deeply organized in ways that are generally unrecognized by users. Indeed, this is true of much linguistic behaviour. However, the concept of spontaneous discourse requires more explicit discussion than I have given it so far.

Although many such terms are used more or less synonymously in the literature, they disguise two rather different distinctions. The first distinction is between (a) language which occurs naturally without any intervention from the linguist; and (b) language which is elicited by the linguist as part of some experiment. Type (b) includes data which are the linguist's own introspections or intuitions: data elicited by the linguist from him or herself. A second distinction is between (c) language which is spontaneous in the sense of unplanned, and which is composed in real time in response to immediate situational demands; and (d) language which is deliberately planned, rehearsed, thought about, altered and edited. Type (c) characterizes most spoken language, including everyday conversation, whereas type (d) characterizes most formal written language. (Cf. chapter 5.) It might be argued that normal conversation is, by definition, unplanned and unplanable, and that it is relatively unpredictable, except sometimes in the short term. Types (b) and (d) often coincide. That is, introspective data are often highly self-conscious and mulled over at great length with reference to a particular theoretical problem, and this constitutes a major limitation in using such data as representative of normal language use (cf. Labov 1975). It means that many examples used in linguistic arguments are stylistically closer to written than to spoken language, because both written language and well-considered introspective data are heavily edited and revised. This is a problem with much data in transformational grammar, despite the fact that it claims to study language, independently of particular varieties of language (cf. Crystal 1980). There is confusion, therefore, over the object of study: characteristics of English or characteristics of restricted styles of English, for example.

There are therefore at least two dimensions along which data can lie, and examples are given in table 3.

Ochs (1979) provides a very useful discussion of the distinction between planned and unplanned discourse, and of many formal linguistic features which characterize speech which is unplanned and relatively unpredictable.

Table 3 Examples of two dimensions along which data can lie

	Naturally occurring	Planned
Everyday conversation	+	−
Much written language	+	+
Introspective data	−	+

She defines unplanned discourse as talk which is not thought out prior to its expression (1979: 55), and has not been prepared, but points out that much discourse falls somewhere between the two extremes of planned and unplanned. It may well be, for example, that, in the data used in this chapter, G has told his story about the haunted house before. The narrative may have been planned and rehearsed overall, but it has clearly not been rehearsed in all its details, since it is locally managed, utterance-by-utterance, to take account of the demands of social interaction.

I have already given examples of many of the features which Ochs lists as characteristic of unplanned speech in general: frequent repetition; simple active sentences with unmarked SPCA word order; the joint construction of propositions over two speakers' utterances. Other features which Ochs notes can also be illustrated from the data, a tendency to string together co-ordinate clauses, often linked by *and*, rather than to use subordinate clauses; the juxtaposition of clauses with no explicit link at all, e.g. (72-4); arguments and predicates not syntactically linked, e.g. (78-80); the deletion of referents, including subjects of clauses, e.g. (41), (52); the use of deictic modifiers (e.g. *this*) rather than definite articles e.g. (29); left-dislocated syntactic structures, in which the subject noun phrase is followed by a co-referential pronoun, e.g. (29). Taken together, several of these characteristics mean that semantic relations between propositions or between parts of propositions (e.g. subject and predicate) are often not explicitly marked. Mere juxtaposition may be used, or an element of information may be deleted altogether. In addition, it means that topic–comment structures are prominent.

These points do not imply that the speakers' language is 'ungrammatical'. However, they do imply that the syntax is significantly different from the syntax of most formal written language. In addition, they imply that the unit of *sentence* is not always applicable to conversational English. There is no difficulty in dividing the transcript into clauses with a basic SPCA structure. However, any attempt to divide the transcript into sentences involves making arbitrary decisions about sentence boundaries, due to the large number of clauses co-ordinated with *and*, and a few other items such as *but* and *then*. Rather than sentences, we have loosely co-ordinated clause complexes (cf. Crystal 1980: 159).

These observations are of central importance to the linguistic description of English, which has tended to be almost exclusively based on styles towards the more formal and planned end of the stylistic continuum. Linguistic description has therefore tended to overemphasize certain syntactic devices, and has often failed to study the function of different syntactic choices.

Native-speaker fluency

The concept of unplanned discourse raises one other issue of very general importance for linguistics, although it is not often discussed. This is the question of what constitutes native-speaker *fluency* in a language. When the concept has been discussed, it has generally been from the point of view of language teaching (Crystal and Davy 1975; Leeson 1975) or language pathology (Dalton and Hardcastle 1977).

A common-sense observation is that native ability in a language involves *speaking* it *fluently*. One would not normally regard someone as having native competence if they were able only to understand written language, however perfectly. The whole of Chomskyan linguistics is, of course, an explicit attempt to characterize the concept of a native speaker's competence in a language. However, the notion of fluency plays no part in this concept of competence. The Chomskyan view is static. Linguistic competence involves the ability to do syntactic and semantic manipulations on isolated sentences or pairs of sentences: for example, the ability to recognize ambiguous sentences, or whether one sentence entails another, or is synonymous with another. This current Chomskyan view therefore ignores two things which are central to the common-sense view of linguistic competence, and also to the view of discourse competence which underlies my discussion here: the ability to handle connected discourse, and the ability to do this in real time without prior rehearsal. In other words, the native speaker can improvise, maintain continuity in speech and comprehension, respond immediately to unexpected utterances, make rapid changes of topic and speaker, and so on. The native speaker has therefore the ability to use language under the communicative stress (cf. Givón 1979: 105) of real time processing. These points hold, even given the generally recognized normal non-fluencies (cf. Crystal and Davy 1969) in unplanned discourse: that is, normal hesitation phenomena, filled pauses, repetitions, false starts, and the like.

There are two main points at issue. First, the kinds of discourse phenomena discussed in this chapter are important to a balanced concept of native-speaker competence in a language. Second, the common-sense concept of fluency is clearly a cover-term for a complex of factors, but is worth consideration alongside the linguist's concept of competence, which is normally very highly idealized.

The implication that syntactic and linguistic organization in general should be studied from the point of view of perceptual and processing strategies is an interesting issue, but has not been studied in detail by linguists.

Conclusions

My presentation in this chapter has been relatively informal, although I have commented in detail on several formal linguistic features of the data. I have shown that spoken discourse is open to analysis. The analysis as it stands is illustrative, rather than systematic: I have not, for example, proposed an analysis which gives a comprehensive description of the data; although I have indicated briefly how one could move further in the direction of such rigorous and comprehensive description. I have also shown that much traditional linguistic description neglects intuitively important aspects of linguistic competence, because it neglects a close study of naturally occurring conversational language. Discourse analysis therefore appears to be both possible and interesting, despite the glimpse into several theoretical chasms along the way.

DATA APPENDIX

This is an extract from an interview with two boys, G and M, aged 12. They are talking about Newhaven, the district of Edinburgh where they live. MS is the interviewer (the author).

```
G    there's quite a lot of they old fishermen's houses -           (1)
     I used to go along there when I was much younger but            (2)
     they've demolished most of the Haveners -                       (3)
M    aye (        )                                                  (4)
G    hardly anything left except the ⌈ harbour                       (5)
M                                    ⌊ (          )                  (6)
G    and the old primary - that - that dates back - that's           (7)
     a hundred and twenty seven years old                            (8)
M    you shoulda seen me once - ⌈ (          )                       (9)
G                               ⌊ all the old houses are            (10)
     knocked down                                                   (11)
M    we were mucking about in the playground -                      (12)
     (several seconds inaudible)                                    (13)
G    I climbed - the roof of the: - what's that height             (14)
     from one roof - you climb onto the one roof and right          (15)
     up the drainpipes about sixty seventy feet isn't it Mike       (16)
M    what the haunted ⌈ house                                       (17)
G                     ⌊ (          ) - no - at the - school         (18)
     once you've got onto that wee roof where the ball goes         (19)
     up - right onto the top on the top s - near the spire -        (20)
     's about seventy feet - isn't it - it's roughly that -         (21)
     I climbed ⌈ up that                                            (22)
M            ⌊ (      brother) up the top of the haunted           (23)
     house - and then on top of that                                (24)
G    I went up the top of the school and I was on                   (25)
```

```
        the spire and this - the school in the centre's got a          (26)
        big huge skylight I just about fell through                    (27)
        that                                                           (28)
M       this haunted house it was burnt out - an' er - folk just      (29)
        go up there and - muck about there and muck about             (30)
        in the rafters                                                (31)
G       I smashed the place up somebody you told me when I            (32)
        was about five - ⌐ or six                    there was m-     (33)
M                       ⌊ there was money there                       (34)
G       money hidden there and I smashed the place in I ju -          (35)
        looking for it I burst down every wall and everything -       (36)
MS      d'you find it (1)                                             (37)
G       I found t two pair o' crutches - old crutches                 (38)
        bloodstained but that was all I found hhh                     (39)
M       I went up ⌐ (              )                                  (40)
G                 ⌊ found a couple of old ⌐ paintings                 (41)
MS                                        ⌊ not much good             (42)
M       I went ⌐ and                    ⌐ I went up with              (43)
G              ⌊ but I di I d I just saw ⌊ they were old paints so    (44)
        I smashed them in they might ⌐ have been something            (45)
M                                     ⌊ I went up with my pal -       (46)
    ⌐ y'know - my pal and myself                                     (47)
G   ⌊ (         )    (         )                                     (48)
    ⌐ I was too young to understand then                              (49)
M   ⌊ (             )                                                (50)
        there was nothing - to do in the afternoon so he just        (51)
        came up there - started knocking the knocking the            (52)
        walls down - never found a thing - all the walls are         (53)
        ripped away - and all you could see is the - (out)           (54)
        the frames o' them                                           (55)
G       I tore the stairs away as well and I got -                   (56)
        a rope and I smashed in at the side of the                   (57)
        wall and I - tugged and I tugged and the stairs              (58)
    ⌐ fell in - and then the wall that was where I found             (59)
M   ⌊ aye there was only about that much (left                       (60)
        of the) stair                                                (61)
G       a pair of crutches - ⌐ bloodstained crutches                 (62)
M                            ⌊ these stairs only about that          (63)
        size ⌐    - and it's                                         (64)
MS       ⌊ mm                                                        (65)
M       just no support there's only about - that much of a          (66)
        support y'know for - thing                                   (67)
G       there was wee bits of what *look*ed like *bone* -            (68)
        scattered all over the house - but - I just - sharpened      (69)
        it up you know you can sharpen up bone -                     (70)
MS      uhuh -                                                        (71)
```

G	I just ⌐ - used it for anything -	(72)
M	└ the rafters	(73)
G	it might have been something -	(74)
	they bloodstained crutches I - I keep thinking in my	(75)
	the night you know - that that might have been	(76)
	something -	(77)
MS	what you think it coulda been -	(78)
G	well s pieces of bone about that size and you c -	(79)
	y'know just - wee bits of bone and it makes you	(80)
	think -	(81)
MS	mm -	(82)
G	cos they were in the wall you know - somebody	(83)
	might have been had - scattered the bits all over the	(84)
	house and hid the crutches and that (2)	(85)
MS	what time does this period end is it ⌐ ten	(86)
G	└ quarter past	(87)
MS	quarter past oh that's all ⌐ right	(88)
G	└ what time is it	(89)
MS	ten past . . .	(90)

ACKNOWLEDGEMENTS

This chapter is a revised version of an article first published as chapter 2 of Michael Stubbs, *Discourse Analysis*, Oxford: Blackwell, 1983, pp. 15-39. A preliminary version, co-authored with Deirdre Burton, was circulated in mimeo in the *MALS Journal* (Midland Association for Linguistic Studies), Summer 1975.

10

Are there disorders of conversation?

Introduction

In chapter 8 I discussed some relations between language and logic, and in chapter 9 I defined discourse analysis as the study of what makes written texts or spoken discourse hang together: what is meant by discourse coherence? Is this a logical matter, or do conversations have their own distinctive kind of organization? This chapter develops both of these topics, by studying data from children who appear to have a linguistic or cognitive disorder: they seem to have particular difficulties in speaking logically or coherently. The chapter uses a type of argument which is common and useful in linguistics and psychology: looking at abnormal language use can illuminate normality. It is often when we study how language can go wrong that we realize the enormous complexity that underlies the apparently simplest of everyday conversational exchanges. The general principle concerns the value of error analysis. By studying, for example, the mistakes made by young children learning their native language, or by speakers learning a foreign language, or by studying slips of the tongue, we can learn a great deal about what is involved in normal native linguistic competence.

This chapter also provides a case where the technical descriptive terminology and concepts which have been developed in linguistics are necessary in analysing a real practical problem. Everyday language just does not have the conceptual distinctions required to provide a precise description of the semantic and pragmatic problems which the children have. And a precise classification of their problems is a necessary first step in diagnosing and then treating their difficulties.

Notational conventions

(A)   attested data.
(A : S)   attested data from school for language disordered children.
(A : name)   attested data from work of scholar cited in references.
(M)   modified data, i.e. attested, but simplified by deleting utterances
             which seem irrelevant to the point at issue.
(I)   intuitive data, invented just to illustrate a point.

T   therapist/teacher/adult.
P   patient/pupil/child.

This chapter is about children[1] who apparently suffer from a language disorder which makes it difficult for them to produce coherent or logical conversation. The reason for my cautious use of the word *apparently* is really the topic of the whole chapter.

The argument may be of interest to three categories of readers. First, some readers may be directly interested in such children, because they have to teach them or try to help them in some way. Second, other readers may be teachers concerned with 'normal' children. Most children clearly do not have the problems described here. Nevertheless, teachers constantly complain that pupils do not write 'clearly' and 'explicitly': but what does 'coherent' writing involve? A look at extreme cases of incoherence may illuminate normality. Third, other readers may simply be interested in what can go wrong with conversation: the glimpse that this gives us into just how complex conversation is, how much we normally take for granted, and how complex are the inferences which we perform on even the simplest of exchanges. By studying what can go wrong in language, we can give some insight into the normal working of the system.

Semantic pragmatic disorder?

Most children who become patients at speech therapy clinics or pupils at special schools for language disordered children, have problems with phonology or syntax; and, compared to the children described here, their problems are simpler to recognize and describe, if not to remedy. However, some children present complex problems in the use of language and in the comprehension of language in context. This can seriously disrupt normal conversation, and therefore social interaction and the children's education. Various terms have been used to refer to such children. One of the most useful is probably *semantic pragmatic disorder* (henceforth SPD), since, intuitively, there appears to be something wrong with the children's semantic and pragmatic systems: that is, the aspects of language which are concerned with the meaning of utterances and their use in social contexts. (The term appears to have been used first by Rapin and Allen 1983.) That is, children who have phonological and syntactic disorders produce language which may be acceptable in terms of meaning and content, but is deficient in form; whereas children with a semantic pragmatic disorder produce language which is acceptable in phonological and syntactic *form*, but appears disordered in terms of *content* and *use*.

Therapists are uncertain, however, whether the term applies to one single identifiable group of children or to different groups with overlapping symptoms. They are also uncertain whether the children have a language disorder per se, or whether they have a disorder in thought or a moderate learning disability which is reflected in their language: that is, it is uncertain whether the disordered language is just an effect of something else.

Bishop (1981, 1984; and Bishop and Rosenbloom in press) has provided a review of what is known about such children, although, in fact, most of the evidence is anecdotal: there is no body of research, and very little in the literature. The first point is that they are children within the normal non-verbal IQ range, and do not suffer from obvious emotional or behavioural disturbance, although their behaviour may be socially odd. The second is that they are strikingly different from other language disordered children. Their articulation may be perfectly normal, and their syntax fluent and complex. (Another term sometimes used is 'fluent language disorder', although this term is hardly helpful or descriptive of anything.) They may have syntactic problems, typically with use of tense and with pronouns. These may appear minor, although errors in verb forms and reference can hide complex semantic and pragmatic problems. However, it is the content of what they say that is most recognizably odd, loose, tangential, unexpected, inappropriate and irrelevant. (I will comment on these impressionistic terms below.) Their comprehension of words and phrases, and of concrete matters, may be good, but they have comprehension problems with connected discourse, and with subject matter at a higher and more abstract level. Their comprehension problems do not therefore become evident in standard picture tests. They can often pass such tests, but have problems in understanding much in real life. On the other hand, they may misunderstand the pictures used in tests and give them bizarre interpretations. Younger children may show signs of echolalia (although the definition of what exactly constitutes repetition is very difficult). Even older children may be fascinated by the sounds of language, with no attention to its meaning on occasion. They may have problems with reading, being able to read aloud quite fluently, but having problems with understanding what they are reading. Their social behaviour may be rather odd: they may have problems with questions of social etiquette; they may be rather withdrawn, and have difficulty in making friends; or they may be over-friendly, appear naive, and show no normal shyness with strangers; they are often fidgety. They often seem to have shown quite severe delay in the initial acquisition of language, sometimes with no speech at all until six or seven years: such extreme delay is very rare. This seems to be the only possible cause about which there is any agreement, although it is not known just how such a delay might cause SPD, nor what causes the delay.

The children show some similarities with other groups of children, but these similarities appear not to be very significant. For example, there is a subgroup of hydrocephalic children with language problems: they can chatter away in superficially good language, and appear bright, but, on longer acquaintance, the superficiality of their behaviour (sometimes known as the 'cocktail-party syndrome') becomes apparent. However, such children have a clear organic, physical cause underlying their language problem. Children with SPD also show some similarities with the behaviour of mildly autistic children, who certainly show deficiencies in the use of language for communicative purposes. But autistic children are typically severely socially withdrawn, and often totally unresponsive to social relationships; their behaviour is ritualistic and obsessional; all of which makes them different from the children discussed here. Autism, however, is not itself a clearly defined disorder. In general, SPD appears not to be an emotional problem: it occurs in children who appear otherwise quite normal. (This seems to render inappropriate another term found in the literature: 'social-emotional disorder'. This may refer to a distinct group of children.)

Other symptoms which are reported by therapists include the following. (But bear in mind that they report that all the children involved are slightly different, and that they have no real confidence that a single group is involved: there are at least many different degrees.) The children's behaviour may be quite normal for longish periods of time: it is possible for strangers to talk to them for some time without noticing anything odd. They respond to the surface meaning of utterances, and not to their underlying intended meaning. They appear naive because they take everything at face value. They have difficulty in making sense of the world, and in connecting language to action. They often appear to understand what is said to them, but they do not act accordingly. They often do not obey instructions, and may therefore be seen as naughty by teachers. They reason along odd lines: often their reasoning is plausible, but somehow is different from the norm. They form odd associations between words and go off at tangents; and they may have difficulty in finding words, when asked to name objects. The children appear to change topic abruptly, to fail to take into account what their hearers know, or to fail to draw simple inferences about sequences of events. (Another term sometimes used is 'association disorder', although, again, this term is used to refer to many different disorders in neurophysiology and is therefore not very helpful.) It is often time and space adverbials which are confused. (This emphasizes the difficulty of separating syntax and semantics: see below.) They lack a common mode of thinking: they just see the world in a different way. They seem unaware of what information is shared and generally taken for granted. They have problems in organizing ideas, and in generalizing.

Although the literature on SPD is sparse, researchers are increasingly reporting problems that lie outside the traditional speech therapy areas, and use terms such as communicative, discourse and pragmatic disorders. McTear (1985) gives a useful review.

What I will try and do in this chapter is to relate such observations to the details of the children's conversational behaviour, and to begin to classify the children's problems in a logical way. Note initially, then, that the comments above amount to saying that the children have problems in relating surface linguistic forms and meanings to underlying meanings, and in relating forms and meanings to both hearers and to the world.

The contribution of discourse analysis?

In summary, the language of such children gives the intuitive impression of being incoherent, confused, contradictory or illogical. Assuming for the moment that this description makes sense, it raises the question of what is meant by coherent, cohesive or connected dialogue, in which speakers co-operate smoothly to construct well-formed sequences of discourse, and in which each utterance is a relevant or appropriate response to the preceding one. Discourse analysis is the study of what is meant by discourse coherence. As such, it faces the problem that the ability to contribute to coherent discourse seems to depend on a range of skills, some narrowly linguistic, but others concerned with a much more general ability to make rational inferences on the basis of everyday knowledge about the world. Is it therefore even sensible to try to define a notion such as discourse relevance?

A specific conversational disorder?

I will take the view in this chapter that the only way to investigate these children's problems is to study closely the details of the exchanges which are perceived intuitively as 'odd' by therapists and teachers, and to try to describe precisely what the oddity consists in. I will try, in other words, to give some precision to terms such as 'odd' or 'illogical' discourse. There appears to be no agreement on any possible medical cause of SPD, and the disorder may be missed on standard tests. We must therefore try to work out what is wrong by studying what the children actually say.

There is one other general point, before I start discussing the data. As I said above, there is disagreement amongst therapists as to whether SPD is a specific disorder of conversation, which can exist independently of other disorders, linguistic or cognitive. There do appear to be individuals who speak fluently with normal phonology and syntax, but whose interactive skills are disordered. It is quite possible, however, that the conversational disorder is only the surface observable symptom, and that it is a reflection of some higher-order cognitive disorder. Put very simply, perhaps the child's conversation is confused, because the child is confused, and has problems in reasoning and thinking. Furthermore it is difficult to disentangle cognitive from social skills, since both involve the ability to make inferences. On the other hand, there may be no way to observe certain aspects of the child's inferential ability, except by a close study of conversational sequences.

Then, as one might expect, some children do show both conversational and other language disorders. In such cases we have the normal problems associated with interpreting a correlation: two things co-occur, and it is unclear whether A causes B, or whether B causes A, or whether both A and B are caused by something else. It is perfectly plausible, *a priori*, that syntactic disorders might cause conversational disorders. For example, syntactic disorders might cause problems in formulating certain kinds of speech act (for example, requests), and this could disrupt discourse. So the conversational disorder would be an effect, not a cause. Equally, it is perfectly plausible, *a priori*, that if a child has problems in interacting with people, then s/he will have difficulties in learning at least some syntactic forms. In this case, the conversational disorder would be the cause, and the syntactic disorder the effect. Equally, it is perfectly plausible, *a priori*, that both are caused by something else, for example, a higher cognitive disorder. In some of the data cited below, it will be clear that the children do have syntactic problems, even if these seem minor compared with the conversational disorder. In other data, it will be clear that the borderline between syntactic and discourse errors can be very difficult to draw. This casts doubt, unfortunately, on the value of the term 'semantic pragmatic disorder'.

Linguistic or cognitive disorder?

I will start with cases where it seems difficult to disentangle the conversational disorder from a more general cognitive problem, since such data point to a problem at the centre of discourse analysis itself. Namely, it is obvious that discourse is structured, but it is not obvious whether this structure is linguistic.
   Consider the following examples:

1 T   what do you do after school
   P   you just play and then you finish your breakfast   (A : S)

What strikes me about this exchange is that there is nothing wrong with the language as such. The child reports an odd sequence of events, which does not coincide with our assumptions about normal daily activities. But the discourse itself is well formed: the child answers the question he is asked in a perfectly grammatical sentence. Similarly:

2 P   so I go home before I get in the bus
   T   I see
   P   so my daddy went to work today because it raining   (A : S)

Apart from a slight oddity in the syntax in the last sentence, these utterances are strange in that they report unexpected temporal and causal sequences. But if that is what the child meant to say, then he has said it successfully. (These examples are from the same conversation with one child.) The question is: does the child have a linguistic problem with conjunctions (*before, after, because*), or does he have problems in relating the sequence of clauses to the sequence of events in the world? (This type of example has also received a lot of discussion in the literature on *because* in normal children. Cf. Perera 1984 ch. 3.)

These examples illustrate the distinction between coherence and plausibility. Whereas coherence is a property of discourse, plausibility is a property of a temporal, causal or intentional framework, which depends on background knowledge about the world (Johnson-Laird 1983: 376-7). Discourse that recounts a bizarre sequence of events can therefore be coherent, but implausible; and, of course, much fantasy literature does just this.

Or consider this example:

3   T   when's your birthday Karen
     P   October the third . . . I don't know why
         I have the same birthday I always have
         the same birthday
     T   it's the same date every year   (M : S)

Again, there seems to be nothing wrong with the discourse as such, although the child seems to be confused about how birthdays are defined. It is a moot point whether this is a matter of real-world knowledge, or a matter of the meaning of a word, and therefore a part of linguistic competence.

Or this one:

4   T   when does it snow
         does it snow in the summer
     P   yeah
     T   does it
     P   yeah sometimes   (A : S)

This example is rather more complex. However, again, there is nothing wrong with the discourse per se. The child answers the questions he is asked, producing normal short-form answers. He just appears to be making an odd or untrue claim. (Although perhaps he has in mind that there are places in the world where it does indeed snow in summer: part of the problem with these data is that it is usually possible to explain away any individual example; it is the cumulative effect of many such examples in the children's language that makes their discourse sound strange. Such data show the need for elicitation in a controlled domain.)

However, T's question is also odd. She is clearly not asking the question because she wants to know the answer. It is a test question: an artificial question designed to find out if P knows the answer. Perhaps it is a trick? Not as obvious as it seems? And her second question is not neutral: it seems phrased in such a way as to expect "yes" as an answer. It is probably impossible in context to ask entirely neutral questions (see Stubbs 1983b: 115). Finally, note that P's second utterance backs down on his initial claim. He clearly recognizes that his initial claim is regarded as inappropriate, although he does not abandon it entirely. And this recognition signals considerable discourse competence. (Teachers' test or pseudo-questions have received a great deal of discussion in the literature: for example, see Stubbs 1983a, for a review. The children discussed here probably receive more than their fair share of test questions, because of the amount of language therapy they receive. Therapists comment that the SPD children seem to have more problems with pseudo-questions than children with syntactic disorders.)

Or consider this one, again slightly more complex to analyse:

5 (T and P are talking about P's holiday)
    T   do you know how long you went for
    P   no
    T   a week was it a week
    P   yeah   (A : S)

Again, T appears to be asking P a question to which she already knows the answer. But in this case it is a piece of information to which P should have privileged access: after all, it was his holiday. P ought to know more about it than T. We will see later that several of these children appear to have difficulty in distinguishing who knows what.

Or consider this one:

6 T   now do you want to see if you can play
           some games with me
   P   yes
   T   they're very easy games
   P   they are indeed
   T   well we'll see   (A : McTear)

It is difficult to state exactly what is wrong with the discourse here. The turn-taking shows no problems: P produces appropriate short-form answers. The problem seems to lie in what P may appropriately claim knowledge of. One might say that P has no personal experience of the games, and cannot know whether they are easy or not. But T has just told him that they are easy, and P simply politely agrees! Suppose the exchange had gone:

7 T   they're all in big boxes
   P   they are indeed   (I)

This seems normal, since the evidence for P's agreement is observable. The problem seems to lie in the varying accessibility of different kinds of propositional knowledge: is it objectively observable and publicly verifiable, or is it inherently a matter of subjective evaluation? What is the speaker's responsibility or justification for an assertion?

Here is a final example, where the problem in the discourse does not seem to be purely linguistic.

8 (conversation takes place in Nottingham, about three hours' travelling time from London)

```
P   we go home every day
T   do you go home every day
P   yes
T   where do you live Stephen
P   London
T   so you don't go home every day do you                    (A : S)
```

Again, there is nothing wrong with the discourse. The child interacts, answers questions, produces normal short-form answers. His turn-taking is normal, with no hesitations. The problem is simply that his answers are untrue! A simple test that there is nothing wrong with his discourse is that if I had been talking to the child, rather than a therapist who knew him, I would not have noticed anything wrong with his answers. The oddity is apparent only to someone who had some real-world knowledge about the child. This distinguishes this example from several above. (Again, note that this individual instance could be explained away: there is an ambiguity about the referent of the term *home*. Perhaps T and P had just interpreted the word differently. Again, there is a need for the controlled elicitation of data.)

In fact, this child seems to put the construction of well-formed discourse *above* the provision of a true account. He appears to have developed a coping strategy: he fulfills the discourse obligations, and gives possible, meaningful answers. The problem is that this seems to take precedence over truth and accuracy. Perhaps he is unable to sustain both at once. Perhaps the problem is that conversation demands the integration of two rather different things: interactional skills, plus the organization of knowledge and its presentation to a conversational partner. (I have taken the term 'coping strategy' from McTear 1984: see this for a discussion of similar data.)

This example also means that we have to develop the distinction above between coherence and plausibility. Here P's discourse is coherent, but implausible to T, since she knows that you cannot reasonably travel from Nottingham to London every day. We might say that the discourse makes *sense* in principle, but not in practice. The internal discourse coherence is maintained: the problem arises in the correspondence between the discourse and the world. Briefly, the additional distinction which we need is between *sense* (i.e. internal linguistic relations) and *significance* (i.e. relations between language and the world, including what the language refers to).

We still have to explain the concept of *plausibility*, however. How do we know what *is* plausible? One hypothesis is that for many relatively stereotyped everyday activities, we have 'scripts': that is, sets of social roles, objects and instructions, which specify normal behaviour (Brown and Yule 1983b and Johnson-Laird 1983 review the literature on 'scripts'). For example, we have a script for getting up in the morning (cf. example (1) above), which contains items such as: get up; wash; have breakfast; brush teeth; go to school; etc. The script embodies our expectations about normal behaviour in this situation. Similarly, we might have scripts for going to a restaurant, taking a rail journey, and so on. The concept of scripts might provide a basis for some teaching or testing material for the children. However, it is evident that we can also interpret discourse about new events: for them, we have no script, but we interpret them on the basis of our general knowledge about the world, which supports more general inferences.

Examples of ill-formed discourse

The distinction I have tried to draw between discourse problems per se and problems which are displayed in discourse should be clearer if I give just two examples where there appears to be difficulty in the construction of well-formed discourse itself.

9 T   are they friends of yours
     P   they are friends of mine   (A : McTear)

10 T   did you go camping in the woods
      P   camping in the woods (shouts)
      T   yeah did you ever do that
      P   yeah he ever do that
      . . .
      T   when are you going home
      P   um he *is* going home   (M : Greenlee 1981)

In these cases, there is something wrong with the construction of the discourse. The child is not producing the appropriate short-form elliptic answers, and in the second case he does not answer two questions at all. In the second case, P also has problems with pronoun reference: *he* probably refers to P himself.

Conversational inferences

I have started with these examples of cases where the oddity does not seem to be located in the language itself, since they raise a serious problem which is at the very centre of discourse analysis. This is that the ability to take part in discourse is not a purely linguistic skill, but involves the ability to make rational inferences. The definition of coherent discourse therefore involves both linguistic skill and the ability to make rational inferences. Consider this example, from a language disordered child, but cited here for its perfect normality:

11 (talking about P's sister)
      T   what sort of dancing does she do
      P   she wears them funny shoes
      T   oh I know   (A : S)

P's answer is indirect, but it is perfectly appropriate and intelligible. The hearer just has to infer its relevance: for example, "you know, that kind of dancing where you wear funny shoes, I've forgotten what it's called". I assume the child means ballet or tap dancing. T seems to know what is meant. In other words, there is a general interpretative principle in conversation: if the answer does not seem immediately relevant, then look for some deeper connection.

This topic has been widely discussed in the work of Grice (1975 and elsewhere). He discusses examples such as:

12   A   hasn't John got a girl friend these days
     B   well he has been travelling down to London a lot recently
                                                              (M : Grice 1975)

There is no linguistic connection at all between what A says and what B says: the connection has to be inferred. Grice uses the term *implicature* to mean a proposition that has to be inferred under the assumption that the speaker is being co-operative and trying to provide relevant, if inexplicit, information. (Cf. chapter 7 for detailed discussion of implicatures.)

One comment which therapists make about these children is that they change topic at random. It is possible that they do not appropriately mark such changes of direction (though this is a very tentative suggestion). What is less tentative is that there are many ways in which speakers can mark indirect answers, and indicate that inferential work will have to be done to recover an implicature. For example, Lakoff (1973) has shown that *well* is a marker of an indirect answer to a question: it warns the hearer that what is coming is related, but not directly, to what has gone before. Hence the oddity of:

13   A   what time is it?
     B   *well, six o'clock.   (I)

But the normality of:

14   A   what time is it?
     B   well, the milkman's just been.   (I)

There are other hedges on relevance such as *anyway* . . .; and also implicature indicating devices such as *Let me put it this way* (Katriel and Dascal 1984).

Questions and answers

There are instances in the data from the children, however, where it seems impossible to find any coherence between question and answer, even after inferential work. For example:

15 T   were these children in it
   P   I saw a baby chick trying to fly   (A : S)

This exchange appears to make no more sense in the discourse context from which it was taken (despite the *children-baby* association). An obvious interpretation is that P is just paying no attention to T. This is a persistent difficulty in interpreting the data: it is often unclear whether P *intends* his/her contribution to be a relevant one at all. A comment which teachers of such children make is that it is often difficult to tell if a child is intending to 'be sensible'. Attention is difficult to gauge, however, and it is difficult to decide whether their language is inappropriate because they do not pay attention, or whether they do not pay attention because the language they hear is not very meaningful to them.

Although I have demonstrated above that there are no necessary surface links between utterances, there are certainly constraints on what may appropriately follow what. There are constraints, for example, on what may follow a yes-no question. This does not mean, of course, that the words *yes* or *no* must appear. It means that there is an expectation that whatever does appear will be interpretable as "yes" or "no". For example:

16 A   is Jim in today?
   B   I haven't seen him.   (I)

B's answer is interpretable as "no, I don't think so".

This shows again that discourse coherence is not a matter of observable linguistic relations between utterances, but has to be constructed via conversationalists' interpretations and planning.

But consider the following data:

17 P   we went on holidays the Lake District
      there was lakes
   T   super where were you staying Karen
   P   for two weeks   (A : S)

18 T   where do you go to bed
   P   before the telly   (A : S)

In both of these example, P answers a *where* question with a time adverbial. Recall that the therapists comment that such children often have problems with time and space adverbials. However, before we could say exactly what the problem in such cases could be, we would have to know how *where* and *when* questions can appropriately be answered in normal conversation. Clearly there are constraints in discourse such that *where* questions expect place adverbials as answers, and *when* questions expect time adverbials. However, the facts are not as straightforward as that might imply. Basically, *where* questions do demand place adverbials, but *when* questions allow both. Consider:

19   A   when did you see him?
    B   in the pub   (I)

The point is, as we have already seen, that connections are not mechanical between utterances, but are constructed by hearers' interpretations; and we readily interpret such a response as "when we were in the pub". (Cf. Stubbs 1983b: ch. 6.)

Presuppositions

So far, I have discussed the way in which the ability to make general inferences enters into the construction of coherent discourse, and therefore the way in which discourse coherence relies on general rationality. I will now discuss a case intermediate between language and logic.

Consider this (perfectly normal) exchange:

20   T   does your brother Jack go to work
    P   he isn't my brother   (A : S)

P here challenges a presupposition: that is, a proposition that is not asserted, but is taken for granted by T. (Cf. chapter 7.) The test for a presupposition in this sense (although this definition will be modified below) is that it remains constant in positive, negative and interrogative sentences. All of the following sentences presuppose that "you have a brother Jack":

21   your brother Jack goes to work
22   your brother Jack doesn't go to work
23   does your brother Jack go to work?   (all I)

Or consider this example:

24   T   I bet your mum was pleased when you used
        all her hair spray - what did she say
    P   not all of it I only use a quarter of
        a bottle   (A : S)

(Note incidentally that T says the opposite of what she presumably means, namely that P's mother was *not* pleased! Discourse sometimes requires hearers to make complex inferences on it.) But P ignores the question and instead challenges the presupposition.

Here is another case:

```
25  T   what else do you do when you're at home
        what do you like to do
    P   play my lego
    T   play with your lego you've got some lego
        at home then
    P   yeah                                        (A : S)
```

Here, it is T who questions a presupposition of what P says, namely: *I play with my lego* presupposes "I have lego to play with".

Consider this more complex example, a continuation of example (4) above:

```
26  T   does it snow in the summer
    P   yeah
    T   does it
    P   yeah sometimes
    T   does it snow in the winter as well                (A : S)
```

Here T begins by questioning P's assertion that it snows in summer, but ends by presupposing it, and therefore apparently accepting P's view. This can be tested by making the utterance positive, negative and interrogative:

```
27  it snows in the winter as well
28  it doesn't snow in the winter as well
29  does it snow in the winter as well                    (all I)
```

All of these sentences presuppose that "it snows at some other time, i.e. in summer". Sometimes, therapists' conversation is also confusing!

Sometimes, however, the child's discourse is odd because presuppositions are not handled correctly. Consider:

```
30  P   we can get in the car and walk
    T   do we have a car
    P   no                        (A : Blank and Franklin 1980)
```

P's first utterance seems odd as cited here, but in context it is likely that P means that first they can travel in a car, and then get out and walk the rest of the way. However P is also logically contradicting one of her own presuppositions. She first presupposes that they have a car, and then asserts that they have none.

This example also shows that presuppositions are more complex than my definition above implied: because there are circumstances in which a speaker can reasonably deny one of his/her own presuppositions, as in:

```
31  we can't go in the car because we haven't
    got one                                                (I)
```

This is a standard argument for saying that presuppositions are not purely semantic (i.e. linguistic) objects, but have to be defined pragmatically. That is, they are distinct from logical entailments, which cannot be cancelled in context. Presuppositions are defeasible by adding new premises. (See Levinson 1983, for a full summary of the arguments.)

Here are some further data from the language disordered children. Here P asserts what is already a presupposition:

32   T   what does she put in the stove
    P   yes she put it in the stove   (A : S)

This type of example is familiar from the literature on the acquisition of *wh-*questions by normal children.

Here T presupposes that mummy is in bed; but P presupposes that she is not:

33   T   so why are they taking mummy breakfast
       in bed
    P   a prize
    T   a surprise what for
    P   cos he cos they want her to go to bed
       early - er late   (A : S)

In summary, in these exchanges the children seem to show difficulty in keeping track of which propositions have entered the discourse. We require the concept of a commitment slate, which is maintained by each speaker. (Cf. Gazdar 1979, following Hamblin.) Suppose someone is in Nottingham and says:

34   I took the train down to London last week
    to see my sister.   (I)

Apart from this assertion, various propositions have entered the discourse. There is a logical entailment: "The speaker left Nottingham". There is a presupposition: "The speaker has a sister". Neither of these could later be logically denied. There is an implicature: "The speaker left from Nottingham". But this could be logically denied: in the case where the speaker, it turns out, left from somewhere else, but had simply omitted to mention it, because it seemed irrelevant. Some speech acts, such as permissions and denials, can also remove propositions from the discourse context. Speakers build up such commitment slates or mental models of what they are committed to, and what other speakers and hearers appear to assume. These children appear to have problems in doing this. Levinson (1983: 212-13, 219-20) discusses sophisticated models, which help to explain how such commitment slates are built up.

These remarks suggest one type of test or teaching material that might be of help to these children. Basically, they could be put in situations that require them, in a controlled way, to monitor the introduction of new propositions into the universe of discourse.

Brown et al. (1984: 70ff) describe just such a task. Two pupils, A and B, each have a map of the same desert island. They cannot see each other's map. A has a route marked on his/her map, and has to guide B, for example, from the coast to some buried treasure, over bridges and past dangerous obstacles, and so on. However, the two maps are not entirely identical, having been 'prepared by different explorers'. It quickly becomes apparent therefore that A and B have incompatible information: for example, only one map has a crucial bridge marked over a river. Each therefore has to build up a representation of what the other knows. This appears to be precisely the kind of task at which the SPD children have problems: constructing representations of the world that accommodate the different knowledge of other people, and therefore co-operating in the transfer of information.

The features of discourse which I have been discussing above concern the internal consistency between propositions: whether they are compatible, logically contradictory, or whether one entails, presupposes or implicates another. They are therefore largely matters of sense relations and discourse coherence. However, they also raise questions of reference. The concepts of presupposition and reference are closely related, as can be seen in an example such as (30). If there is no car, is the utterance *We can go in the car* untrue? Or is it neither true nor false? Do you make untrue statements by referring to things that do not exist? Or do you produce a different kind of nonsense?

Logical and pragmatic connectors

Another case that is intermediate between language and logic is provided by the so-called 'logical' connectors, or co-ordinating and subordinating conjunctions. Consider these data on one child's use of *but*:

```
35  P    I've got a gerbil
    T    oh that's nice
    P    but his name's Peanuts
         . . .
    T    it's a good name
    P    but I said Peanuts (laughs)
    T    (laughs) that's nice                              (M : S)
```

Clearly T is confused by the end of this exchange! Like me, she can presumably see no contradiction between having a gerbil and calling it Peanuts. Yet P's use of the connector *but* implies that there is some incompatibility in these two facts, or that the second is unexpected. *But* is used to cancel a plausible proposition, which need not be asserted, but is assumed to have been made. (Since it can be cancelled, it is an implicature.) Consider uses such as:

36 He's got a big house but no car.
37 John came but his girlfriend didn't.   (both I)

Here are further examples from the child:

38 (talking about the child's holiday at the seaside)
    P I've got my own bucket and spade
    T yes you've probably got a good spade too
    P mm but it's a yellow one   (A : S)

Being good and yellow are not incompatible, but the spade's yellowness is
presented as though it was unexpected. P denies an assumption which I
would not have made.

39 (talking about an overnight car journey)
    T did you sleep in the car
    P yeah . . . fast asleep . . . but in the
       morning I was still fast asleep   (M : S)

Again, there is no expected contrast in the propositions, and *and* would have
been normal.

40 P my mum didn't come
    T couldn't she come
    P but she came   (A : S)

Here P first denies, then asserts a proposition, and in addition uses *but* wrongly.
Consider an appropriate use in an exchange such as:

41 A I couldn't talk to her since she didn't come
    B but she did come   (I)

But is used to deny a previous assumption. That is, it introduces an utterance
for a particular purpose; and has to do not merely with syntax, but with the
relationship between different propositions, and with what A assumes that B
assumes.

Stereotyped use of sentence-initial *but* is also found in normal language
acquisition studies.

Underlying the correct use of *but* is some quite complex reasoning. A *but*-
clause does not contradict a general assumption, but only the applicability of
the general assumption to the particular case under discussion. Consider
example (36). The underlying reasoning is:

A He's got a big house.
B People with big houses are well off.

C Therefore they usually have other possessions which
   go with such a life-style.
D *But* he is an exception to this generalization.

Therefore, *but* does not question the truth of A, which is asserted; nor of the expected norm B; nor of the conclusion C; but only the validity of the generalization in this particular case, D. (Cf. Bublitz 1978: 49.)

Here is more complex example:

42	1	T	and what kind of things do you like to build	
	2	P	cars	
	3	T	mm	
	4	P	lorries	
	5	T	mm	
	6	P	but I haven't built a lorry yet . . .	
	7		I haven't built a yellow one . . .	
	8		I builded another one	(M : S)

Utterance 4 could mean that he would like to build lorries, but he has not yet done so: therefore, 6 could be compatible with 4. However, 8 cancels this interpretation, and becomes logically contradictory.

Both *and* and *but* are complex items, and have to be considered together. They have the same truth conditions. That is, suppose *and* can be substituted for *but* in a sentence, or vice versa, and still give a grammatical sentence; then if one sentence is true, the other sentence will also be true. The difference between them is that *but* implies a contrast or something unexpected between the propositions. Consider:

43 He's got a big house and/but no car.
44 John came and/but his girlfriend didn't.   (both I)

There are other complications with *and*, however. *And* can have a symmetrical interpretation. For example, the following two sentences might be entirely synonymous.

45 She parked the car and he rang Susan.
46 He rang Susan and she parked the car.   (both I)

In these cases, *and* behaves like the logical connector &: in the propositional calculus, $p \& q$ means the same as $q \& p$. But the following example would normally be interpreted as reporting a sequence of acts in the same order as the clauses; reversing the clauses therefore tells a different (and in this case rather odd) story.

47 She parked the car and walked into the shop.

The following sentence would normally be interpreted as telling of a sequence of two events, where A occurs first and causes B.

48 She parked the car and knocked over the old lady.

The basic principle of interpretation is that if two events can be seen as occurring in temporal sequence, then they will be; and if they can be further interpreted as being causally related, then they will be. This means that the interpretation of conjunctions depends to some extent on our knowledge of typical relations between events. Again, we are talking of propositions that are not explicitly asserted, but have to be inferred. Consider the following examples (developed from Johnson-Laird 1983: 366):

49 He had taken the drug, and he died.
50 He had taken the drug, but he died.
51 He died, and he had taken the drug.
52 He died, but he had taken the drug.   (all I)

I think the normal interpretation of the first would be:

53 "He died because he took the (poisonous) drug."

Whereas all three other sentences would normally be interpreted as:

54 "He died, although he took the (beneficial) drug."

The general point I am making is that these children appear to have problems in interpreting temporal, causal and intentional sequences. But the way in which such sequences are signalled in discourse is subtle, and not by any means well understood by linguists. Nor is it evident even to thoughtful practitioners. Having presented the data on the child above to a group of therapists, one commented that she would just have to teach him to use *and* instead of *but*. This is an understandable reaction, but it simply demonstrates that 'normal' speakers can grossly underestimate the complexity of the language they use every day. And it therefore demonstrates that therapists and teachers need theory as well as practice.

The other connectors are also complex. I will not discuss them in detail here, but just consider the non-logical or pragmatic use of the conjunctions in the following. Basically, they relate an utterance to a justification for the utterance: they do not relate the events in the two clauses directly.

55 He must have been drunk, because he fell off the pier.
56 There's some food in the fridge, if you're hungry.
57 There's a good film on tonight, or don't you fancy
    going out?

(Chapter 8 discusses such examples in more detail, and some educational implications of their correct analysis.)

Different logics

One general point which derives from all this discussion is that the logic of everyday conversation is not always the same as the logic of the propositional calculus. If we are trying to discover how such children think, and are then concerned to help them to understand normal discourse, we have to keep clear just what some of these differences are. It is easy to illustrate some of the different types of logical relation between utterances by using an adapted version of what is known to philosophers as Aristotle's Square. This sets out the relations between sentences of the following type: that is, between particular and general statements:

some *x* are *p*   some *x* are not *p*
all *x* are *p*   all *x* are not *p*

A more normal way of stating the last of the sentences is *No* x *are* p. Figure 7 is a version which suits my purpose here. The square illustrates three types of relationship between statements: logical entailment (E), induction (Ind) and implicature (Imp).

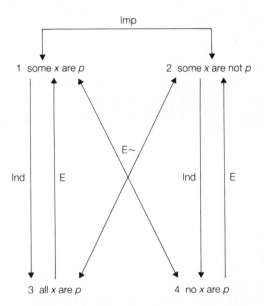

Figure 7 Adaptation of Aristotle's Square, illustrating different types of logical relation between sentences

Logical entailment (*E*).   Statement 3 entails statement 1, and statement 4 entails statement 2. If it is the case that all the students play football, then it cannot logically be denied that some of them do. Furthermore, statement 3 entails the denial of statement 2, and vice versa; and statement 4 entails the denial of statement 1, and vice versa. Or, if you prefer, statements 1 and 4, and 2 and 3 are logically contradictory. If it is the case that all the students play football, then it cannot be true that some do not; etc. Such deductive logical inferences are not defeasible, that is, they cannot be cancelled:

58   *All of the students play football, but some of them don't.

Induction (Ind).   One might induce statement 3 from statement 1, and statement 4 from statement 2. That is, on the basis of the observation that some students play football (i.e. all the ones you have seen), you might jump to the conclusion that they all do. This might or might not be justified, but it is certainly not a logical entailment, and it would not be logically contradictory to say either:

59   Some of the students (if not all) play football.
60   Some of the students (but not all) play football.

Such arguments are therefore defeasible.

Implicature (Imp).   Normally, statement 1 would be interpreted as implicating statement 2, and vice versa. But as the sentences just quoted show, this is not a logical entailment. The interpretation works on the assumption that it is communicatively uncooperative to make a less informative statement (i.e. about only some x), if you are in a position to make a stronger one (about all x).

With reference to *but* again, in example (60) note that the *but*-clause confirms the implicature (that some x is not p) and denies the generalization (that all x are p). Implicatures appear to be the only type of inference that is freely reinforceable in this way. (Cf. Levinson 1983: 114-16.) In example (59), the *if*-clause suspends the implicature.

What is to be done?

The most useful approach to the diagnosis of these children would seem to be to study carefully the details of utterance sequencing in their conversation. One stage must be to identify, on purely intuitive grounds (that is, relying on native-speaker intuition), places where their discourse is odd. These oddities then have to be described as carefully as possible: as I have tried to show briefly in this chapter, there is recent work in semantics and pragmatics which can help with a precise description. This work derives from the discovery that there are at least half a dozen different types of inference that are performed on utterances in conversation. The intuitive report of therapists is that the children have problems in organizing ideas and in being aware of what information is shared by others. The most relevant work by linguists may therefore be studies of the relations between propositional information which is asserted, entailed, presupposed, assumed to be shared, and so on. (Recent surveys of relevant work include Brown and Yule 1983b; Levinson 1983; Stubbs 1983b.)

The first task must therefore be to attempt a linguistic description of the 'odd' exchanges. The other aspect of this attempt in which linguists should be able to help is in construction of an overall profile or category system to classify the errors. In other words, we need the type of profile that has been developed for phonology, prosody, lexical semantics and grammar. (Crystal 1982 summarizes work by himself, Garman and Fletcher.) I do not think it is particularly difficult to construct the beginnings of a profile that consists of half a dozen broad categories to be later refined. No such profile could be as detailed or as certain as the profiles we have for other levels of description: we just do not know enough about discourse. But it could be of initial help in establishing whether a child has problems in specific areas of conversation, and whether indeed they are specifically linguistic problems or cognitive problems.

Recall, first, that these children's language is relatively normal in form, but abnormal in content or meaning. We therefore require a classification that allows us to discuss at least the relations between forms and meanings, and their relations both to the hearer and to the world.

I do not discuss in any detail in this chapter the relations between surface syntactic forms and surface meanings. I take this for granted because, although it is itself a very complex area, it is in effect the whole topic of standard grammars of English, and the basic descriptive information is therefore available elsewhere. In figure 8, I therefore concentrate on the relations between surface and underlying meanings (i.e. intended meaning in context), and on the relations between forms, different levels of meaning and extra-linguistic context (i.e. hearers and the world). Figure 8 is a very crude model, but one which may allow initial identification of where a child's problems lie.

We want to be able to answer questions such as:

1 Does P relate appropriately to the hearer? (e.g. Does P show the motivation to interact at all?)
2 Does P relate surface forms and meanings correctly to underlying meanings? (e.g. Can P correctly interpret indirect utterances?)
3 Does P choose the appropriate forms for the hearer? (e.g. Does P use appropriate forms of politeness?)
4 Does P choose the appropriate meanings for the hearer? (e.g. Does P take account of what the hearer already knows?)
5 Does P relate meanings appropriately to other meanings? (e.g. Does P recognize contradictory propositions?)
6 Does P correctly relate meanings to the world? (e.g. Does P make true statements?)

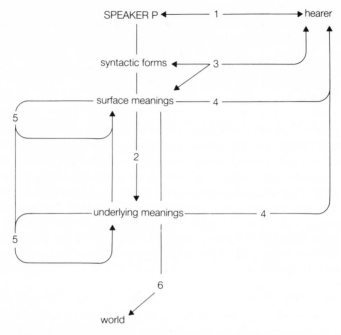

Figure 8 Profile to classify errors in some language disordered children

Cross-cutting these relations, we need to study also whether the competence is linguistic or whether it depends on non-linguistic principles of inference and general rationality. This will be particularly difficult with questions 2, 4 and 5.

I will comment in more detail on each of the categories. They clearly overlap to some extent, but I think clear instances can be found for each category, and fuzzy boundaries do not necessarily invalidate categories.

Category 1: speaker and hearer

This question is asking about P's interactional competence per se. Sub-questions are: does P participate, respond, and co-operate in the joint construction of conversation? Or conversely, does P fail to respond, ignore the hearer, keep talking on his/her own track, irrespective of what the hearer says? Does P both initiate and respond? Does P have more difficulty with one or the other? (There are reports, for example, of children who ask the same question repetitively, with no apparent interest in the answer that they receive. It is reported of other children that they answer their own questions.) Does P have problems with turn-taking, for example, with recognizing the potential end of utterances and with a smooth changeover between speakers? Does P use attention-getting devices, which would show communicative intent? (It is reported that autistic children characteristically do not use them.) Does P have the ability to repair conversational breakdowns? For example, does s/he correctly use requests for clarification? Does P construct well-formed exchanges? For example, P may recognize that a response of some kind is required, but not recognize what content is required. (Even extreme echolalia may be a recognition of the social obligation to respond, although P may not recognize that s/he has echoed.) These are questions about interaction, independent of the form or content of its utterances.

Category 2: forms and meanings

Can P recognize speech acts: for example, can s/he interpret interrogatives both as questions and requests according to context? Can P recognize only highly conventionalized requests, or also requests that require inferential work to be done? More generally, can P correctly interpret the communicative intent and underlying meanings of utterances? Does P understand only surface meanings, or can s/he correctly interpret implicatures? Does P have more difficulty in interpreting declaratives, which are more ambiguous than interrogatives? Imperatives are less ambiguous still.

Category 3: forms and hearers

Can P select the correct forms of politeness to maintain social relations according to the social status of the hearer? The expression of politeness in English requires a very complex set of lexical, syntactic and semantic surface forms. (It is reported that many children with SPD have difficulty with very simple aspects of social etiquette, and have to be taught to greet people.) Can P disagree politely, as well as arguing or accepting others' views passively? (Though do not forget here what is normal: many children have problems with such aspects of social behaviour for a long time.)

Category 4: meanings and hearers

Can P take account of the hearer's point of view? Does P talk just of his/her own interests, with no account of the hearer? Can P assess the hearer's state of knowledge, and not tell him/her too much or too little? Can P ask for more information, if s/he needs it? That is, can P correctly estimate if another speaker has misgauged P's state of knowledge? Is P's discourse repetitive or redundant? Can P distinguish between old and new information? Are new topics correctly introduced? Can they be correctly rephrased to take account of the hearer's needs? Does P provide for the continuation of discourse beyond minimal responses (cf. category 1). Can P provide explanations and instructions to suit the hearer's state of knowledge?

Category 5: meanings and meanings

Can P recognize the logico-semantic relations between utterances: entailments, presuppositions; propositions which are compatible or logically contradictory? Can P recognize the similar relations between words: synonymy, antonymy, hyponymy; and the relations between words in the same semantic field? (The lexical relations can be defined in terms of logical entailment and incompatibility; cf. chapter 6.) Can P recognize particular statements as examples of general or more abstract statements? Can P keep track of new propositions as they are introduced into the discourse, and integrate different propositions into a single mental model? These are questions about discourse coherence.

Category 6: meanings and the world

Are P's statements true? Do they correspond to plausible beliefs about normal events in the world? Does P have the 'scripts' for various everyday situations? Can P make correct predictions about sequences of causes and effects? Can P do this equally for predictions about concrete, abstract and hypothetical events? That is, can P operate with imaginary worlds, which have been constructed entirely through language? Does P make correct reference to things in the world? (It is widely reported that the children have problems with pronoun reference.) These are questions about plausibility and signification.

I think that these categories are clear enough on the most general level. However, I have to admit that I am much less confident about whether they can be developed into anything resembling the kind of profile available for phonology and syntax. More detailed descriptive categories are at best available for small areas.

Don't you have friends like that?

One final point occurs to me. This is that the conversation of 'normal' adults can be disrupted in various ways when they are under different kinds of communicative stress (cf. Brown and Yule 1983b). Studying the ways in which 'normal' discourse can be disrupted may give some insight into the children's problems.

For example, most adults find it difficult to talk to telephone answering machines. The problem appears to be that the machine gives no feedback. It demands the production of monologue, which in turn demands advance planning, of a much more elaborate type than is normally required for spoken language production. (Cf. category 1 above on interaction problems.) My students often misinterpret my comments as requests or commands. If I say, intending a comment, 'I think you would find it interesting to have a look at this book', they say 'Do you want us to read it for the next essay?' (Cf. category 2.) An unfamiliar social setting will often leave people 'tongue tied', because they are afraid to put their foot in it, and therefore say nothing. (Cf. category 3.) If you are unsure of your audience, this can also cause problems. Problems can occur if you are talking to a mixed audience, in which some hearers have already heard all your favourite jokes and stories, and some haven't. (Cf. category 4.) An unfamiliar topic can disrupt the ability to spot logical inconsistencies between propositions. I read many student essays that contain blatantly contradictory claims. (Cf. category 5.) Finally, if you are talking in a foreign language, which you speak up to casual tourist standard, but not much better, there is often a tendency to say what you know how to say, rather than what is entirely true. (Cf. category 6.)

These final points may also suggest some ways in which the communicative stress may be lifted from children in teaching and testing situations.

NOTES

1 The data cited in this chapter come mainly from children aged 9 to 10 years. Clearly, many exchanges which I identify as anomalous would pass unnoticed with younger children. On the other hand, other children, much older than those cited here, may show similar problems. I have not commented specifically on the age of different children cited in the chapter, since the initial aim here was to discuss ways of understanding and classifying their problems.

FURTHER READING

Crystal, D. (1980) *Introduction to Language Pathology*. London: Edward Arnold.
Crystal, D. (1982) *Profiling Linguistic Ability*. London: Edward Arnold.

ACKNOWLEDGEMENTS

This chapter is published here for the first time. It is a revised and expanded version of an invited paper read to a conference of speech therapists at Dawn House School, Nottingham, 27 October 1984. I am very grateful to Corinne Haynes, Chief Speech Therapist at Dawn House School, for providing me with much of the data cited in this paper and for getting me interested in this topic in the first place; to Mike McTear, University of Ulster, for discussing some of the ideas in the paper with me and for providing me with further data and some of his unpublished work on children with conversational disorders; and to Dorothy Bishop, David Crystal, Eva Grauberg and Nigel Shadbolt for comments on a previous draft.

Written Language

11

What writers know:
written language and society

Introduction

A peculiar feature of much writing on education is that it seems unable to answer apparently fundamental questions (where often a common-sense view sees no problem at all): for example, what is meant by reading? or literacy? However, the reasons for such confusion on questions of definition, which appear basic to the concept of education itself, are not difficult to see. First, as I argue elsewhere in this book (especially in chapters 1, 2, 4 and 5), topics in language in education require a very broad range of different types of facts for their proper analysis. Thus literacy has aspects that require to be understood in a relatively narrow linguistic and psycholinguistic way (cf. chapter 12). But we also require a sociolinguistic theory of the relations between written and spoken and between standard and non-standard language (cf. chapter 5), and of people's perceptions of literacy in different communities and cultures. Second, as soon as we recognize this last point, it is evident that literacy simply means different things to different people in different communities using different languages. One of my general themes in this book is that language diversity is typically underestimated. What we assume to be 'normal' is merely what we happen to know about, and is the result of a particular local, ethnocentric or class-based construction of what is important or prestigious. The preoccupations of the Western education system are less widely shared than many teachers would like to assume.

In this chapter, I discuss some of the social and cultural background to different perceptions of literacy in Britain.

Europeans and Americans may . . . feel that it is somehow 'natural' that writing should be evaluated more highly than speech; although a little thought will make it clear that this category is by no means universal. (Milroy 1980: 98-9).

Some peculiarities of written language

A peculiar feature of some academic articles is that it is not certain who their audience is going to be. If the articles are on topics of potentially wide general interest, such as reading and writing, they are likely to be prepared with ill-defined social groups in mind, such as teachers, researchers or even the person the street. This problem is acute in a collection of articles on language in education, where many different disciplinary perspectives are likely to be represented among readers: practising teachers, educational researchers, psychologists, sociologists and linguists – all with different assumptions and interests, and probably not even agreeing on what reading and writing mean.

Some academic articles, in particular those published in specialist journals, are of course written for a relatively small, well-defined and homogeneous group of fellow professionals, who are actively working in some academic specialism: say, acoustic phonetics, low-temperature physics, or the study of Old Norse. This in itself causes confusion. Readers with a general interest in the area may try to read such articles and find them impenetrable, because they were not designed for general readers in the first place. This may not often happen in most specialized areas, but it often happens when readers with a general interest in some aspect of language try to read articles on linguistics that were primarily intended for fellow academic linguists.

I raise these problems at the outset of this chapter not only because they touch on practical problems faced by the author of a collection such as this one, but because these problems point to peculiar features of written language in general. Spoken language is usually addressed to particular individuals, but written language only has very marginal functions of this kind: notes to the milkman and postcards to grandmother. The vast bulk of printed material has no well-defined addressee. It will often have a mythical social group in mind as an audience: beginning teachers, working mothers, sociology students, the educated layperson. But once language has been written down, it has to stand on its own, strangely institutionalized and decontextualized. Writers are uncertain what they can assume their readers know, and readers are usually unable to ask the writer for clarification. These are features of written language that often cause problems for children learning to read and write.

Conference papers are even more peculiar, in that they are a strangely mixed mode: written down, with a view to being spoken aloud, and hopefully designed at this stage for oral presentation. Like written language, they are likely to be condensed, highly edited, with a high information load and low redundancy. But listeners cannot use the kinds of comprehension strategy they can with written language. They cannot reread unclear sections or skip sections they know already; they are condemned to follow the speed of spoken presentation. The spoken version may suffer from having been composed on paper; the version later written up for publication may suffer from having been adapted from an oral presentation.

In this chapter, I want to discuss reading and writing as sociolinguistic activities. They are obviously psychological activities, involving the processing of visual information and various kinds of problem solving. But they are also linguistic activities; people read and write meaningful language. And they are activities that serve particular social functions in different communities.

It is possible to think of the problem of 'what writers know' within such a framework. It then becomes clear that writers must have knowledge of the wider writing community in which their written product becomes an artefact. This involves socio-cultural knowledge of, for example, the high value that is placed on written language, particularly formally published language, by the Western academic community. However, these values are not universal, as I shall show in the following.

Some introductory anecdotes

Since I am not sure of the disciplinary background of my readers, I would like to try and create a small amount of context by mentioning very briefly half a dozen recent personal incidents, which have led me in various ways to think about the different roles that written language serves in modern societies, and the different relationships it may have with spoken language.

Recently, I was waiting for a train in a station in a city in the English Midlands (Leicester), and noticed a poster advertising an estate agent. The poster was written in three versions: in three non-Roman scripts, and presumably in different Asian languages, with no English translation. Even as a professional linguist, I could identify only two of the scripts, and none of the languages with any certainty, although I could guess what a couple of them probably were.

Some time ago, I had to attend a barmitzvah in a synagogue in London. Being a fairly traditional synagogue, the service was conducted throughout in Hebrew, except for the sermon in English (for which I was grateful). Even though I had a bilingual prayer book, I could not follow the progress of the service. This was not very surprising, but what surprised me rather more was that many of the congregation seemed unable to follow it either, and were constantly asking each other what page we were at in the book.

I used to do some adult literacy tutoring. On one occasion, one of my pupils rang me at home, and the telephone was answered by someone else in the house who took a message. When they passed on the message, they asked me who had telephoned: I said it was one of my pupils. They looked surprised and said: 'But he sounded quite normal.'

I once asked this particular pupil how he managed to get along in everyday life, without being able to read - something I could hardly imagine. He explained that he just has a strategy for most contingencies. He had a friend who always filled out his tax-return. If he went to a restaurant, his girl friend always ordered the meal from the menu. Since he could not read a telephone directory, he would ring directory enquiries and say it had been stolen from the telephone booth. He said he had no real problems. He wanted to learn to read, incidentally, because he wanted a driving license for heavy good vehicles, and needed limited literacy for this purpose.

Another of my adult literacy pupils was an agricultural worker from the north-east of Scotland, on an involuntary stay in the south, in prison. His accent and dialect were so marked that I had real difficulty understanding him in conversation for several months. I had no problem, however, understanding him when he was reading aloud to me, since he then switched sharply into a variety of Standard Scottish English very close to my own. He had no difficulty in understanding my Standard English, of course, since he was familiar with such a variety from radio, television, the education system, and so on.

One final incident. When the renowned British broadcaster Wilfred Pickles died in March 1978, interesting facts were revealed about his work for the BBC during the Second World War. Pickles was well known for his Yorkshire accent. In the early 1940s, when it was feared that Germany might invade Britain, he was moved to London to read the news on radio. The reason, which was not advertised at the time, was that it was felt that the Germans might be able to imitate a southern English accent and mislead people with false news broadcasts, but they would not be able to imitate a Yorkshire accent. Pickles was popular in the south, but in the north, people complained that they sent their children to school to learn to talk properly, only to have them hear the BBC news being read with a local regional accent.

These incidents are all commonplace in themselves, but they could be multiplied ad infinitum from other everyday observations. And they raise a large number of questions about the role that written language plays in society: what it means to be literate in a multilingual society; the changing and increasing demands on literate members of modern societies; the different attitudes toward literacy in different social groups; the peripheral part that literacy plays in many people's lives; the concept of partial literacy, in one or more languages, for restricted purposes; the confusion in many people's minds between literacy and intelligence, or between literacy and normality; the complex relations between written language and standard spoken language; the prestige and stigma associated with different regional and social varieties of language; the social and educational forces that maintain the standard language. I think such examples show already, therefore, that any coherent theory of reading and writing cannot be purely psychological. For questions of individual psychology may be swamped by powerful social attitudes concerning regional and national values, group solidarity, and so on.

The relation of spoken and written language

Written language cannot be fully analysed in isolation from spoken language. There are cases (further discussed later) where a person may be able to read a language (for example, a dead language such as Latin or Sanskrit) that they cannot speak. But in general our understanding of written language clearly draws on our knowledge of the corresponding spoken language and on our linguistic competence in general. It is obvious that reading and writing are not merely psychological activities, involving the visual interpretation of word and letter shapes, but that this interpretation involves linguistic knowledge.

One thing that is central to any theory of literacy is an understanding of the relation between spoken and written language. Unless we know what this relation is, we do not know what it is that children learn when they learn to read, since we do not know the relation between the spoken language that they bring to school and the written language that they learn there. This is perhaps obvious, and it is something that is being taken into account more and more in the preparation of basal readers for young children.

What is rather less obvious perhaps is that the relationship between spoken and written language is not well understood. It is easy to assume, in fact, that there is one set of relationships that can be easily stated. But if we look at the place of written language in different societies at different times, we find that many different relations are possible.

I will take three types of case in Britain that show that the linguistic diversity of industrialized countries is often underestimated, and that the relation between spoken and written language may vary widely. I will take examples from the Gaelic-speaking community in north-west Scotland, working-class communities in Belfast in Northern Ireland, and various examples from immigrant communities; and make various more general points on the basis of these examples.

Some of the geographical, historical and social facts in what follows may seem of purely local interest, and rather a long way from the immediate concerns of the nature of written language. But this is because I wish to argue that such local facts are crucial, if we wish to understand the relationship between spoken and written language in different communities. The gist of the argument is that we require an ethnography of reading and writing, and although this has been proposed by scholars (for example, by Basso 1974), the required fieldwork has hardly been started.

Gaelic in Scotland

I will take first the case of Gaelic-speaking Scotland. (Some of the facts cited in the following are from MacKinnon 1977, the first substantial sociolinguistic study of an area of the Scottish Gaidhealtachd; others are from Thomson 1976, and from my own observations. Trudgill 1984b also contains articles on Gaelic in Scotland.) There are around 80,000 Gaelic–English bilinguals in Scotland, with no remaining monolinguals, except among the very young, or a few very old women in the most remote districts. The men have traditionally been very widely travelled and have therefore been bilingual with English. A large number of Gaelic speakers live in the industrial city of Glasgow, in the centre of the country, but when one refers to Gaelic-speaking Scotland, one is usually thinking of the Gaelic-speaking community that is concentrated on the islands off the north-west coast of Scotland. This is a day's drive plus an hour in the ferry from Glasgow and Edinburgh, and around 600 miles from London – not far in absolute distance, but a long way in psychological terms from the Westminster parliament in London; the area has very low priority for British politicians. Unemployment is the highest in Britain (around 25 per cent), and educational opportunities are very poor. The only institution of higher education in the whole of the Highlands and Islands area is one technical college. Even the Scottish Nationalist Party only formulated a policy on Gaelic in 1974. Given the failure of attempts at Scottish devolution, and the decline of SNP Members of Parliament at Westminster in the 1979 general election (which voted in the Conservative Thatcher government), this fact is of little practical importance in any case.

Gaelic in Scotland has been retreating under pressure from English for a thousand years. Around AD 1000, Gaelic was probably spoken over the whole of Scotland, although there is some dispute over this. By the 1300s, English was already the normal language in central areas of the country. In the 1700s, Gaelic was still the normal language of the Highlands. But in the second half of the eighteenth century, the collapse was dramatic. A major demographic fact about the area is its continuing depopulation. The serious depopulation started in the mid-eighteenth century, when the Highland clan system collapsed after the Battle of Culloden in 1745. This was the battle in which Prince Charles Edward Stuart (Bonny Prince Charlie or The Young Pretender) so mismanaged things that the Highlanders were defeated in less than half an hour. The collapse led to large-scale emigration, mainly to North America.

All in all, this was a very unromantic period of Scottish history – the romantic picture of the kilted Scotsman being largely a later creation of authors such as Sir Walter Scott. In deliberate attempts to dismantle the clan system, Highlanders were forbidden to wear tartan, carry arms, or play the bagpipes. There was also continuing official condemnation of Gaelic. For example, in 1872, the Education Act (Scotland) made no reference to Gaelic. As late as the 1930s, pupils in the Scottish islands were punished for speaking Gaelic in school. One punishment was to wear the maidecrochaidh, a stick on a cord, worn around the neck. (The same device was used in schools in Wales for pupils caught speaking Welsh.) The device was passed from pupil to pupil, to whoever was caught, and the pupil left wearing it at the end of the day was beaten.

Given this thousand-year history of decline, it is amazing that Gaelic is still as vigorous as it is. But it is still the everyday language in the Outer Isles, with up to 90 per cent of the population fully bilingual in some areas. On the mainland, Gaelic is hardly heard at all: that is partly due to very strong norms of politeness, which forbid Gaelic to be used in front of English-speaking tourists. On the Inner Isles, tourists can often hear Gaelic spoken, by listening to men in the public bar of pubs (not the lounge bar!). On the Outer Isles, Gaelic can be heard almost anywhere.

One of the major theoretical problems for sociolinguists is this often un-expected capacity of low-prestige languages to survive what appears to be the relentless pressure of major world languages. We require therefore an ex-planation of how Gaelic has managed to survive so well, and this requires some further basic sociological and demographic data. The social organi-zation of the Scottish Outer Isles is very unlike most of the rest of Britain. They comprise rural crofting and fishing communities, with no true middle class. The community is very strongly religious and Sabbath observance is absolute. In almost all the islands, the religion is Presbyterian, Calvinist and austere; this is a central factor in the maintenance of Gaelic. Late marriage, after the age of 30 or 40, is normal. And this late marriage and continuing depopulation lead to a low birth rate, and to an ageing and declining popula-tion. The young often leave to get a good education on the mainland or to find work. The maintenance of the language is helped by the nature of the tradi-tional communal society and by its geographical isolation.

In schools in north-west Scotland today, initial literacy is taught in Gaelic where appropriate. But English is the official language, and Gaelic rapidly becomes a subject on the curriculum, comparable to geography or mathe-matics or whatever. Despite the high level of language maintenance, and the fact that literacy in Gaelic is general, very little written Gaelic is in evidence. There are, for example, almost no bilingual roadsigns. I have only ever seen two in the Highlands and Islands area (on Skye), and I suspect that they are for the benefit of tourists. I have also seen a Bank of Scotland (in Tarbert, Harris) with a redundant Gaelic sign: *Banca na h'Alba*). This is simply not an issue, in contrast to the situation in Wales, for example, where people have been jailed over the question of bilingual roadsigns.

It would be easy to assume, in fact, that the situations of Scottish Gaelic and Welsh in Britain would be very similar, but they differ in significant respects. Welsh has official status in Wales and is required by law to be used alongside English for various purposes. Gaelic has no official status in Scotland at all. Wales has developed a system of bilingual schools, but there is nothing com-parable in Scotland. And it is evident in general that the speakers of Welsh and Scottish Gaelic have very different attitudes toward their languages. Even with situations that are superficially so similar - two Celtic languages spoken in different areas of Britain - the relation of these languages to English cannot be taken for granted. Unlike Wales, in Scotland there is simply no language dimension to politics in general, although there has been, more recently, some language activism in the Gaelic-speaking area itself.

In the Scottish islands, even notices in shops about local events are in English. There are probably two reasons for this. First, it caters for some people who are literate only in English; the young acquire literacy in Gaelic at school and the old learned on the Gaelic Bible, but some middle-aged people have missed out. Second, it caters for the English-speaking incomers: the minority, who are nevertheless the ones who are active in local politics and in charge of the committee structure on the islands. The norms of politeness are such that incomers are not required to learn Gaelic. (It is much more import- ant that they observe the Sabbath.) English is therefore the language of com- mittees and bureacracy. It is possible, in principle, to use Gaelic in matters of business, politics and law, but impossible, in practice, since documents are in English, there are few Gaelic-speaking lawyers, and so on.

A factor in the inevitable decline of Gaelic is therefore that English is being used in more and more domains, particularly those that require institu- tionalized written language, such as business and commerce, law, technology and tourism. One other very simple factor in Gaelic literacy is that, as with all minority languages, there is only a small market for books. Printing and publishing are uneconomic, with small print-runs, which push up the prices of books and restrict the market even further. Arguably, there are far too many books published in English, but not enough in Gaelic.

To summarize, the factors contributing to the decline of Gaelic are high emigration; an ageing and unbalanced population; the break-up of the Gaelic-speaking area, now spread across many different islands with poor communications between them; the number of English-speaking incomers; the lack of official status for the language; and the increasing use of English in technical and bureaucratic domains. The shift of English is therefore geographical, social and functional. Factors contributing to the maintenance of Gaelic include not only rather obvious ones such as the geographical isola- tion of the area. They include also factors that are not immediately apparent to outsiders, because they involve the local value system, which revolves around the traditional communal society and religious beliefs.

Written language and institutionalized communication

The relationship between written language and bureaucracy, which I have pointed to briefly before, is an important one. Many of the functions of written language depend on its ability to create durable and accurate records. These recording or storage functions are obvious enough to us as fluent and practised readers, but they were not obvious, for example, to the early printers. It was about a hundred years after the invention of movable type before books were regularly printed with page numbers, yet only then could they be fully exploited for reference and the easy retrieval of information (McLuhan 1960). It is a common experience that beginning readers have to be taught explicitly to exploit the permanence of written text. Children have to learn to process written text in ways not possible with spoken language: to read faster or slower depending on the purpose of reading, to re-read, skim read, use indexes, and so on. At a higher level, it is a common complaint that students often have no idea how to exploit the information storage potential of big libraries. This is not surprising, since modern library systems are very complex, involving different systems of cataloguing and indexing, systems of abstracting services, and computer-assisted search systems relating different libraries across the world. The investigation of methods of indexing or abstracting articles, for example, is now no longer concerned merely with rather crude attempts at picking out key words. It is drawing on recent ideas about formal representation of the discourse structure of written texts (Hutchins 1978).

The storage functions of written language lead, of course, to its central role in running any modern organization, from a small business to a state. And the bulk of written material has institutional, administrative and bureaucratic functions.

As an international language, English has unique roles in the world-wide recording and transmission of information, in business and commerce, science and technology, education, and government. Not only is English the native language for some 400 million people. There are millions more who use English as a second language in areas such as India, West Africa and Malaysia, where governments have retained English as an auxiliary language of wider communication after independence. There are still more millions who have learned English as a foreign language for various purposes. These figures lead to other startling statistics on the role of written English in conveying and recording information. It is estimated that 75 per cent of the world's mail is in English (Strang 1970: 73) and that 50 per cent of the world's scientific literature is in English (Quirk et al. 1972: 4). (Cf. chapter 4.)

It is possible to compare the world's languages in a very general way, by comparing their utilization in writing. Ferguson (1962), in a widely quoted taxonomy, proposes four levels of utilization: W0 - no use, that is the language has no writing system; W1 - normal written purposes; W2 - use for reporting original research in the physical sciences; W3 - use for translations and résumés of scientific work in other languages. This taxonomy obviously requires to be made finer grained for some purposes, but the general point is clear.

Consider the following more detailed examples of the relationship between written English and other languages. If we want to understand fully how written English works, we cannot study it in isolation, but have to look at the relations between it and other writing systems. It is obvious, first of all, that there is a striking correspondence between the major writing systems in use in the world, and major political and religious blocs: Roman, Cyrillic, Arabic, Chinese. We need therefore the concept of the wider writing community (Berry 1968) within which a writing system is used.

One feature of English spelling is that it often differentiates native words from foreign borrowings. For example, *llama* is recognizably foreign. There is a rule of English spelling that words do not end in -*i*: words which do are recognizably foreign, for example, *ski, pi, khaki, timpani*, and so on. Further, there is a growing international vocabulary shared by a large number of languages, especially in fields such as politics, sport, science and technology. Often such words are recognizable in a wide range of languages precisely because the spelling is not too closely related to the different pronunciations. An understanding of the writing conventions of one language therefore requires a study of its relations with other languages that are culturally important to the speakers.

I emphasize these peculiar facts about written English for two reasons. First, they mean that English puts enormous pressure on minority languages with which it comes into contact. For example, Scottish Gaelic is maintained to an impressive degree at the level of everyday life in a traditional community, but is increasingly restricted in the functions it serves outside local life. This is one of the ways in which a language dies. The incoming language takes over more and more of its functions. Second, when we investigate the functions that written language serves in the real world, we find that many of them are institutionalized and depersonalized, and clearly beyond the needs and experience of children. It would be quite impossible, for example, to explain most of the points I have just made about the world-wide distribution of English to young children learning to read. Young children, in a rather literal sense, have no need of written language, and this constitutes a great teaching problem. Several of the points I have made about the uses of written English in bureaucratic and technological areas are also beyond the experience even of older students.

More on the relation of spoken and written language

A common view of the relation between spoken and written language is illustrated in figure 9. Both spoken and written language show stylistic variation from formal to informal. Spoken language shows more variation than written. It ranges from the formal language of lectures and speeches to casual and intimate conversation between individuals who know each other well and share background knowledge. Written language shows relatively less stylistic variation, since it is used predominantly for rather formal purposes. Casual written language, such as personal letters between individuals, are a relatively minor use when compared with the massive amount of formally published material that characterizes modern industrial societies. The written and spoken scales overlap. In other words, more formal spoken language is more similar to written language. Some styles of formal spoken language are of

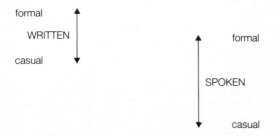

Figure 9 Relation between spoken and written language

course based closely on written language. For example, a lecture may be based on written notes. But spoken language is rarely, if ever, as formal as the most formal written language of public notices, legal documents, and the like.

It has even been suggested that styles of language can be ranged along a single, linear continuum from casual to formal, and that this continuum simply ignores the distinction between spoken and written English. Labov, in a large number of well-known studies (1966, 1972b, and elsewhere), has collected speech data by recording speakers in different social settings: casual conversation, interviews, reading connected texts, and reading lists of words. In research in the United States, mainly in New York, he has found that informants' language shifts consistently in a single direction along this linear stylistic continuum, which is illustrated in figure 10. Labov argues that there is a single linear measure of the amount of attention which speakers pay to their speech, and that as the social situation becomes more formal, this monitoring increases, and the style changes.

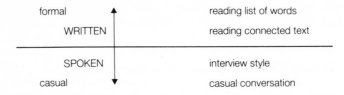

Figure 10 Linear stylistic continuum for some varieties of English

It is tempting to regard this model of a linear continuum as a theoretical statement about the relation between spoken and written language. However, it is, first of all, a statement about people's reactions to different kinds of language: how they *read* lists of words, for example. Second, the correct interpretation would seem to be that the linear relation is not a necessary statement about the relation between spoken and written language, but an empirical finding that holds for Labov's New York data, but which does not hold everywhere. It seems, in fact, that this continuum depends on speakers being highly literate and therefore having a particular view of the relation between spoken and written English.

Consider further what may happen to figure 9, if one adds (still in a highly simplified way) the distinction between standard and non-standard spoken language, and attempts to show how these three dimensions interact: formal versus casual; spoken versus written; and standard versus non-standard. One kind of relationship is shown in figure 11.

All written language is on the standard-language side of the line. This represents the norm for contemporary English, rather than being literally true. That is to say, non-standard written English, in dialect poetry for example, is very much the exception rather than the rule. And often when non-standard English is written, in novels for example, it is between quotation marks, as the written representation of spoken English. In other words,

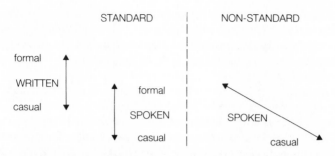

Figure 11   Relationship between spoken and written, formal and casual, and standard and non-standard English.

there is a special relationship between writing and the standardization of the language. Standardization almost necessarily implies writing. Full standardization implies deliberate codification by generations of printers, publishers, dictionary makers, grammar-book writers, schoolteachers, and the like. Further, there is stylistic variation within non-standard dialects of any language, just as there is within spoken standard dialects. But this style-shifting will often involve dialect shifting, toward the standard dialect in more formal social situations. (Cf. chapter 5.)

Since the standard versus non-standard distinction is also related to the social-class stratification of modern societies, all this might also imply a linear model of another kind: that people often aspire to be like people above them in the social-class scale; and that they often aspire to *speak* like them. The basic notion is therefore of a single prestige norm, where there is a correlation between middle-class language, standard language, written language and stylistically formal language. However, although this model fits some cases, including what one might roughly refer to as Western middle-class society, it does not fit all societies, as the next case study shows.

English in Belfast

As a second case study of the different place that literacy and written language may play in communities, I would like to discuss very important sociolinguistic work that has been done in Belfast, in Northern Ireland, by James and Lesley Milroy (Milroy 1980; Milroy and Milroy 1978; Milroy and Margrain 1978). They have done detailed fieldwork in lower-working-class communities in decaying inner-city areas in Belfast. Like tight-knit working-class groups elsewhere, the local community networks they have studied are relatively self-contained and isolated from the upwardly mobile mainstream society. In fact, the groups studied might best be regarded as being marginal: outside the industrial class structure rather than occupying the lowest position within it (Milroy 1980: 74-5). They are closed communities, characterized by multiplex networks, in which people interact in more than one capacity: that is, a man's neighbour is likely also to be a kinsman and a fellow employee. Being relatively isolated from mainstream society, such communities appear to impose their own linguistic norms on their members. There is evidence, for example, that they are relatively unaffected by, and ignorant of, the norms of Standard English.

The Milroys have collected extensive data on how written and spoken language are perceived in these Belfast working-class communities. They carried out the same kind of procedure as Labov, recording people in casual and formal interaction, and in reading tasks. But they propose that reading is perceived as quite a different activity from conversation. They found predictable style-shifting from casual to formal conversation. But this direction of shift was not always maintained in reading out lists of words. Here the style often shifted back to a vernacular style of pronunciation.

Many of their informants were illiterate or semi-literate: able only to read the three-letter words on the lists. Many other informants simply refused to read connected texts at all. They said they never read anything aloud normally, excepting possibly instructions on a can of food; they sometimes argued that it is wrong to read aloud what someone else has written, since it is wrong to take on someone else's role in this way. They were happy to read lists of unconnected words, and did this rapidly, with a characteristic rhythm and rise–fall intonation: *bág, bàd, rág, stàb*. It seems that, for these informants, reading aloud is a speech event that is partly outside the norms that govern other speech events. It might not even be recognized as a speech event at all. The informants do not normally do it, and will do it only with embarrassment, if at all. The view of speaking and reading as lying on a stylistic continuum may apply only to confident, highly literate speakers.

More generally, the Milroys argue that not all language communities have a single, easily identifiable prestige norm. The notion of a single norm, in which formality, written medium and middle-class standards coincide, is a product of middle-class European and American societies, but is not universal.

In other work, Labov (1973) has warned against the bias introduced into linguistics by the fact that most linguists are white, middle-class, socially and geographically highly mobile individuals, who are not members of any natural speech community. The Milroys are pointing out that Labov himself has been misled by this bias in some of his own work.

Finally, the Milroy's work provides a detailed study of a case where a low-prestige language has shown an unexpected capacity to resist the relentless pressure of a standard language. They point (for example, Milroy 1980: 178) to the close-knit network structure of the community as an important mechanism of language maintenance.

Attitudes to written language in other communities

It would be possible, of course, to find in other communities totally different beliefs again about the value of reading aloud. For example, there are many places, particularly in the Middle East, where children are taught to read aloud a foreign language that they do not understand at all, because of the religious significance of the language (Ferguson 1971a). Such teaching at least used to be common in synagogues in Britain, although the practice is probably changing. Learning to read aloud in Hebrew can be a formidable task, if there is no understanding of the language, since in the scrolls Hebrew is written unpointed, with no indication of the vowels.

Different cases of this kind imply very different cultural beliefs about what is meant by literacy and the functions that it can serve. Goody (1968) presents papers on what he terms 'restricted literacy' in many countries. He points out that, although many peoples have been in contact with written language over the past 2,000 years or more, most of them have only been marginally affected. This is still the case with many people in the world. There are fewer and fewer countries left in which people do not have access to written language in some form. But individuals may not have access to literacy in their own language or dialect.

In addition, there are now many reports available of the high value that is given to oral traditions in many parts of the world by social groups who stand outside the mainstream middle-class culture (Bauman and Sherzer 1974; Labov, 1972a; Opie and Opie 1959). As Milroy (1980) argues, the view that written language is to be more highly valued than spoken language is not a generally held belief, but a belief that has particular historical roots in Western culture.

In this chapter, due to my ignorance of other cultures and other writing systems, I am only able to discuss a few cases of the functions of written language in different social groups in Britain. Although Britain might appear superficially rather homogeneous, I am arguing that there is unexpected diversity even here. I could make my case much stronger, if I were competent to discuss more exotic cases involving, for example, Eastern languages, which use writing systems very different from ours (for example, Chinese).

Many of our ideas about language in general and about written language in particular have not only the middle-class bias discussed previously, but a more general Western bias. This has occasionally been pointed out. For example, J. R. Firth's theories of non-segmental, prosodic phonology were explicitly influenced by his knowledge of Indian languages, with their various writing systems. And Bugarski (1970) has discussed in general terms the ways in which Western linguistics has been biased by the particular segmental analysis of language foisted on us by our alphabetic and word-based writing system.

Literacy in multicultural Britain

As I have shown already, there is often unexpected diversity in the native British population. Sociologists often give the impression that Britain is all rather homogeneous, and often seem to think that they may as well do their fieldwork in London or the big English cities. They seldom seem to get as far as Scotland or Ireland. However, the major source of linguistic diversity in contemporary Britain is the recent immigration into London and the big conurbations in the Midlands, such as Birmingham, Nottingham and Leicester. The whole linguistic configuration of many areas of Britain has changed radically in just 20 years. There are not even accurate statistics on the languages spoken by immigrants, since census figures refer only to country of birth: this can only give a very rough indication of language for someone coming from a multilingual country such as India or countries in West Africa. Questions about racial, ethnic and linguistic origins are clearly questions about very sensitive areas, and there was a great deal of debate over whether such questions should be asked in the 1981 British census (HMSO 1978; Saunders 1978). In the event, no such questions were asked in the version of the census used in England. The debate is now continuing over the next census in 1991.

Since the whole linguistic configuration of large areas of Britain has changed profoundly since the period of large-scale immigration in the 1960s, it is unfortunate, but understandable, that both politicians and educators are often ignorant of the facts and issues involved. Of course, even census data on the language backgrounds of immigrants would not reveal how immigrant groups actually use different languages.

The first major report on the teaching of English in England was the Newbolt Report, published in 1921 (HMSO 1921). It simply makes no reference at all to any language other than English. A more recent and very influential report is the Bullock Report, published in 1975 (DES 1975). It does discuss the problem, although it refers to 'children of families of overseas origin', and is very sparse on statistics. The Bullock Report also supports the principle of bilingual education, but it does not specify what is meant by this or how it might be put into practice. An estimate (Campbell-Platt 1976) of the most widely spoken immigrant languages in Britain, in descending order, is:

Punjabi, Urdu, Bengali, Gujerati, (i.e. northern Indian languages), Polish, Italian, Greek, Spanish and Cantonese or Hakka.

To this could be added (from Rosen 1980), in alphabetic order this time:

Afrikaans, Arabic, French (including French creoles), Hausa, Igbo (West African languages), Japanese, Malay, Maltese, Persian, Portuguese, Pushtu (Iranian), Sinhalese (from Sri Lanka), Serbo-Croat, Swahili, Tagalog, Tamil (from Southern India), Twi (from West Africa), Turkish, Yoruba and others.

The most detailed statistics, for five areas of England, are in the Linguistic Minorities Project (1985). It is now common for teachers in some English cities to have classes where native English-speaking children are in a minority. Nursery and infant classrooms in schools in English cities are now among the most linguistically varied and interesting environments to be found anywhere.

A large number of children in Britain's ethnic minorities now attend evening or weekend classes outside the school system, in their mother tongue. Little is known about the extent of such provision, or how effective it is (but see Saifullah Khan 1976, 1978, 1980, for discussion). Classes are held in these languages, at least:

Arabic, Chinese, Greek, Gujerati, Hebrew, Hindi, Hungarian, Italian, Latvian, Polish, Punjabi, Spanish, Ukrainian and Urdu.

Such classes are also held in other countries: for example, one estimate for Australia (Grassby 1977) is that 100,000 children attend such ethnic schools in 25 languages. There are many motivations for this demand for instruction in the mother tongue. Children may be more fluent in English than the parents, and the parents are worried about being able to communicate with their children. The parents may plan to have the children marry within the community in the native country. They may fear forced repatriation, or wish to return home at some time. Or there may be parental pride in the language and culture. Or there may be religious reasons.

Few teachers have much idea of the existence of such schools; nor do they generally have any knowledge of the mother tongues of their pupils or the implications of acquiring literacy in these languages. This is not surprising, given the linguistic complexity involved. At least a couple of dozen languages are involved, if we are talking of the situation in London and the conurbations in the English Midlands, and several different writing systems, including:

Arabic, Chinese, Cyrillic, Devanagari, Greek, Gurmukhi, Hebrew, Urdu.

The linguistic complexity in a single case may be considerable. For example, Punjabi speakers from Pakistan will write their language in the (Perso-Arabic) Urdu script (not the Gurmuhki script which is used in the Punjab). Their religious book, the Quran, is learned in Arabic. In schools in Birmingham, Punjabi teaching has been organized for some children by Asian members of staff (Chapman 1976), but parents are not always in favour. They argue that their children would be wasting less time if they were learning English. In addition, English-medium education is prestigious. They may nevertheless send their children to mosque evening classes to learn Arabic. In addition, it is quite possible for someone to speak Punjabi and English fluently, but to be literate only in English.

A problem now is that many immigrant children opt for the language of their peers, and refuse to use their mother tongue at all, even with parental encouragement. For example, Wiles (1979) documents the case of an immigrant boy, who lived in India until he was 4 years old. His preferred language was Bengali, which was the language of his father and friends, but he was also in contact with Hindi and English. At the age of 4 : 2 (4 years, 2 months), he was in Britain, clearly recognizable as a foreign speaker of English. At the age of 4 : 6, he was attending a play group in West Sussex, and had acquired some local accent features. At age 5, he was in a primary school in north London. The West Sussex features were giving way to London features. By now he was reluctant to speak Bengali, despite parental encouragement, and English was clearly his dominant and preferred language. It is an important socio-linguistic finding that the peer group is usually the most powerful influence on children's language. Children grow up talking like their friends, and not like their parents (cf. Labov 1973). This fact should, of course, be exploited in classroom teaching, as it is more and more in the development of types of collaborative learning.

The state of the art

I will finish with some brief comments on the state of the art in research on literacy and on written language. Concentrated research on reading has been underway since the end of the nineteenth century. In Britain, the Education Acts of 1870 and 1872 made the first requirements of universal literacy for schoolchildren, and set off a large amount of research. There are several terms and concepts that appear to have a modern ring to them, but have been used for a long time. The term 'congenital word blindness' was first used as long ago as 1896, for example, in the *British Medical Journal* (Morgan 1896). Despite a hundred years of research, we would have to admit, however, that there is nothing even approaching a coherent theory of reading and writing.

It is a generalization, but a fair generalization, to say that the dominant approach to reading over this period has been an experimental psychological approach. Reading has tended to be seen as a perceptual process involving the recognition of word and letter shapes, eye span, eye movements, and so on. It has again been known since the nineteenth century that, in reading, the eyes move in a jerky fashion (Javal 1897).

Again, it is a generalization, but a fair one, that research on reading has tended to ignore various things. First, it has often been ignored that what is read is language. People generally read meaningful texts, and texts are linguistically organized. Competent readers can, of course, read nonsense syllables, if they are required to do so, for example, as part of a test; and this ability has to be accounted for. But, by and large, readers settle down with a good book, and not with a string of nonsense syllables. We have to distinguish, therefore, between a peripheral activity that readers can perform in response to a special request, and the activity of reading that readers engage in naturally. This distinction is important for several reasons. It is at the centre of many disputes over just what 'reading' means. Is it what fluent readers do naturally? What they can, in principle, do? What young children should be taught to do?

The fact that readers usually read connected meaningful text is, of course, not ignored in all research. It is central to approaches that take reading to be a 'psycholinguistic guessing game', to use Goodman's phrase (1982). And the real uses to which reading is put have been emphasized by researchers such as Lunzer and Gardner (1978), who have investigated the way in which children actually handle written material in real classrooms.

Second, the relation between spoken and written language has often been ignored. Not always, of course: there are some excellent reading schemes that begin very explicitly from the child's own spoken language. One example is the British *Breakthrough to Literacy* scheme (Mackay, Thompson and Schaub 1970). More accurately perhaps, the relation between spoken and written language may now be taken for granted and regarded as uncontroversial. But as I have illustrated, the relationship between spoken and written language differs in unexpected ways in different cultures.

Third, there has been a tendency to ignore the social functions of written language: the reasons why people read and write. Again, as I have shown, this cannot be predicted, but needs to be studied within different communities.

The neglect of such topics is partly the fault of linguists. Due to particular historical reasons, twentieth-century linguistics has given priority to spoken language. This has been partly a reaction against previous language study, in which spoken language was despised and literary language was regarded as the high point of linguistic development. One apotheosis of this view was represented by Dr Johnson in the Preface to his famous dictionary of 1755. He took a view, which is still often held today, although often not as explicitly or clearly stated as he expressed it: spoken language is 'wild and barbarous jargon' that has to be given order by being 'reduced to an alphabet'.

The high value attributed to written language continued throughout the period, when the study of classical languages took precedence over the study of English and other modern European languages in Europe and America. However, a significant change began to take place at the end of the nineteenth century. This was the period in which several different trends came together, not least the invention of mechanical ways of recording speech, and led to the development of phonetics as a serious academic discipline in England. There had been a long history in England of interest in different forms of speed writing and shorthand. Generally these were based on the conventional orthography. But Isaac Pitman's system, published in its first form in 1837, was based on a new analysis, and was fundamentally phonemic in the way it related directly to spoken English. A. J. Ellis, along with Pitman, was interested in questions of spelling reform, and published important work on phonetics in 1847. Further influential work on representing spoken language was Bell's ideas on 'visible speech', published in 1867. This used symbols that were conventionalized diagrams of the vocal organs. The system was used by Henry Sweet (the model for Professor Higgins in Shaw's play *Pygmalion*), who published important work on phonetics and the theory of transcription in 1877 and 1890. And the Phonetic Teachers Association (later to become the International Phonetic Association) was founded in 1886. Practical mechanical methods of recording speech were only becoming available during this period. Edison's phonograph was first demonstrated in 1877. Disc records did not become available until years after that. Radio spread in the 1920s and convenient, portable tape recorders were not available till the 1940s.

As a result of these various advances, a significant shift took place towards the study of spoken language in England. In the United States, a shift toward studying spoken language also occurred, in particular after 1900, although in the United States other factors contributed to this study. A major factor was the intensive study of American Indian languages. These languages were often on the point of dying out and required to be recorded as rapidly as possible. They were, of course, largely unwritten languages, and they were despised as being primitive. A lot of effort therefore went into showing how complex they were, and we find aggressive statements by American linguists asserting the primacy of spoken language.

The most famous statement is probably Bloomfield's (1933: 21) that 'Writing is not language, but merely a way of recording language by means of visible marks.' Such comments are, as I say, understandable in view of the intellectual climate of the time. On a charitable interpretation, Bloomfield's statement is very ambiguous. On a literal interpretation, it is both muddled and simply false. That 'writing is not language' is true only if we assume that 'writing' here refers to one medium in which language may be realized. The same is true of speech, of course: speech is not language. But written language *is* language. The statement is ambiguous in so far as it fails to distinguish explicitly between language as an abstract underlying system, and the different media in which language may be realized. However, the second half of the statement is wrong in its implication that the recording has no effect on the language: writing is not 'merely' a record.

Just to emphasize that such attitudes have not really changed even now, consider this statement from Trudgill, a leading British sociolinguist, which is more or less a paraphrase of Bloomfield's statement, with the added confusion of the claim that spoken language comes first and is then recorded by being written down. 'Writing is parasitic upon speech in that it is simply a way of recording the spoken language in an enduring visual form' (Trudgill 1975: 20). To see how the debate continues, one might also look at R. A. Hall, Jr's review of Josef Vachek's book on *Written Language* (Hall 1975; Vachek 1973). Hall was one of the American linguists who was most vociferous, in the 1940s and later, in defence of non-prescriptive attitudes to non-standard and unwritten language. The result of views such as Bloomfield's was the virtual abandonment of the study of written language in mainstream American linguistics from the 1920s to the present. It is also simple to check just how few references there are to written language or literacy in most contemporary textbooks on theoretical linguistics and sociolinguistics. Only a few individuals, such as Martin Joos and Dwight Bolinger, published the occasional article on problems of written language. In recent Chomskyan linguistics, the focus of interest was on the nature of human language. It was not interested in the relations between spoken and written language. Two main strands of linguistic work on written language have, however, continued. One strand has been work by European linguists, working mainly in Prague. The main name here is Josef Vachek. Second, there is the enormous amount of work on creating writing systems for unwritten languages done by the missionary linguists working with the Summer Institute of Linguistics. (See Gudschinsky 1976, for a review of this work.)

I do not think it is special pleading, however, to argue that the study of language does have particularly awkward problems associated with it, which are not encountered in other scientific pursuits. Linguists constantly have to decide whether to study particular languages or human language in general, and also whether to study language (or *a* language) or its realizations in speech or writing. The first distinction has been referred to as the difference between first- and second-order theories (Sampson 1975). First-order theories are theories, descriptions or grammars of particular languages. They tend to give prominence to idiosyncrasies, and on what makes, say, English different from Eskimo. Second-order theories are theories of the nature of human language. They are theories of linguistic universals, of ways in which all human languages are alike, and ways in which they differ as a whole from, say, animal communication systems. Other sciences do not have this problem, but all linguistic descriptions are distorted in some way by having to make a choice between concentrating on what is unique to a language or on what is universal. (Stubbs and Berry 1980 discuss this in more detail with reference to a particular current debate in English grammar, about whether features of the English verb should be described in a way that brings out the idiosyncratic behaviour of English verbs or in a way that relates the description of English to universal grammar: cf. chapter 14).

The second distinction is between a language and the medium in which the language is realized. The medium will usually be speech or writing, but could also be, for example, manual signing for the deaf. One could study the relation between the medium and the language (for example, whether a writing system is consistently alphabetic-phonemic, morphophonemic or syllabic), or differences between the syntax of spoken and written English, or such problems. Or one can write a grammar of a language with no reference to its realization, since the grammar of written and spoken English is, after all, largely shared.

In practice, the two distinctions are often related to each other, although, as far as I can see, they are logically independent. Thus an interest in the second-order theory of linguistic universals often goes along with a lack of interest in the particular realizations of a language. Chomsky, for example, is interested in linguistic universals and never discusses the relations between spoken and written language. Bloomfield, on the other hand, is especially interested in particular exotic languages, and concentrates on their spoken versions (although this is due mainly to practical, not theoretical, reasons; and, as I have said before, he does not give a satisfactory account of the relation between the spoken and written language).

The shifts of interest between written and spoken language can also be seen in shifts of fashion in foreign language teaching, which has often been influenced by current trends in linguistics. The traditional *grammar-translation* method was based firmly on written, and usually literary, language. This approach was perfectly understandable and appropriate, in so far as it was long used for teaching dead classical languages, such as Latin and Greek. It has always been more evident, with reference to learning foreign languages, that written and spoken language can be kept separate, at least for some purposes. It makes perfect sense to say of someone: he has a reading knowledge of German, or whatever, but cannot speak it. And if the language in question is a language that is no longer spoken and is studied primarily for its literary or historical interest (for example, Latin, Greek, Old English or Sanskrit), then there is no obvious alternative to the grammar-translation method.

However, by the 1920s it was becoming evident that teaching grammatical rules explicitly and translating written texts from one language to the other was less appropriate for modern languages. The grammar-translation method began to be replaced by the *direct method*, which advocated learning by hearing the spoken language. Bloomfield and American structuralist methods, together with behaviourist psychology, led to *audio-lingual* methods, most obviously represented in many language laboratory courses. Here, the emphasis is on spoken language. In extreme forms of language laboratory drills, nothing is explained explicitly to the learners. They are expected to repeat over and over again the model on the tape, and to induce the correct patterns. The behaviourist-structuralist approach assumes that skill in handling the written language comes after, and is dependent on, command of the spoken language.

More recently, there has been interest in teaching *reading ability* in foreign languages, with or without teaching ability in the spoken language. This has been related especially to the teaching of English for special purposes: for example, teaching English for scientific and technological purposes. This approach has seemed particularly appropriate with older learners, where it is possible to foresee their communicative needs. For example, they may be university science students in the Middle East or India, who need to be able to read scientific papers.

Concluding comments

One comment about research: a sociolinguistic theory of literacy will have to be based on a great deal of observation of the uses to which written language is put in a wide range of social settings. These uses are by no means always obvious to outsiders, since they may differ widely in different communities, and the kind of observational and ethnographic work required has hardly been started. And one comment about teaching practice: a major principle in teaching any language skills is that work should, as far as possible, have some genuine communicative purpose. The kind of understanding of the many different functions of reading and writing, which I have discussed, should therefore also underlie such teaching.

The chapter is tidily packaged, as is the convention for written academic articles, between headings, subheadings and references. However, this cannot disguise the fact that the argument is often rather formless, jumping between details of Scottish geography, the history of linguistics, English spelling, and so on. This is because I have tried to argue that a coherent theory of written language must be much less narrowly based in its facts than many studies in the past. I have dealt in more detail elsewhere (Stubbs 1980) with some of the topics that I have dealt with scantily here. But I am only too aware that my own knowledge is narrowly restricted, and that I have said almost nothing at all, for example, of the different kinds of writing systems and their uses in other parts of the world. Such a range of reference will be necessary, if we are to have the basis for a general, second-order theory of the universal characteristics of written langauge. At present we can do little more than document some surprising local idiosyncrasies.

'What writers know' is always different when they finish writing a book or article, from when they started. I know from personal experience that formulating ideas in written language changes those ideas and produces new ones. But problems writers have include deadlines, and a less formless argument will have to wait. What readers know when they come to the end of a chapter may or may not be the same as when they started!

ACKNOWLEDGEMENTS

This chapter is a revised version of an article first published as 'The sociolinguistics of literacy', in T. Bessell-Browne et al: (eds), *Reading into the Eighties*, Adelaide: Australian Reading Association, 1980, pp. 99-113; and then expanded for publication as 'Written language and society: some particular cases and general observations', in M. Nystrand (ed.), *What Writers Know*, New York: Academic Press, 1983, pp. 31-55.

12

The sociolinguistics of the English writing system: or why children aren't adults

Introduction

One area of language in which inadequate everyday models abound is English spelling, which is typically believed to be illogical, inconsistent and irregular. Many adults assume that because they know how to spell, they also understand the underlying principles. However, as with other aspects of native linguistic competence, our spelling habits may be too close to be observed accurately: they may be too automatic after years of practice, and they may have been wrongly explained by teachers in the first place. As with other aspects of linguistic competence, speakers may think (consciously) that they do one thing, but in fact they do another. Clearly, the English spelling system contains many irregularities, but many fewer than is often thought. Indeed many of the supposed irregularities are due to an underanalysis of how the system actually works. It is often assumed that it is sound–letter correspondences that must be regular. This, however, is only one possibility: there are regularities not only in the relations between letters and sounds, but also between letters and meanings. An analysis of English spelling also demonstrates the need for adequate descriptive linguistic concepts, such as phoneme and morpheme. These explicit concepts are for the teacher, of course: the pupil needs to be shown the patterns, but probably does not need the linguistic terminology.

This chapter is about some characteristics of the English writing system that I suspect may cause problems for children learning to read. The basis of my suspicion is that the same characteristics seem to cause problems for some of my university students . . . (Of course, it does not necessarily follow that what causes problems for my university students will also cause problems for 5- or 6-year-old children!)

For example, a fair number of my students use the spelling *grammer*. This is always embarrassing around examination time: it cannot impress external examiners to find students who cannot even spell *grammar* after two or three years studying it. But, of course, the real point is that if you spell *grammar* with an *e* (like *hammer*), then this betrays a fairly fundamental lack of understanding about how the English spelling system works. I should make clear immediately that I do not attach particular importance to good spelling in itself. It is easy to erect spelling into something which has value in its own right, but there are more reliable indices indices of high intelligence or social worth. However, there are powerful social conventions connected with being able to spell. And there are interesting general principles which explain many apparent irregularities in English spelling, and which are not as widely known as they might be.

Why children aren't adults

I want now to develop my main argument, by making some comments about the subtitle of the chapter. A traditional argument has developed in linguistics over the past fifteen years or so, that children are remarkably skilled and rapid in language acquisition, and that they gain their linguistic competence in an amazingly short time, with no special training, and apparently no great effort. By the age of 4 or 5 years, they have acquired the vast bulk of the phonological, syntactic and semantic systems of their language. More recently, similar arguments have been applied to the ability to carry on dialogues or conversation, and children as young as 2 or 3 years can be shown to adapt their language according to who they are talking to.

The general trend in such work is to push back children's linguistic competence further and further. Now, this is a very important argument for teachers to appreciate: that the language of any normal 4-year-old is already so complex that linguists are not able to describe it fully. This is an amazing fact about children which has to be accounted for. However, I assume that no one would question that 4- to 6-year-olds do not have all the linguistic competence that adults do. And it may be that aspects of competence that they have not acquired are particularly crucial in learning to read.

There are several aspects of linguistic competence that develop relatively late. Although the bulk of grammatical competence is acquired by the age of 4 or 5, a great deal of communicative competence is still being acquired into the teens and later, including competence in a range of different styles, from informal to formal. This is important for reading, since written material is conventionally much more formal in style than most spoken language. Next, there is vocabulary competence: speakers go on increasing their vocabularies during the whole of their lives, and there are more words in English than any one individual knows. (See chapter 6.) *Collins English Dictionary* (Hanks, ed., 1979) has over 162,000 entries, and unabbreviated general dictionaries have up to half a million. This is the kind of unlimited proliferation of words which is due to a long literary tradition; but no-one knows half a million words. An important feature of English spelling is, however, that one of its major principles is only fully accessible to someone with a wide vocabulary of rather erudite words. This is illustrated below. A third example is that children have limited experience of the functions to which written language can be put. These are characteristically bureaucratic and administrative purposes, and therefore of no interest to young children. This too is illustrated.

The English spelling system

One area of difficulty for children learning to read is the English spelling system. This is not because the system is *irregular* or *illogical* - this is not a satisfactory explanation - but because, in order to understand how the system works, readers require knowledge about English which young children may not have. In order to take the argument further here, I need to make some general comments about English spelling. This is now fairly well understood, and a consensus view has, I think, developed amongst linguists that it is not *irregular*, but that its regularities are more abstract and less obvious than is often assumed. (Albrow 1972 provides a useful introduction to the principles of English spelling, and Venezky 1970 is a detailed scholarly study. My comments here owe much to these two books. Several of the points below are also developed at greater length in Stubbs 1980.)

English spelling is based on sound-letter correspondences, that is, it is basically phonemic. (A phoneme is a functional sound unit which can distinguish between different words.) Sometimes there is good sound-letter correspondence, as in *behind*. But even in a word like *through*, where there are seven letters and only three phonemes, it is still clear which letters correspond to which phonemes. However, the system is obviously not consistently phonemic, and the phonemic principle is often overruled by other principles: English spelling is a mixed system. Sometimes letters relate to sounds, but they also relate to other linguistic units, grammatical and semantic: in particular to morphemes. A morpheme is the smallest meaningful unit. So, *spelling* and *mix-ed* consist of two morphemes each.

A major principle in English is: one-morpheme-one-spelling, whether or not the sound is the same. Conversely, different morphemes are spelled differently, whether or not the sound is the same. An alternative formulation is same-meaning-same-spelling, different-meaning-different-spelling. For example, in pairs such as *scene, seen* or *rough, ruff* there is the same sound, but different meanings and therefore different spellings. Whereas in pairs such as *sign, signature* there are different sounds, but related meanings and therefore related spellings. Another way of putting this point is to say that spellings are more sensitive to ambiguities in meaning than spoken English is. Therefore, homophones (same sound, different meanings) such as *rough, ruff* or *bow, bough* are common. But homographs (one spelling, different sounds, different meanings) such as *bow* or *read* are relatively rare. An estimate (Perera 1984: 179) is that there are over a thousand homophones in English, but less than two hundred homographs.

Yet another way of thinking about the point is to regard English spelling as a visual system. It marks visual identity between items that mean the same, and visually distinguishes items that mean different things. This is perfectly reasonable, since writing is designed to be seen and not heard. It does not have to be read aloud, and there is therefore no reason why it should necessarily represent sounds.

Consider, as another example, the way the past tense morpheme is marked in written and spoken English, in words such as:

want-ed /id/ after /t,d/
bang-ed /d/ after voiced sounds
kick-ed /t/ after unvoiced sounds

(Phonemes are conventionally written between slash brackets.) In each case, the spelling marks the past tense with *-ed*, maintaining visual identity between items that mean the same, although they are pronounced differently.

In this case, the spelling can ignore the variation in pronunciation because this is predictable, an automatic consequence of the last sound in the word. If this alternation is predictable, then it cannot affect the meaning. This is an elementary point in information theory. There is only meaning where there is uncertainty, unpredictability, the possibility of something different, some choice. English spelling, however, is usually sensitive only to contrasts in meaning. Incidentally, how do readers know that *-ed* is a morpheme? One reason is simply that it has the letter *e* in it. Compare: *-ed, -es, -est, -er, -en*. But contrast *solid*, where the *-id* does not mark a separate morpheme, although *solid* rhymes with *wanted*.

Now, consider the problems this may cause for learners, especially young children. The one-morpheme-one-spelling rule is only really obvious if you know a large number of pairs of words such as:

sign, signature; paradigm, paradigmatic; medic, medicine; romantic, romanticize; cognitive, cognition; existence, existential.

The problem letters (italicized) are clearly fixed in one member of each pair. But these are rather erudite, mainly Latinate words, which are most unlikely to be known to young children. The principle operates elsewhere (for example, in past tense forms), but it is particularly striking in hundreds of pairs like these. Such words are unlikely to be known by young children, since they are precisely the kind of words that are often learned through reading. Once you can read, then this becomes a major source of new vocabulary. I have to beware of paradoxical argument here, and of implying that you can only learn to read, if you can read already. Obviously, it is possible to get into the system, but things become easier once you *are* in.

Written and spoken language

The functions of written language are quite outside the experience of young children. But there are also much more basic functions of written language that may be opaque to children. More generally, there are functions of written language that are obvious to literate adults, but outside the needs or experience of people with limited experience of literacy. For example, it is obvious to us that written language can record and store messages for reference in the future, but this was not obvious to the early printers. It was about a hundred years after the invention of movable type that page-numbering was regularly introduced into books. Clearly, only with page-numbering can books be used conveniently for reference. Similarly, early manuscripts were often learned by heart. This rather misses the advantages of the medium: like the early days of educational television, which often merely showed a teacher standing in front of a blackboard.

The permanence of the written medium is also obvious to skilled readers in a different way. Written language does not have to be understood at the first reading: it can be re-read, skimmed, sections can be omitted and referred to later. This is very different from spoken language, which has to be processed in real time, in lockstep with the speaker. The evidence is that children require a lot of practice in processing written texts in appropriate ways.

Since it is permanent, written language can be transmitted across time and space. Again, this is obvious to us, but may be beyond children's experience. It also has a peculiar result. Apart from occasions like radio talks or lectures (which are probably based on notes or written scripts anyway), spoken language generally has a specific audience. But most written (i.e. published) material has only a mythical audience, such as *second-year sociology students* or *the intelligent layperson* for books and articles, or *car drivers* or *the general public* for items such as forms, questionnaires or notices.

Features deriving directly from the permanence of written language affect its form, and explain certain differences in the linguistic organization of written and spoken texts. Permanence has contradictory effects on the comprehensibility of written language. On the one hand, written language should be easier to understand than spoken: (a) it can be planned in advance, re-drafted, and edited, and should therefore be more logical and better organized; (b) it should be more explicit – since it has to stand on its own, things should be explained more clearly. On the other hand, written language should be more difficult to understand: (c) it does have to stand on its own, and therefore has less support from the context than spoken language does; (d) it assumes that the reader will refer back, re-read sections, and so on, and will therefore typically be more condensed, less redundant, less predictable and with a higher information load.

Relative to spoken language, written language is highly planned, explicit, context-free and unpredictable. Spoken language is not planned in advance, less explicit, context-bound and more predictable. If the differences between written and spoken language are formulated in this way, they come out sounding very similar to Bernstein's distinctions between elaborated and restricted codes. Several people have suggested that Bernstein has put his finger on a useful distinction, but has put the distinction in the wrong place. He suggests that schools are *predicated upon elaborated code*: but one might equally well say that they are predicated upon written language. Yet nowhere in Bernstein's work does he discuss written language or literacy. (Cf. chapter 5 for more detailed discussion of such speech-writing differences.)

Conclusions

The main points I have made are as follows. Certain aspects of written English are: (a) peculiarly adult, in that they are beyond the needs or experience of young children; (b) peculiarly English, in that they assume native knowledge of the English language; and (c) peculiarly literate, in that they assume a highly literate reader with a wide vocabulary; and also in that the system is a visual system biased towards fast, silent reading, and not designed for reading aloud. English spelling is a good system for its fluent, native English-speaking adult users, but not so good for young learners.

If you are teaching someone to read and write, you should do at least two things. First, tell them how the English writing system does work. The way I have explained it here will not, of course, be appropriate: pupils will not want to be told that English spelling is a mixed morphophonemic system. But the one-spelling-one-meaning rule can be displayed by setting out relevant examples to show the visual regularities involved. It is clear that no one has ever pointed out these regularities to many of my students. Second, learners will need a lot of practice in dealing with permanent written text, which involves skills not required in processing spoken language. They will require a lot of practice in reading at different speeds, re-reading, scanning, skimming, using indexes and reference books, and so on. Otherwise, they will never fully profit from the information storage potential of written language.

Again, this is something that many of my students never fully appreciate. They often never come to appreciate and exploit the massive technology which now underlies the production of the printed language, rolling off the printing presses at millions of words a day. And they often never discover the full potential of reference books, catalogues, abstracting journals, microfilm, the network of lending libraries, translation services, and so on. In other words, they often never learn to exploit the information storage capacity of a big library, which is the logical extension of the storage function of written language in books. But then it takes some students years to learn how to spell *grammar* . . .

So why is *grammar* not spelled like *hammer?*
Because the *a* maintains the visual relationship with words such as *grammatical* and *grammarian*.

And I have never found any of my students who were tempted to put an *e* in those words.

ACKNOWLEDGEMENTS

This chapter is a revised version of an article first published in the *Australian Journal of Reading*, 5(1): 30-6, 1982. It is also reprinted in M. Stubbs and H. Hillier (eds), *Readings on Language, Schools and Classrooms*, London: Methuen, 1983, pp. 279-86.

Educational Research

13

Scratching the surface: linguistic data in educational research

Introduction

Several chapters in this book discuss the superficial nature of the linguistic analysis in much educational work on language. In this chapter, I discuss the way in which language is used as data in educational research on the classroom. Educationalists are not interested in language for its own sake: they want to know how language relates to learning and teaching. However, this can lead to a premature jump from relatively surface features of language to psychological, social psychological or sociological features of the context: ignoring the organization of the language itself. This means that educationalists may be ignoring a much richer source of information about learning and teaching. The term 'superficial' is a loaded one, of course. Linguists themselves are accused of superficiality and of lack of sociological sophistication in their analyses. Just because workers in different disciplines all talk about language, it does not mean that they are talking about the same object of study. One of my main points in this chapter, however, is that linguists are correct in their insistence that language must be explicitly studied in its own terms: it is not possible to skip this stage in the analysis.

Since the late 1960s, an increasing amount of educational research has been concerned with language in education, and in particular with language in the classroom. This chapter discusses some problems that arise when such studies attempt to use language as *evidence for educational statements*. It does not discuss any practical problems of collecting or analysing linguistic data, but considers problems involved in relating linguistic data to educational statements in a principled way. It suggests that many studies that do select aspects of language as data for educational statements have no principled basis for this selection, since they ignore the depth of organization of the language itself. They often merely scratch the surface of the available linguistic data, restricting their attention to superficial characteristics of language in use.

We are, then, concerned with the question: how can language be used as data in educational research, in ways (to use J. R. Firth's phrase) that will avoid 'loose linguistic sociology without formal accuracy'? The argument in this chapter will be based on examples from educational research, but the argument could be made more general by substituting 'sociology' for 'education' throughout.

Although this chapter will be entirely at a theoretical level, its argument has developed from empirical analysis of sound recordings of classroom language (Stubbs 1976) and other types of discourse (chapters 9 and 10; and Stubbs 1983a). In this data-based work, I often commit the sins of which I here accuse other researchers.

Language as evidence

Language as a 'marker' of educational processes

There is now a large volume of work which uses linguistic data as 'markers', 'indices', 'indicators' or 'evidence' for social-psychological statements that are of interest to educational theory and practice. Much of this work is concerned with studying classroom language: with recording, observing and analysing teacher–pupil interaction and using the language as evidence about teaching and learning processes and outcomes.

Between the fieldwork and the published report, some sequence of decisions such as the following inevitably takes place. Researchers return from the field with video-recordings, audio-recordings, notebooks or other data. From these recordings or notes, they *select* for quotation and discussion short *extracts* of, say, teacher–pupil dialogue. From these extracts, and probably more generally also within the corpus of data, they further *select* particular *features* of language which they regard as *evidence* for educational statements. However, precisely how such extracts do illustrate claims about the educational process is often not discussed. It is often simply assumed that particular details of what teachers and pupils say can be quoted, and can serve unproblematically as demonstrations of some educational process. Readers are expected to be able to recognize a particular teacher–pupil interchange or sequence of utterances as, for example, an instance of a 'closed teaching style', a 'democratic teacher' or a 'divergent pupil'. The fact that extracts of talk are quoted does, of course, mean that readers are free, to some extent, to form alternative interpretations. However, I want to question whether quoted utterances or surface features of language do provide evidence of anything non-linguistic.

Work of the type I have in mind includes many excellent individual studies which provide close, perceptive analyses of the ways in which language is used in schools and classrooms; and some generalizations have emerged about the relationships between 'language' and 'education'. But it is difficult to see in what way such studies are cumulative or even comparable. Certainly, they do not constitute a paradigm (Kuhn 1962) tackling a well-articulated set of problems in well-defined ways, with agreed standards of solution and explanation, and drawing on a consensus of theory. As a whole, the studies lack coherence.

I am referring to studies of classroom language by researchers such as Adelman, Barnes, Cazden, Delamont, Flanders, Hammersley, Hawkins, Keddie, Mishler, Rosen, Sinclair, Stubbs, Torode, Walker and many others. I am not, of course, implying that these researchers think that they have much in common. But it is perhaps disappointing that such studies have very little in common beyond a loose notion that somehow 'language' is important in 'education'. I emphasize that individual researchers usually have well-defined notions, but overall there is nothing more than this loose consensus. The fact, for example, of studying language *in the classroom* provides no principled basis for relating such research. The fact that different pieces of research are carried out in similar physical settings can provide no rationale for them (Atkinson 1975: 180 argues this point very clearly).

Unprincipled selection of data

The very tenuous and unprincipled relationship between the kinds of studies I have cited is evident from two things.

First, different studies claim to relate features of language to a very mixed collection of social-psychological concepts, including: the educability and cognitive orientation of pupils (Bernstein 1971a); teaching strategies, for example 'open' versus 'closed' (Mishler 1972); the teacher's role, for example democratic versus authoritarian (Flanders 1970); methods of social control in the classroom (Hammersley 1974; Torode 1976); different types of classroom organization (Walker and Adelman 1976); pupils' and teachers' differing concepts of classroom knowledge (Furlong 1976; Keddie 1971). These are a few examples of rather different types of educational process for which language is used as evidence: the list could, of course, be extended.

Second, different studies select a wide range of not obviously related linguistic units, both formal and functional, as 'indicators' of these social-psychological and educational processes. These include: different teachers' use of pronouns (Mishler 1972; Torode 1976); the complexity of nominal group structure in children's language (Hawkins 1977); the functions of teachers' questions and different types of question–answer exchanges (e.g. Barnes, Britton and Rosen 1969; Mishler 1972); functional categories of speech acts (Stubbs 1976); intonational and paralinguistic features (Gumperz and Herasimchuk 1972); the overall structure of teaching 'cycles' (Bellack et al. 1966). This list could also be extended.

It is not unfair to say that many researchers seem to feel justified in picking out, as evidence, any feature of language which appears intuitively to be interesting. Mishler (1972: 297) is one of the few researchers to admit that he has been 'relatively eclectic in the types of linguistic units used in drawing inferences'. Less misleading terms than 'eclectic' might be *ad hoc* or *unprincipled*. Given how little we know about the communicative functions of different aspects of language, it would clearly be a mistake to *restrict* enquiry to any one particular type of linguistic feature, and I am certainly not proposing that. Walker and Adelman (1976) have demonstrated very clearly that utterances with educational significance may be found in unexpected places. However, this is only to admit that research is still proceeding along heuristic and therefore unprincipled lines, still searching for the socially significant features of language. This does not mean, however, that one is condemned to pick and choose linguistic items at random, unrelated to the organization of the linguistic data as a whole. This would, in any case, merely lead to the unending task of looking for more and more particular features of language, unless these particulars are related to a coherent framework. I am, then, using the term 'unprincipled' to refer to studies in which surface features of language are picked out at random and not related to underlying linguistic statements and descriptions.

Two things might immediately strike the linguist about such research. First, linguistic items are selected, usually with no explicit justification, from several different levels of language - including lexis (i.e. individual words), syntax (i.e. grammatical structure), semantics (i.e. meaning), language function, and discourse (i.e. overall conversational structure). Second, these items, either as unique items or according to their linguistic class membership, are then often related directly to social-psychological categories, rather than being first *related to the linguistic and sociolinguistic systems and structures in which they are terms.*

For example, the fact that a teacher uses pronouns in a certain way has been said to be evidence of his style of social control (Torode 1976) or of his pedagogical message (Mishler 1972). And the fact that children use pronouns in a certain way has been said to be evidence of their intellectual orientation (Hawkins 1977). It is not obvious, first, that the use of pronouns can be considered apart from other characteristics of the speaker's language. Nor, second, is it obvious that the use of pronouns relates *directly* to social and psychological processes.

These two related points amount to the criticism that such studies characteristically attempt to relate isolated linguistic variables to social-psychological categories, *as though the language had no organization of its own.* This point is well made in an article by Coulthard and Ashby (1976). They argue, with reference to sociological studies of language, that 'sociological categories should not be used to classify stretches of speech as though [the speech] had no other organisation'. This means that these studies often attempt to relate concepts at quite incompatible levels of abstraction and generality. Isolated, surface features of language are taken as indicators of deep, general and highly abstract social-psychological categories.

One body of work that does explicitly discuss how to relate linguistic and sociological categories at an equal depth of generality is Bernstein's. His work is an attempt to state causal relationships between a theory of educational transmissions and pupils' social class, family type, cognitive orientation and use of language. He accuses other researchers of not having recognized the depth of abstraction of the problem (Bernstein 1975: 25). Unfortunately, the deep, underlying principles and categories which Bernstein proposes are unrelated to any naturalistic linguistic data. Bernstein has never made any statement which formulates precisely either how sociolinguistic codes or the concepts concerned with educational transmission (e.g. 'framing') are realized in language.

Atkinson (1985) provides an extremely useful and clear interpretation of Bernstein's work, in which he argues that linguists and others have simply failed to see the type of highly general and abstract social theory which Bernstein proposes. But it seems to me that Atkinson still does not tackle the problem of how Bernstein's theories can be tested on particular cases, to see whether they fit the empirical data. In fact, on his own admission, Atkinson does not discuss the large body of empirical studies done by Bernstein's research colleagues in London. Bernstein is clearly not interested merely in a theory of linguistic variation; he is not, as Atkinson points out, a sociolinguist *manqué*. Nevertheless, the relation between the broad structuralist social theory and the linguistic data remains unclear.

Reductionist descriptions

Much important twentieth-century work in linguistics has been concerned with the complexity of surface and underlying systems and structures in language, and has consequently ignored the relations between language and its social contexts of use. (This is true at least of mainstream American linguistics in the Bloomfield to Chomsky tradition, but less true of British work from Firth to Halliday.) However, recently much attention has been paid to the importance of relating language to its social contexts of use. Within linguistics, Hymes (1964) and Labov (1970) in particular have led the attack on the Chomskyan concept of a grammar that is independent of social context and on the concept of context-free grammatical competence. In addition, within sociology, much attention has been paid to the importance of studying social contexts. The arguments here are well known: that a failure to study contexts reifies the object of study, by neglecting the interpretative procedures by which situated meanings are constructed, and by failing to treat as problematic the ways in which social order is successfully accomplished by members. The arguments usually amount to the criticism that context-free studies of language are reductionist: they reduce praxis to process; they reduce the study of meaningful behaviour to the study of ideal-typical structures, taking for granted how such structures are interpreted and used in context; and they refuse to study the essential meaningfulness of human behaviour, and how people make sense of social interaction.

I have also discussed elsewhere (Stubbs 1975) how studies of classroom language are often decontextualized by being treated in strange isolation from other types of social interaction, such as casual conversation, doctor–patient consultations or committee meetings, which are organized by comparable sociolinguistic rules; and also in isolation from sociolinguistic findings about radically different kinds of classroom organization in other cultures. Again, just the fact of collecting data in the physical setting of classrooms does not mean that the study will be an adequate account of language in context. Studies of classroom language will remain theoretically *ad hoc* unless they are related to general sociolinguistic principles of language behaviour and draw on observations of everyday life in other settings.

It is therefore no solution to reductionism to make loose references to context and to interpretative procedures, *if this ignores the inherent structural and systemic complexity of language.* To proceed directly from isolated features of language to social-psychological categories is itself severely reductionist, for it ignores the partly autonomous, complex organization of the language itself. Many levels of organization are simply bypassed.

I use *systemic* in this chapter in its technical linguistic sense, as the adjective corresponding to a linguistic *system*. A *system* is a closed set of choices or options in a language which are mutually defining. Thus, English has a number *system* comprising two *terms*, singular and plural. Old English had a three-term system, comprising singular, dual and plural. Clearly, plural means something different in two-term and three-term systems. Most linguistic systems are, of course, much more complex than this. Languages are then regarded as systems of systems. Systems may be identified at different *levels* of description. Linguistics traditionally uses the term *level* to refer to phonology, morphology, syntax and semantics, but usage here is variable. (Cf. chapter 2.)

Two examples

To make these points clearer, I will discuss briefly two extreme and well-known examples of studies that pass directly from isolated, surface features of language, to social-psychological statements, whilst entirely ignoring the inherent linguistic organization of the data.

Flanders's (1970) work on teacher-pupil interaction in classrooms is well-known and has been very influential. The basic research procedure involves coding teachers' and pupils' utterances, every three seconds, into a series of discrete categories in a pre-prepared category system. There are now a large number of articles that criticize Flanders, and similar research, for bypassing all the interpretative problems involved in 'coding' language data. A linguistic version of this criticism is that such a coding scheme necessarily ignores any inherent linguistic organization which the talk itself has. Flanders's interaction analysis categories (FIAC) require utterances to be coded directly as pedagogical acts (e.g. lectures, praises). The codings of these acts are then taken as immediate evidence of 'indirect' or 'direct' teaching: the teacher's 'I/D ratio' being computed directly from the simple addition and division of utterances coded into different categories (Flanders 1970: 102). This I/D ratio is then further taken, by implication, and with no further intervening argument, as evidence of a teacher's social role, for example, 'democratic' or 'authoritarian'. This procedure thus takes us directly from utterances (the language data) to social role (a very high-level social–psychological concept), with no intervening discussion of *how the language itself is organized.*

Specifically, the sequential organization of the classroom dialogue is ignored. Flanders (1970: 2) claims to study the 'chain of small events', in the classroom. But FIAC cannot be used to study the structure of classroom talk, because 'events' are defined arbitrarily as 'the shortest possible act that a trained observer can identify and record'. That is, the 'chain of events' has nothing to do with the autonomous organization of the talk itself. This organization is taken for granted in the observation. Briefly, we have to know where an event occurs in structure before we can know what kind of event it is.

A second study that passes directly from surface linguistic features to deep social–psychological categories is the well-known experiment by Bernstein's colleague Hawkins (1969) on how young middle-class and working-class children talked to a researcher about a series of cartoon pictures showing some boys kicking a ball through a window. Hawkins found that the working-class children used more pronouns, whereas the middle-class children used more nouns and complex nominal groups in their narratives. Hawkins takes this finding about the complexity of the nominal group as direct evidence of different cognitive orientation in the two groups. His argument is that the middle-class children have more possibilities of elaborating and differentiating what they are talking about (since one cannot modify a pronoun with an adjective: one can say *good boys*, but not **good they*).

An alternative interpretation is, of course, possible: the pronouns used by the working-class children take account of the conversational context in which the language is used. The hearer can see the pictures and does not need to be told explicitly who *they* are and where they kick the ball. That is, the pronouns do not necessarily have any cognitive function: they might have a discourse function, that is, a *linguistic* function. The data could be explained with reference to factors in the conversational context: that is, they could be given a *sociolinguistic* explanation. They do not have to be accounted for in psychological terms. When Bernstein himself discusses the experiment (1971a: 219), he relates the different language use to context, and not directly to intellectual potential.

More recently, Hawkins (1977) has written a book in which he himself provides a very considerable reworking and reinterpretation of the data in his 1969 article. In his book, Hawkins takes, like Bernstein, a much more cautious line, and admits that in his earlier work he has crucially ignored the social context and the functions of the language. He has, for example, entirely dropped all references to cognitive ability, claiming now simply that working-class and middle-class children talk differently in the interview situation (which, it is pointed out, is broadly similar to test situations in school). The point is that the working-class child assumes a different relation between speech and situation, and therefore operates with different ways of reporting and constructing social reality (Atkinson 1985: 121). Hawkins further claims (pp. 200 ff.) that the children talk differently because of speech differences in their home backgrounds. This would be interesting if it could be docu-

mented, but the only evidence presented (pp. 64, 202) is hypothetical interview data: mothers were asked how they *would* talk to their children in different situations.

There are, however, major points to be gained from the book. First, it emphasizes the widely divergent interpretations which can be placed on data
about social-class variation in language use. Second, it demonstrates that
everything is vastly more complex than popularized accounts of an elaborated
/restricted dichotomy suggest. Hawkins's analysis is careful and painstaking:
what we are dealing with is differences in relative frequency of items which all
the children use, and therefore with performance, not competence (pp. 108,
186-7). The care which has gone into the linguistic analysis of the nominal
group is considerable, and if readers get nothing else from the book, they
ought at least to see the sophistication required of such analyses, and therefore
the total inadequacy of impressionistic comments on working-class and
middle-class language. Finally, however, as a result of this detail, Hawkins's
analysis could be interpreted as data against the codes theory altogether, on
the grounds that if no absolute and clear-cut differences exist between
children's language, and if it is all a matter of relative frequencies in usage,
and is all highly context-dependent, then there does not seem to be much support for the notion of two discrete underlying codes. At most we have (that
characteristically Bernsteinian term) 'orientations' (pp. 183, 203 and elsewhere). (See also Stubbs 1978.)

Sociolinguistic work on language and social context

The question arises, then, of what kinds of relationship linguists have found
between language and its social contexts of use. I will take some examples
from Labov's work to illustrate the depth and complexity of these relationships.

In his original work on the social stratification of English in New York,
Labov (1966) found strong correlations between speakers' social class and
their use of phonological variables. (Labov 1966 is now out of print, but most
of the material has been revised and included in Labov 1972b.) For example,
simplification of word-final consonant clusters (e.g. *tol'* for *told*) correlates
more strongly with working-class than middle-class membership. Such
linguistic variables therefore have predictive power: they are socially significant and can be interpreted as an index of social structure. Note two complications, however.

First, Labov found a great range of absolute values of such phonological
indices, but agreement in the pattern of variation. When he looked only at the
speech of individual speakers, he found oscillations, contradictions and alter-
nations which were inexplicable. On the other hand, the language turned out
to be highly determined, when charted against the overall social variation between speakers. In other words, the language of a speech community turns
out to be more regular and predictable than the speech of an individual. Thus

the absolute use of an isolated linguistic variable tells us nothing: correlations are found only by looking at the relative frequency of use of linguistic variables across a speech community. What one finds is that, if speakers are rank-ordered both in terms of their use of selected linguistic variables and in terms of their social class, these rank-orders coincide (apart from various 'cross-over phenomena' connected mainly with particular linguistic sensitivity in the lower middle class to features of language in the course of change).

Second, some linguistic variables are entirely ambiguous as indices either of the social class of speakers or of the formality of the conversational context. That is, some linguistic items serve both as demographic and as stylistic markers. One can therefore draw no inferences from a speaker's language about his or her social class, unless one also knows whether the social, conversational context was formal or informal. In Labov's words, one cannot tell a casual salesman from a careful pipefitter.

Labov distinguishes, in fact, between different types of linguistic item. An *indicator* correlates with some demographic characteristic of the speaker, say, social class; but does not vary in the speech of the individual. *A marker* is evidence of, say, social class, but also varies stylistically according to the formality of the situation. Empirically, both types of item are found.

In other work, Labov (1973) has studied the language for pre-adolescent Black gangs in New York. He has found the boys' language to be a sensitive *index* of how closely the boys are involved in the street culture. The language of core members of the gangs (discovered independently by sociometric techniques) turns out to be different in describable ways from the language of peripheral members ('lames'). But the important point is that the language is not different on the surface, for example, in the use of particular words or isolated items. There is, in fact, no absolute difference between the language of the groups. That is, for any feature of Black English Vernacular that core members use, lames will also be found to use it. What is different is the whole system. Labov's finding is that the core members' language is more consistent in its use of the rules of Black English Vernacular. Thus, they might delete the copula in 100 per cent of cases (in sentences like: *He my brother*), where lames will follow the rules only some of the time. The *index* of membership of street culture is therefore provided only by the *overall consistency of the whole grammatical system*:

> the consistency of certain grammatical rules is a fine-grained index of membership in the street culture.
> . . . It must be remembered that all of these boys appear to speak BE [Black English] vernacular at first hearing.
> . . . All groups use the same linguistic variables and the differences in the system are internal variations in the organisation of similar rules: differential weightings of variable constraints. (Labov 1973: 81, 88).

Labov also points out the severe practical and theoretical problem that the core members of the subculture, whose language is most consistent, are precisely those who are most inaccessible to researchers. It is the lames, whose knowledge of the subculture is inadequate, who are most likely to be informants for educational researchers.

The main warning from such work is that, if language is to be used as evidence of social structure and processes, then the language must be examined *as a system*, not as isolated items. Relationships are found between linguistic *systems* and sociological categories. Therefore, the language data must be studied for their own linguistic, systemic organization. In general, then, the relation between language and educational statements is much less direct and more abstract than many educational studies assume.

Sociolinguistic studies of the relationship between language and context also recognize the importance of speakers' attitudes and perceptions of language, as an intervening link in the chain between language forms and social processes. Much recent sociolinguistic work has concentrated not only on features of how language is used in context, but on the social values which speakers attach to language. (For American studies of language in education that emphasize this, see especially Cazden, Johns and Hymes 1972.) Labov (1969) has suggested that a speech community is defined by speakers who hold the same linguistic attitudes and stereotypes. The phonological variables which are indices of a speaker's social class are often raised to the status of stereotyped and stigmatized features for speakers themselves. But there is a complex relation between speakers' perceptions of other speakers' speech and actual behaviour. Labov's general finding is that people perceive in categorical terms what is, in fact, variable speech behaviour. Thus, a speaker who simplifies word-final consonant clusters in some linguistic environments some of the time may be perceived as doing it all the time, if the frequency of consonant-cluster simplification rises above a critical perceptual threshold.

There has been little work on the institutionalized attitudes to language transmitted by Colleges of Education and schools. But what little there has been suggests that schools and colleges often take highly prescriptive attitudes to pupils' language. (See Milroy and Milroy 1974 for data on Belfast, and Macaulay 1977 for data on Glasgow).

I now move on to discussing one particular level of linguistic organization whose study cannot really be avoided by educational researchers.

Classroom language as a discourse system

Much classroom research is actually concerned with studying classroom dialogue: in terms of teachers' questioning strategies, pupils' responses to teachers' questions, the kinds of exploratory discussion amongst groups of pupils working on tasks, and so on; if not immediately concerned with studying the dialogue itself, much work nevertheless draws its data from such sources. And much other work admits that it ought to be concerned with teacher-pupil interaction, or that study of teacher-pupil interaction would be required to provide empirical substance to theoretical points (see Keddie 1971: 156, and many other examples).

The organization of classroom discourse

Most studies of the classroom are, then inevitably concerned with how teachers and pupils interact; that is, with aspects of teacher-pupil dialogue, conversation or discourse. There are now many studies which demonstrate in detail that discourse (multi-party conversation) is a complex linguistic system: a highly patterned, rule-governed activity describable in terms of several interrelated ranks of description. That is, *discourse has its own organization*. Major studies of how spoken interactive discourse 'works' are by Sacks (e.g. 1972) and his colleagues in the USA; and by Sinclair and his colleagues in Britain (Sinclair and Coulthard 1975). This latter work is on teacher-pupil discourse amongst other discourse types. Many quite specific proposals have now been made concerning how spoken discourse can be analysed structurally and systemically, in terms of the linguistic 'mechanisms' which make it 'work'. Much work has been done, for example, on minimal interactive units, at the rank of question-answer pairs. (Cf. Sinclair and Coulthard 1975, on exchanges; Sacks 1972, on adjacency pairs; Goffman 1971, on interchanges.) Often classroom researchers (e.g. Barnes et al. 1969) have worked with an intuitive notion of such discourse units. Larger discourse units are also discoverable. Schegloff and Sacks (1973) suggest ways in which whole conversations are structured. The most specific suggestions have come from work in Birmingham (Sinclair and Coulthard 1975) which proposes several hierarchically ordered ranks of structural units into which discourse can be analysed on formal grounds. The details of such analyses are not important here. What is important is that any attempt to relate isolated linguistic units to non-linguistic categories completely bypasses these levels of conversational organization.

The general point is as follows. Language is a relatively autonomous system, or more accurately a system of systems. Within language, discourse or conversation constitutes a relatively autonomous level of linguistic organization. That is, it is possible to formulate discourse structures (including two-place structures such as question-answer) and systems of choices (if A says x, then B will say $y1$ or $y2$, and will not say z). In order words, it is possible to begin to specify how conversation works. It is also possible to specify how different discourse types work, for example, how teacher-pupil dialogue typically differs from a doctor-patient consultation. Treating teacher-pupil interaction as a linguistic discourse system means studying the formally recognizable linguistic 'mechanisms' by which the talk is organized and made coherent. That is, studying, amongst other things, how topics are introduced, sustained and closed, or how one speaker's talk is related to another's. Many formally identifiable markers of discourse cohesion have now been identified, including lexical repetition, parallelism of syntax and intonation, anaphora, ellipsis and sentence continuations. (Halliday and Hasan 1976 include a very detailed discussion of these topics.)

If language data are selected from observations or recordings of classroom language, these data are necessarily abstracted from their context in discourse structure. Any principled study of such data must therefore take account of their own organization.

The transmission of educational knowledge

There is another powerful reason why educational researchers should be interested in such linguistic organization. In ignoring it, they are in fact ignoring a vast resource, much deeper and richer than surface linguistic items. Studying teacher-pupil interaction as a discourse system can provide educationally interesting insights which are not available to studies that bypass this organization. One example is as follows.

Much recent educational research has been concerned with the sociology of knowledge: with how educational knowledge is socially defined, selected and made available to pupils. Much of this work raises 'predominantly conceptual issues' (Young 1971: 2) and provides no detailed specification of how knowledge is actually transmitted from teachers to pupils. There is much theorizing, but few case studies. (Case studies based discursively on classroom interaction include Furlong 1976; Keddie 1971.) Studies in this area can usefully be done at different levels: one can study, for example, how the curriculum defines knowledge (e.g. Hamilton 1976). However, description of how teacher-pupil discourse is sequentially organized could also provide much information for the educationalist interested in how teachers control the knowledge which is presented to pupils. By studying discourse sequencing, one can study in empirical detail: how teachers select bits of knowledge to present to pupils; how they break up topics and order their presentation; how these discrete items of knowledge are linked; how distinct topics are introduced and terminated; how pupils' responses to questions are evaluated; how pupils are made to reformulate their contributions; how bits of knowledge are paced and allowed to emerge when the teacher considers it appropriate. I cannot see how such topics could be studied, other than in an *ad hoc* way, by looking at isolated utterances of features of language. But by studying the overall structure of the teacher-pupil interaction as a discourse system, these topics are inevitably studied.

Studying teacher-pupil talk as a discourse system would, for example, provide one way of studying how classroom knowledge is 'framed' (Bernstein 1971b). Only by studying how teachers control the classroom discourse itself can one then study how this also controls the transmission of educational knowledge. Only preliminary studies have so far been done on how the concept of framing may be grounded in sound recordings of classroom language (Stubbs 1983a: ch. 7; Walker and Adelman 1972, 1976).

Such topics of study are simply not available to researchers who treat language at the level of isolated surface features, ignoring its abstract, underlying, sequential and hierarchic organization.

Pots and kettles

It often happens that educationalists, and sociologists in general, accuse linguists of ignoring the contexts in which language is used. 'Contexts' here generally mean social and cultural contexts. Such accusations are often true. (The fact that they are also no news to linguists, who are quite aware of the idealizations they make, and have strong reasons for making them, is often ignored by critics, but this is another matter which does not concern us here.) But in this chapter, I am accusing educationalists, in their turn, of ignoring contexts. By 'contexts', *I* mean levels of linguistic organization in the data: one such level is discourse sequence.

I am not claiming that, by taking account of linguistic organization, everything can be explained. This would clearly be factually wrong. Reference to the social context is often necessary in order to account for how langauge is used.

Nor am I arguing that the social functions of language ought to be related explicitly to the linguistic forms that realize them: the problem of the relationship between language forms and functions is a quite separate issue, which I have only mentioned in passing in this chapter. It is well known, in academic debate as in everyday life, that we often think people are saying what we expect them to say. When linguists talk about language, they are often heard as insisting that educational and social researchers pay more attention to language forms. But this is only one concern of linguists, and it has not been my concern in this chapter.

What I am arguing is that it is often tempting to proceed directly from language to social context, bypassing levels of organization in the middle. As a principle, and even if it does not always work, one ought to try and account for linguistic data on its own terms, before turning to sociolinguistic, sociological or psychological explanations. The argument is not that one ought to study language as a system *instead of* studying the social context; but that one ought to study language as a system *before* trying to relate it to the social context. Linguists and educationalists both accuse each other of being reductionist.

Conclusion

I have discussed some theoretical problems in relating linguistic data to social-psychological statements in a principled way. There are various ways of thinking about these problems.

First, it is the problem of how researchers can place some control on their intuitions. What is to stop researchers picking out isolated linguistic items or classes of items and taking these as 'evidence' of democratic social control, closed learning sequences, or whatever? Second, it is the problem of idealization. Descriptions of phenomena have to simplify and idealize: otherwise they would merely reproduce the features of the original under study, rather than make hypotheses about what it is significant to describe. Third, therefore, it is the problem of how to avoid reductionist statements. Clearly descriptions of language which ignore its social context of use and social meanings are severely reductionist and unlikely to be of any interest to the educationalist. But in concentrating on the use of language in context, one must not ignore the complexity of the language system itself, by reducing the linguistic data to a string of isolated features.

As a whole, studies of language in education have attempted to relate a mixed collection of surface linguistic features to a mixed collection of deep social-psychological categories. This is a prima facie indication that such studies are unprincipled in that they treat the linguistic data as a mere resource, as though it had no organization of its own. I suggest finally that classroom researchers are inevitably concerned with using teacher-pupil dialogue as a source of data, and that they should therefore be concerned with how the dialogue works: that is, with teacher-pupil discourse as a linguistic system in its own right. To ignore teacher-pupil talk as a discourse system is, in any case, to throw out the baby with the bathwater, and to ignore a much richer source of data than isolated and surface linguistic items.

I find it difficult to see what direct relationship there could possibly be between isolated, surface features of language and learning and teaching strategies. For example, the cognitive complexity of an argument will never be computed merely by calculating the number of subordinate clauses it contains, the mean length of its sentences, the complexity of its noun groups, or the rarity of its adjectives. Nor can a teaching style ever be defined merely in terms of the number of closed questions the teacher asks or the number of pupil initiations. The relationship between language and educational processes is much less direct than this, and seems to depend crucially on a notion of the organization of the language as a *system* of communication. This is a much deeper, more powerful and more interesting concept of language. At present, many educational studies are only scratching the surface of the language data which they use.

ACKNOWLEDGEMENTS

This chapter is a revised version of an article first published in Clem Adelman (ed.), *Uttering, Muttering*, London: Grant McIntyre, 1981, pp. 114-33.

14

Analysts and users: different models of language?

Introduction

An important trend in educational thinking is that teachers should be 'their own experts' (see Eyers and Richmond 1982). The basic argument is that experts such as professional linguists are not the sole repository of authority and knowledge about language. Teachers have perceptions about classroom experiences which are not available to experts in the usual sense of someone who stands back from immediate experience in order to gain a magisterial overview. Children also have legitimate perceptions about the functions of language which have been forgotten by many adults (see Halliday 1969; and chapter 1). The basic debate is therefore about different kinds of authority: everyday versus specialist, analytic versus experiential, abstract and rational versus concrete and practical. The general argument seems clear enough: that no single group could possibly be the sole source of all that is worth knowing about language, and that language study must be a collaborative exercise in which teachers and linguists (and others) work together. However, this general argument must also be made more precise. In this chapter, I try to show, with specific and sometimes fairly technical examples from syntax, semantics and pragmatics, that linguists' descriptions can be strengthened by taking account of everyday perceptions of language – and in some cases that linguists are missing essential knowledge about language by ignoring common-sense perceptions.

This chapter is theoretical. However, it is concerned with the kind of linguistic theory required for pedagogical practice; and with ways in which linguistic theory should take more account of practice. It tries to bring together several rather different aspects of language, where users have their own legitimate perceptions and where these differ from the professional linguist's perceptions. Sometimes these users' views are of central practical concern in first or second-language teaching, but they may also be of theoretical value to the analyst in constructing better models of language. In recent linguistics, analysts have been prepared to accept the judgements of 'linguistically naive' informants in only some areas of language. For example, grammaticality judgements may (sometimes) be accepted as legitimate, but judgements of correctness are rejected: although such a distinction between different types of intuition would not be recognized by most naive informants. In general, I will argue that the division between professional linguistics and folk linguistics is not as clear-cut as linguists have often implied.

A conceptual basis for language teaching

There is a great deal of fragmentation between the different branches of language teaching, and often a sharp opposition between mother tongue and foreign language teaching. Nevertheless, there is increasing support for the idea that this fragmentation is unfortunate, and that a common conceptual basis for these different branches should be developed. (This is a recommendation, for example, of NCLE 1980).

Chomskyan work is one obvious influence here, since it has emphasized similarities between first- and second-language learning by emphasizing the systematic nature both of any language learning and also of learners' errors. Error analysis has therefore been an important technique in both recent mother tongue and foreign language teaching; it has been both pedagogically useful and theoretically interesting in the way it has shifted attention to the learner-user.

Paradoxically perhaps, another trend which has helped to break down the opposition of mother tongue and foreign language teaching (FLT) is the increasing specialization of the branches with their various labels: English mother tongue teaching (EMT), English as a second dialect (ESD), English as a second language (ESL), English as a foreign language (EFL), and perhaps especially English for specific purposes (ESP), including English for academic purposes (EAP) and English for science and technology (EST). A major reason behind the specialization has been the increasing attention paid to non-native users' needs in language learning, and the specification of these needs has typically been in terms of communicative goals.

Both recent FLT and recent EMT are characterized by an emphasis on communicative goals and creativity, in various senses of this term. The notion that language is a medium of learning is emphasized by much current EMT, and also by ESP, where courses are designed for adults who require English in order to have access to academic materials. Such ESP courses often resemble well-prepared study skills courses more than they do traditional language teaching materials (cf. chapter 3). In addition, they blur the distinction between native and foreign speakers: for example, in a special purposes course, say German for chemists, French for caterers, or English for economists, it is likely that native speakers would not themselves be fully competent in the varieties of language involved (Sinclair 1978). ESP materials also reflect a general movement towards a greater explicitness in what is intended to be achieved in language teaching. The concentration on users' communicative purposes and the blurring of the distinction between native and foreign speakers is also evident in ESL courses, especially for immigrants in Britain; ESL therefore provides a mid-point between EMT and EFL. An even more ambiguous central point is provided by the teaching of ESD to speakers of an extreme dialectal variety of English, say an English-based creole. (See Wight 1974, on the relation between Standard English and Jamaican creole in Britain; and papers in Brumby and Vaszolyi 1977, for a discussion of teaching Standard English to speakers of Australian creoles and non-standard Australian Aboriginal English.) Various work of this kind therefore draws into question the concepts of mother tongue and native speaker, which are often taken for granted in theoretical linguistics. Again, this comes about due to an increasing interest in the learner-user's own competence or needs.

Finally, there is increasing support for the view that a study of language should underlie both EMT and FLT in British schools. This general view covers rather different proposals about possible relations between a study of language and more traditional subjects on the school curriculum: that there should be a separate curriculum study of Linguistics (Tinkel 1979), of Language (Hawkins 1979, 1984) or of Modern English Language (see chapter 4); that such a study should be a preparation for later FLT (Cross 1979); that FLT can no longer be justified on the grounds that it provides British pupils with a useful instrument of communication, and that the principal concern of FLT should be to improve understanding of the phenomenon of language in general (Byram 1978); or that the Bullock Report suggestion of language across the curriculum is still an appropriate one (DES 1975).

So these various *rapprochements* are apparent. Their general basis is fairly clearly established within a communicative and functional view of language, and this view is theoretically grounded in the ethnography of communication and speech act theory. Further, there is a general trend, which has given more importance to learners' and users' own competence, requirements and perceptions of language. However, this still all provides only a very general view of language and not the kind of precise and coherent conceptual basis asked for by NCLE (1980).

Models for applied linguistics

I now want to try and develop an argument put forward in various papers by Widdowson (1979c, 1980a, 1980b), that one aim of applied linguistics is to develop a model of language that is relevant to language learners. We cannot simply assume, he argues, that such a model can be derived from theoretical linguistics, because theoretical studies tend to ignore or even deride users' models of language, and it is plausible that language learning has to be based on a user's model rather than on an analyst's model.

In fact, Widdowson's view of the relationship between theoretical and applied linguistics has changed over several articles. In a previous paper

(1979b), he had adopted a widespread view that applied linguistics should be a mediating subject, with the aim of interpreting theory for the language teacher. But he subsequently (1979c) adopts an independent position, arguing that applied linguistics should aim to develop its own coherent model of language, designed with its own purposes in mind. He admits that he has 'no very definite idea about what such a model might look like in detail', except that he would expect it to embody the users' concept of language, and therefore to be based on a communicative approach, since this is in accord with the learner's experience of language. Similarly, he argues (1980b) that applied linguistics can develop its own non-conformist theory, its own relevant models of description. In a fourth article (1980a), he takes his argument another stage further, arguing that the analyst's model of language and the user's model are radically different, and actually incongruent in principle. The main reason, he argues (1980a: 83), is that analysis must be precise to be valid; but communication must be imprecise to be effective. And users' perceptions of language will focus on communicative uses.

As an example of a more radical view again, one could cite here Labov's (1973) well-known argument that professional linguists are 'lames', and are inevitably always outside analysts, even of the language variety which they regard as their native dialect. He has pointed to the many ways in which academic linguists lose contact with the vernacular: including their characteristic social and geographical mobility, and the very linguistic self-consciousness which is inevitable, due to their training. (Note here, again, the way in which this questions the concept of native language.)

I find myself largely in agreement with Widdowson's view that applied linguistics should develop its own theory, but I think that his argument requires considerable development, if it is to be entirely convincing. In this chapter, I will try, therefore, to develop the argument that Widdowson proposes, and also add some new kinds of argument. On the other hand, I am not so convinced by the claim that analysts' and users' models are necessarily incongruent. Even if they are at present, then this is arguably a defect in our analytic models, which we should try to remedy.

To some extent, I may be simply repeating ideas that are now very familiar in language teaching, making well-trodden points about discourse and pragmatics, and filling in the odd hole or two. However, it seems to me, first, that some of the general argument in applied linguistics is not as explicit or as secure as it might be. There are, after all, constant swings of fashion in language teaching. Corder (1980) not only provides a very useful synthesis of recent research in second-language acquisition and the conclusions that can be drawn from it, but also argues that this research has been done almost entirely by applied linguists, and that a more explicitly theoretical approach would do no harm. Second, whereas Widdowson is concerned with the relevance of linguistic theory to applied linguistics, I am also concerned with the relevance of applied matters to a more adequate linguistic theory. I want to argue that the language user has also been left out of analysts' descriptions.

Analysts' and users' models

The distinction between analysts' and users' models has of course often been drawn, via variously phrased dichotomies, which differ in detail, but which point in one way or another to a potential clash of interests between theory and practice.

One related distinction is between theoretical and pedagogical grammars. A basic assumption underlying this distinction is that different grammars may serve different purposes or different consumers. (Cf. chapter 1.) (This basic assumption is itself often questioned by theoretical linguists, who object to the weakening of linguistic theory implied in the view that different models are not strictly comparable, because they are designed for different ends, and therefore a decision procedure cannot decide which is the best grammar. An argument in favour is that a bus is neither a better nor worse vehicle than a sports car: they serve different ends and are better or worse only at specific tasks.) Candlin (1973) draws the theoretical-pedagogical distinction, and then proposes, plausibly, but without any very explicit argument, that pedagogical grammars should be based on semantics, discourse and the pragmatics of language use, rather than just on syntax.

Another related distinction is Corder's (1980) contrast between conscious, analytic knowledge and implicit knowledge. He argues that much of a foreign language must be learned implicitly, since (a) there is much that is not understood by analysts, and this cannot therefore be explicitly taught, and (b) there is much that is simply too complex to be learned consciously. To some extent, then, the learner must call the tune. Newmark (1966) argues further that in those areas where analysts have developed their knowledge of language, this may itself interfere with language learning, since teaching materials may be developed to reflect this finely detailed knowledge, whether it is helpful to the learner or not. The analytic tail may wag the dog: the teacher ends up teaching something because the teacher knows it, not because the learner needs it or wants it (a hazard of all teaching, of course!). Corder argues that some things are too complicated to be taught; Newmark argues that some complicated things are taught because they are known. In either case, the relation between learners' requirements and analysts' knowledge is uncomfortable.

Hymes (1972) argues, with reference to the ethnography of communication that participants must be their own ethnographers. He draws distinctions between insiders and outsiders, participants and observers, and between two kinds of authority for knowledge which derive from activity or analysis.

Many other comparable linguistic distinctions could be listed, but these are perhaps representative. However, such distinctions are also much more widely debated. For example, in the context of a detailed critique of contemporary views on the history and philosophy of science, Feyerabend (1975, 1978) develops distinctions between participants' and observers' views, practice and reason, the layperson and the scientist, and democratic judgement and expert opinion. Participants want to know what to do; observers want to know what is going on (1978: 18). He is attacking the views of Popper and Lakatos, who, he thinks, give too much credit to rationality in the historical development of science. And he argues that they have ignored the rich and well-articulated practices of participants, such as speaking a natural language. He argues further, however, that reason and practice are not distinct, but that both are kinds of practice, and that people have been deceived into thinking that so-called scientific rationalism is something special.

This apparent dichotomy between reason and practice has also been questioned by the ethnomethodologists, who point out both that so-called scientific reasoning depends on many inexplicit practices, and also that everyday life depends on 'practical reasoning'. The dichotomy between 'science' and common sense is therefore invalid. In their detailed analyses of conversational data, the ethnomethodologists have also laid great stress on analyses that take account of participants' orientations (cf. chapter 9).

Within mainstream linguistics, analysis has tended to ignore or deride speakers' own models of language. However, one striking exception is Ferguson's (1971b) work on the ways in which native speakers simplify their language when speaking to foreigners or young children (cf. chapter 6). Theoretical linguistics has had little success in developing a simplicity metric: the notion of simple versus complex sentences is often an artefact of the theoretical model being used. However, speakers seem to have a built-in awareness of what is simple to process psycholinguistically, and the study of such automatic rhetorical adaptations has had great interest for topics such as pidginization of languages and also language teaching (Corder and Roulet 1977). This is a striking, and possibly unique, example where attention to speakers' models of language has increased our understanding of a topic where an analyst's approach has made little progress.

The different though related dichotomies listed above locate the distinction between theory and practice in different places. This itself emphasizes that the boundary between academic linguistics and folk linguistics is not as evident as linguists often imply. Further, some scholars argue that there is no definable boundary at all. However, even if the boundary is fuzzy, this does not mean that the opposition is not important. Nor does an emphasis on users' perceptions mean that analysts' views should be undervalued. An onlooker may have a clearer view of the game than an individual player. What we have to guard against, however, is the armchair critic who passes judgement on the game on the basis of only the half-time score on the radio.

Some syntactic examples

Widdowson (1979c) gives two examples from syntax, where linguists have dismissed language users' intuitive knowledge about language. First, he notes the way in which Chomsky (1965: 18) decides to abandon the concept of kernel sentences, whilst admitting that they have 'an important intuitive significance'. Widdowson argues that this is a 'really rather remarkable state-ment', which denies the user's intuitive sense of language, just because this is inconvenient to the analyst's model. Second, he notes that traditional seman-tic or notional definitions of a noun (as the name of a person, place or thing) have been derided or dismissed as irrelevant by linguists. However, one can take the view that a noun is not a well-defined discrete category, but that words can be ranged along a continuum, to include core nouns (e.g. *boy, table*) and items that share only certain characteristics of nouns (e.g. *shooting*). If one takes the view that such a 'squish' is a legitimate descriptive device, then it turns out that the traditional definition corresponds to the most typical, core nouns, and that it has something to recommend it after all. Lyons (1977: 423ff, 448) also recognizes, for this reason, the value of traditional semantic definitions of verb and adjective.

An area of major current debate in syntax, where some linguists' rejection of traditional definitions is very clear, is the debate over the status of AUX as a category of universal grammar, and consequently over the status of auxiliary verbs in English. Auxiliary verbs are usually taken to be: *have, be* and *do*; plus the modal auxiliaries: *must, can, could, shall, should, will, would, may, might,* and sometimes *ought to* and *used to*. Main verbs are any other verbs. There are many tests which can potentially distinguish between main and auxiliary verbs, but very briefly:

both auxiliaries and modal auxiliaries form questions by a simple inversion of subject and verb; main verbs do not:
   has he? should he? *eats he?
only modals have no -*s* ending on third-person singular present tense forms:
   he could; *he coulds; *he have; he has; *he sleep; he sleeps.

These statements apply to Standard English: such verb forms are often heavi-ly loaded with social meaning and distinguish Standard English from non-standard regional and social dialects (cf. chapter 5).

Ross (1969) put forward what is now referred to as the main-verb hypothesis, arguing that the distinction between main and auxiliary verbs is merely a surface phenomenon of some languages, and that auxiliary verbs should be derived from underlying main verbs. This position is supported in many subsequent articles, including Huddleston (1980) and Pullum and Wilson (1977), but it is attacked by Palmer (1979) and others.

This debate is interesting because it brings out several more general issues about the relation between traditional or common-sense views of language form, and linguists' models. Pullum and Wilson (1977: 742), for example, simply dismiss the distinctions between modal, auxiliary and main verbs in English as 'certain morphological facts and minor syntactic phenomena which have certainly obscured the picture'. Similarly, in the debate between Huddleston (1980) and Palmer (1979), the main point at issue is the significance of idiosyncratic facts of English. Huddleston dismisses the surface facts of the English auxiliaries, because they are idiosyncratic to English and do not reflect linguistic universals. Palmer counters with the point that all languages are idiosyncratic in some ways and this cannot be ignored. There is an unresolved dispute between the relative claims of describing individual languages and the universals of human language.

The debate has become extremely complex, since it is related to other debates over the relative importance of deep and surface structure, generative semantics and autonomous syntax, and transformational grammar versus other models. The debate as it stands is, in fact, probably doomed to stalemate whilst the arguments remain so embedded within long chains of argument within different rival syntactic models. Some outside impulse is probably necessary.

If we accept as relevant the users' view of the phenomena, then this appears to tip the balance against the main-verb hypothesis of Ross, Pullum and Huddleston, and in favour of the position taken by Palmer. This is the view taken by Stubbs and Berry (1980), where we discuss these issues at some length, in the context of devising an appropriate syntactic model for teaching either linguistics or English language to native speakers or advanced foreign learners. In other words, we are concerned with the problem of devising a model of linguistic description designed specifically for learners of different kinds. Our model is developed from scratch, and not derived from any particular theoretical framework. We argue in favour of a model that maintains a distinction between modals, auxiliaries and main verbs, partly on the grounds that such distinctions are fairly striking and easily observed by linguistically naive students. Conversely, some of the 'facts' that Pullum and Wilson (1977) attempt to account for would hardly even be recognized as facts by such learners. I think this model of the English verbal group would constitute one detailed example of what Widdowson (1979c) is asking for: namely, a model that has been developed for teaching. It is probably quite inappropriate for foreign language teaching as such: it is entirely formal, with no reference to the meaning of the forms. But foreign language teaching is only one kind of teaching about language that requires models to be designed for users.

Idiosyncrasies

As I have noted, one major feature of the debate over AUX is the dispute over how much significance should be given to facts that are idiosyncratic to English. The general trend in contemporary linguistics has been to fight against the idiosyncrasies of individual languages. American structuralist linguistics of the 1920s to 1940s emphasized how much different languages could differ from each other. But much mainstream contemporary linguistics, with its emphasis on a homogeneous object of study, emphasizes what all languages have in common; further, it idealizes away variation within languages.

However, if we regard language from the users' point of view, then it is precisely the idiosyncrasies and peculiarities which people tend to notice. What often fascinates people about language is regional accents and dialects, the jargon of different social groups, linguistic taboos, strange etymologies, oddities and irregularities in spelling, and so on. In fact, the only linguistic book which most people are familiar with is a dictionary, and the lexicon is, in Bloomfield's (1933: 274) phrase, a 'list of basic irregularities'. Users of dictionaries are clearly often confused about the origin and status of its entries, regarding them as prescriptive when they are a record of usage; and the theoretical linguist may criticize the uncontrolled listing of irregularities. But there is currently a revival of interest in lexicography in linguistics (cf. chapter 6); and since teaching must start from where the learner is, then such views must be seriously considered.

In fact, dictionaries raise an interesting version of the problem of the relationship between observers' and users' views of language, and of the observers' paradox. Speakers and writers use words, and lexicographers observe and record (some of) them. The lexicographer describes usage, although the description is inevitably selective and therefore a prescriptive bias may be built in. However, even if intended to be descriptive, the product is most likely to be treated prescriptively. This does not always mean that the user of the dictionary is confused, since the very act of recording words changes them. The paradox is most obvious with taboo or obscene words. Obscene words are unrespectable: that is part of their meaning. But dictionaries are one of our most respectable institutions. Therefore, if a dictionary records a word, it cannot be entirely unrespectable. It is given a stamp of respectability by the very fact of being recorded.

Some semantic examples

There is, then, a whole range of such syntactic and lexical examples where there is dispute about the weight that should be given to intuitively striking phenomena that have been at the basis of traditional grammatical categories for centuries. No one would argue, I presume, either that such intuitions should be entirely ignored, or that they should be accepted without question. But just which natural interpretations should be retained and how much weight should be given to them, in the face of other kinds of data, is a question that is not often asked, much less answered.

In addition, the whole of current semantic theory is involved with such a debate over the relationship between natural human languages and the ideal, logical languages (of the propositional calculus, predicate calculus and modal logic). Some scholars have argued that there is no important difference between natural and logical languages. Others have argued that there are significant differences, and that the meanings of natural language utterances can be accounted for only if a narrow logico-semantics is combined with a wide-ranging pragmatics. The main debate is over how many facts of natural language a logical semantics can account for. But closely related to this problem is the importance that should be attached to intuitively obvious semantic facts.

A central problem concerns the value of the concept of *presupposition* (cf. chapter 7), where there is considerable debate over whether this intuitively appealing concept can be accommodated within a traditional two-valued truth-conditional semantics by being reduced to the concept of entailment; or whether it requires setting up a new kind of three-valued logic. Confronted with the classic example:

1   The King of France is bald.

the common-sense users' reaction would probably be, not that the sentence is false (as one would have to say within a two-valued logic), but that there is something strange about the sentence, since its existential presupposition ("There is a King of France") fails. In other words, it is this presupposition that is false, whereas the assertion is not false, but void or inoperative. This commonsense reaction leads to three-valued logic, in which such statements may be said to be neither true, nor false, but third-valued or truth-valueless.

The term *presupposition* is used in many different senses in the literature, including semantic and pragmatic senses. But the sense above is arguably the central one: in which a presupposition is defined as a proposition that remains constant under negation and interrogation. Thus example (1) above, and also examples (2) and (3):

2   The King of France is not bald.
3   Is the King of France bald?

are all said to presuppose

4   "There is a King of France."

(I indicate propositions by enclosing them in double quotes.) And, centrally to my argument here, this also corresponds to the intuitive, pretheoretical sense of the term, where a speaker might say in reaction to (1), (2) or (3):

5   But you are presupposing that there is a King of France.

The first problem is that this concept of presupposition, which seems both intuitively appealing and clear (there are clear tests for it), appears to disintegrate under more careful examination. The second problem is whether this is sufficient justification for abandoning the concept altogether.

There are many recent discussions of the main facts at issue. A succinct statement is by Kempson (1977: ch. 9), and for convenience I will restrict my comments to her types of example. A thorough review is provided by Levinson (1983).

The most commonly cited test for presupposition is constancy under negation, and this predicts therefore that positive and negative sentences behave symmetrically in this respect. However, this turns out not always to be the case. For example, the presuppositions of *wh*-questions such as the following are arguably different:

6   What did John do?
7   What did John not do?

Further, the behaviour of positive and negative compound sentences that contain a factive verb in the matrix sentence appears asymmetrical, and Kempson discusses such examples in detail. The problem arises with sentences containing a factive verb such as *regret*, which entails the truth of the proposition in the embedded sentence. Thus example (8) entails (9):

8   Edwin regrets that it is raining.
9   "It is raining."

However, Kempson argues (p. 146) that sentences such as (10) are contradictory, whereas (11) is not:

10   *Edwin regrets that the King of France is bald, but there is no King of France.
11   Edwin doesn't regret that the King of France is bald, because there is no King of France.

Kempson makes several points about possible interpretations of example (11). She argues that (11) depends on an interpretation of the first clause that is 'not normal', since the first clause would normally presuppose the existence of the King of France. However, she then admits the possibility of its being quite normal, if it is used to deny a preceding utterance such as

12   Edwin regrets that the King of France is bald.

But she later (p. 153) argues that this special denial use of negation is not clearly distinct from the normal use of negation. The presuppositional analysis, she argues, assumes that negative sentences are ambiguous between natural and special denial senses (p. 147), and she questions the validity of this distinction. She appears therefore to admit the possibility of intuitive distinctions between the functions of utterances in discourse, but then argues that these intuitions are unclear and to be disregarded. Givón (1978) argues in more detail that positive and negative sentences perform different speech acts.

Another type of sentence which Kempson considers (p. 150) is:

13   John is married and he beats his wife.

The second clause, considered on its own, could be said to presuppose:

14   "John has a wife" or "John is married."

However, this proposition is not presupposed, but asserted, by the first clause. Therefore, argues Kempson, the whole sentence does not presuppose what the second clause does, and the presuppositional analysis is contradictory. However, one thing which Kempson fails to consider is why one should ever use a sentence such as (13). One rather obvious use is in a discourse exchange such as:

15   A   Married men are kinder than bachelors.
     B   Well, John is married and he beats his wife.

She fails to consider in what discourse circumstances speakers may state the obvious, or assert what might normally be presupposed. One discourse function is to establish common ground for a point in an argument, and to provide the basis for a topic-comment structure.

The situation, in summary, appears to be as follows. Kempson admits (a) that the presuppositional analysis is intuitively appealing, (b) that it is supported for simple sentences, and (c) that negative sentences may have a characteristic use in denying a preceding utterance in a discourse sequence. Nevertheless, she prefers the entailment analysis, because it provides a single explanation for both simple and complex sentences. Yet, the entailment analysis appears to provide a less satisfying analysis for the simple sentences, and an analysis which contradicts the user's pretheoretical understanding of the issue. In addition, the complex sentences on which the argument rests appear artificially contrived, especially when they are considered largely outside the discourse contexts in which they can be seen to have particular speech-act functions: it is well known that sentences that are anomalous from a logico-semantic point of view (for example, tautologies and contradictions of various kinds) are nevertheless used in conversation. Thus, Kempson appears to undervalue both users' intuitions about the phenomena and also the discourse uses of the utterances which she is discussing. The question of how much significance should be attached to such phenomena appears to be largely a question of faith: I agree with the details of Kempson's arguments, but disagree with the general conclusions she draws from them.

Practical semantics

Linguistic semantics has not been conspicuously concerned with practical issues, but arguably it could both contribute to and learn from practical problems of meaning.

For example, factive verbs have obvious rhetorical uses in argumentation, where they can function to introduce key propositions in the presuppositions of a sentence, and thus make them less noticeable or more difficult to attack. It is a characteristic of Chomsky's style, for example, that he often embeds central propositions in his argument in this way. The following example is from *Aspects*, with the factive italicized:

> Modern linguistics . . . has not explicitly *recognised* the necessity of supplementing a 'particular grammar' of a language by a universal grammar . . . (Chomsky 1965: 6)

Many other examples could be cited from this source. Such stylistic techniques can, of course, also be studied elsewhere; for example, in the rhetoric of politicians or in the way in which news is presented in the media.

Another area where such recent linguistic work could contribute to users' concerns is the current attempts to monitor or assess children's 'oracy'. (I discuss this in detail in chapter 8.)

Conversely, theoretical semantics could profit from studying the practical semantic problems which arise in the everyday use of language. Michaels (1980) provides an interesting discussion of the semantic problems that arise in contract law. In an attempt to guarantee objectivity, the law of contract depends on acts, usually speech acts and therefore on forms of words, and denies the relevance of the intent of the parties who make the contract. Nevertheless, problems arise when the interpretation cannot rest solely on the words in the text of the contract, but requires extrinsic evidence of how words are normally used, say in a particular trade or profession. Contract law therefore provides examples of the issue currently at the centre of semantics: how does strictly linguistic (lexical and logico-semantic) meaning interact with pragmatics? How much is meaning a function of situation as well as of texts? Michaels (1980) provides a detailed analysis of one particular dispute over the meaning of the word 'chicken' in a contract.

Some functional examples

The development of ESP has emphasized the issue of users' views of language in a different way. ESP explicitly rejects the view that there is one global function that a second or foreign language serves. Learners differ in their motivation for learning a language and learn for their own widely different purposes. Further, ESP recognizes that these purposes may be very different from the functions the language characteristically serves for the majority of its native users in everyday life. For example, an adult learner of English may require the language only to be able to read academic texts in some fairly restricted area, say economics or biology. These issues arise in ESP because of the functions that English serves as an international language, with its particular uses in academic, scientific and technological communication, and its uses as an auxiliary language in many countries. These questions of the specialized functions of language clearly have both practical implications in the preparation of language teaching materials, and also theoretical implications for the sociolinguist interested in studying the increasing formal and functional diversity of English world-wide. (Cf. chapter 4.)

Brumfit (1978) has raised the following version of the problem, that foreign learners of English may have their own participants' view of EFL. He discusses (p. 15): 'what criteria [we should] use for defining inappropriate English when English is being used to express a foreign culture' by giving examples of the kind of English that occurs in the People's Republic of China, in language teaching textbooks, the English language press, Marxist writings, and similar contexts. He makes the point that foreign users may wish to use English precisely to express cultural differences, which may be wide, between China and the West. Lehmann (1975: ch. 5), in a study of English language teaching materials in use in China, also makes the point that the materials focus on domestic socio-political and cultural matters; contain little information about Britain or the USA; and that students are usually more confident in discussing the Legalists and Confucius than the life of the people whose language they are studying. There are, of course, very special reasons for this focus on Chinese content and lack of information about the West, which lie in the way in which China was almost completely closed to outside contact, especially during the Cultural Revolution.

From the point of view of language teaching and the description of modern English, there would appear to be two main issues. First, a characteristic of modern English is its increasing diversity. This includes the development of regional varieties of world-wide English (such as the fairly well standardized West African or Indian Englishes), and the extreme diversity represented by English-based pidgins and creoles and the proliferation of institutionalized varieties of English (such as the specialized registers of air-traffic controllers, technical manuals and so on). As Brumfit (1978: 16) points out, there is increasing tolerance of this diversity and the recognition that there is more than one model of English for the learner. The issue is therefore over the boundaries of English (cf. chapter 4). Second, there is the question of how semantic and lexical well-formedness can be defined, when English is being used to express concepts from a foreign culture.

The kinds of examples pointed out by Brumfit (1978) and Lehmann (1975) could be illustrated from many recent English language textbooks produced in China. I will take a few examples from Tang and Chen (1979). Here is the beginning of the authors' introduction to their textbook, which provides a fairly clear statement of the kinds of functions that they see English as serving for their students (my translation):

> English is one of the most widely used languages in the world, and has international functions, as well as being an instrument of science, technology and cultural exchange. Studying and practising English, with regard to improving friendly relations between our country and every other country, promoting friendship, and with regard to studying the advanced technology of foreign countries, will speed up the

realization of the four modernizations, and all these things have very important significance.

Many of the lessons in the book provide explicit discussion of these topics. For example, one dialogue entitled 'Hail the establishment of China-US diplomatic relations' concludes with one speaker saying (p. 226):

16   I wish the friendship between our two peoples evergreen!

What comments might the theoretical or applied linguist make about this piece of English? Apart from the slightly odd syntax, the most striking feature is probably the word *evergreen*. This appears to be an over-literal translation of the expression *wàngǔchángqīng*, given in the text, and strikes the English reader as slightly archaic. There seems no reason why the text could not read *Long live . . .*, since this expression (*wàn suì*) is very common in Chinese political rhetoric. Notice, however, that an English equivalent is required which does *not* turn the language into perfectly natural English, since part of the stylistic message is that this *is* specifically Chinese political rhetoric. The proper question is not only what the words mean, but what the users mean.

There are more interesting problems with the term *friendship*, which would probably pass unnoticed by the average English reader. The problem here is that this word (and its Chinese term *yǒuyì*) has particular connotations, which are only apparent if its uses in contemporary China are studied. It occurs characteristically in uses such as *Friendship Hotel* (*Yǒuyì Bīnguǎn*) and *Friendship Shop* (*Yǒuyì Shāngdiàn*), where it means specifically international friendship, and, to all intents and purposes, "reserved almost exclusively for foreigners". What would seem to be required, therefore, is a semantic study of the word in its Chinese contexts of use.

The problems which such examples raise for the theory of translation, for the description of lexical meaning, and for the description of stylistic variation have only started to be discussed. As regards my main argument here, such examples provide a clear case where users have an effect on English usage, and also where users' perceptions raise interesting theoretical problems.

Some other examples

In order to be specific in this chapter I have concentrated on the details of a very few particular examples. However, the issue of the significance which should be given to users' views of language is a very general one, although it is not often given serious attention by linguists. I will conclude simply by listing a further selection of widely different examples of some of the ways in which the problem crops up, in order to try to indicate how general the issue is.

It would generally be admitted that the very notion of 'a language' cannot be defined on strictly linguistic-structural criteria, or even with straightforward reference to observable national and cultural boundaries, but requires taking into account what speakers themselves regard as 'a language'. Similarly, a speech community is now generally defined not on observable criteria such as frequency of interaction, but on the basis of the shared attitudes and values that are held by its members towards linguistic forms. Lambert and his colleagues have shown the importance of such attitudes towards languages and cultures with respect to foreign language learning in many countries. It would probably now generally be admitted that, when it comes down to it, learners' motivations and attitudes are the most important factor in success or failure in language learning. And in all areas of applied sociolinguistics, the importance of speakers' attitudes has proved crucial. There are particularly clear and well-documented cases of the importance of users' attitudes in the development of orthographies for previously unwritten languages (see Stubbs 1980, for a review).

The debate over the psychological reality of the phoneme is no longer central in linguistics, but the question of the perceptual salience of different phonological units (for example, phonemes versus syllables) is actively debated in research on reading. One plausible suggestion is that young children require to develop an analytic view of language forms, if they are to succeed in initial literacy. The more general question of the psychological reality of grammars is also currently unfashionable in linguistics, although it is still sometimes raised (for example, by Hudson 1976: 179). And the kind of pragmatic expectancy grammar proposed by Oller (1979), if it could be formalized, would be a strong contender for a psychologically plausible grammar with obvious applications in language teaching. It would fit well, for example, with Goodman's influential concept of reading as a psycholinguistic guessing game, as well as with current thinking about listening comprehension (cf. chapter 3).

It has been seriously proposed that only Black linguists can ultimately produce definitive descriptions of Black English, especially if the description is to include communicative aspects; and similarly, that only women (or feminists?) can analyse the male bias in language. These are, after all, only specific examples of the usually uncontroversial argument that only native speakers have full access to all the relevant facts for more than a superficial description. But the problem is obviously crucial where ideological issues of social identity are involved in the variety of language being described.

Conclusions and summary

The relation between theory and practice, and between analysts' and users' models of language, is central to all applications of linguistics, including both mother tongue and foreign language teaching. In this chapter I have tried to bring together a wide range of examples where users' views of language should be taken seriously. I have given some detailed syntactic and semantic examples where native speakers' intuitions appear to run counter to linguists' models; and also an example where foreign users' views raise interesting problems of defining correct or appropriate English. A serious study of native and foreign users' perceptions of English therefore raises problems of the relation between language functions and syntactic and semantic well-formedness, problems of the appropriate form of the description (which the theoretical linguist should not ignore), and problems of the increasing formal and functional diversity of English as an international language (which the theoretical sociolinguist should not ignore), as well as problems on which the language teacher has to take practical decisions.

There is a widely held view that common-sense knowledge is inadequate, and that the findings of psychology, linguistics and so on (as well as physics, chemistry and the 'hard' sciences) are incompatible with and superior to naive realism. There is a counter-argument that even hard science relies irremediably on common-sense practices and everyday reasoning. This does not leave us on the horns of a dilemma. On the contrary, we are now in the privileged position of being able to see the merits of both arguments, and that practice and reason, everyday knowledge and expert opinion must collaborate, if we are to understand the nature of human language in use.

ACKNOWLEDGEMENTS

This chapter is a revised version of an article first published in René Richterich (ed.), *Relations entre l'Enseignement de la Langue Maternelle et des Langues Etrangères*, Berne: Institut für Sprachwissenschaft (in press).

For comments on a previous draft of this paper I am grateful to Margaret Berry, Ron Carter, Andrew Gilling, Walter Grauberg and Henry Widdowson.

References

Adelman, C. (ed.) (1981) *Uttering, Muttering*. London: Grant McIntyre.

Alatis, J. E. (ed.) (1968) *Contrastive Linguistics and its Pedagogical Implications*. 19th Round Table Meeting. Washington, DC: University of Georgetown Press.

Albrow, K. H. (1972) *The English Writing System*. London: Longman.

Alexander, R. (1980) A learning-to-learn perspective on reading in a foreign language. *System*, 8(2): 113-19.

Allen, J. P. B. and Widdowson, H. G. (1974) *English in Physical Science*. London: Oxford University Press.

Allwright, R. (1979) Language learning through communication practice. In C. J. Brumfit and K. Johnson (eds), *The Communicative Approach to Language Teaching*, London: Oxford University Press, 167-82.

Ammon, U. and Loewer, U. (1977) *Dialekt/Hochsprache Konstrastiv. Sprachhefte für den Deutschunterricht*. Düsseldorf: Schwann.

Asimov, I., Greenberg, M. H. and Olander, J. O. (eds) (1978) *100 Great Science Fiction Short Short Stories*. London: Robson Books/Pan (1980).

Atkinson, P. (1975) In cold blood: bedside teaching in medical school. In G. Chanan and S. Delamont (eds), *Frontiers of Classroom Research*, Slough: National Foundation for Educational Research.

Atkinson, P. (1981) Ethnomethodology and applied linguistics. In H. Eichheim and A. Maley (eds) *Fremdsprachenunterricht im Spannungsfeld zwischen Gesellschaft, Schule und Wissenschaften*, Munich: Goethe Institute, 64-89.

Atkinson, P. (1985) *Language, Structure and Reproduction: an Introduction to the Sociology of Basil Bernstein*. London: Methuen.

Austin, J. L. (1962) *How to Do Things with Words*. Oxford: Oxford University Press.

Australian Department of Education (1977) *Education in Australia*. Canberra: Australian Government Publishing Service.

Bailey, M. (1979) *Oilgate*. London: Hodder and Stoughton.

Barnes, D. and Todd, F. (1977) *Communication and Learning in Small Groups*. London: Routledge and Kegan Paul.

Barnes, D., Britton, J. and Rosen, H. (1969) *Language, the Learner and the School*. Harmondsworth: Penguin.

Bartlett, F. C. (1932) *Remembering*. London: Cambridge University Press.

Basso, K. (1974) The ethnography of writing. In R. Bauman and J. Sherzer (eds), *Explorations in the Ethnography of Speaking*, London: Cambridge University Press, 425-32.

Bates, E. (1976) *Language and Context: the Acquisition of Pragmatics*. New York: Academic Press.

Bauman, R. and Sherzer, J. (eds) (1974) *Explorations in the Ethnography of Speaking.* London: Cambridge University Press.

Bellack, A., Kliebard, H. M., Hyman, R.T. and Smith, F.L. (1966) *The Language of the Classroom.* New York: Teachers College Press.

Bennett, J. (1976) *Linguistic Behaviour.* London: Cambridge University Press.

Berlin, B. and Kay, P. (1969) *Basic Color Terms.* Berkeley, Ca: University of California Press.

Bernstein, B. B. (1971a, 1975) *Class, Codes and Control,* vols 1, 3. London: Routledge and Kegan Paul.

Bernstein, B. B. (1971b) On the classification and framing of educational knowledge. In M. F. D. Young (ed.), *Knowledge and Control,* London: Collier Macmillan. Also in B. B. Bernstein, *Class, Codes and Control,* vol. 1, London: Routledge and Kegan Paul.

Berry, J. (1968) The making of alphabets. In J. A. Fishman (ed.), *Readings in the Sociology of Language,* The Hague: Mouton, 737-53.

Birdwhistell, R. (1970) *Kinesics and Context.* Philadelphia: University of Pennsylvania Press; also Harmondsworth: Penguin, 1971.

Bishop, D. V. (1981) Varieties of childhood language disorder. *Journal of the Northern Ireland Speech and Language Forum,* 7: 20-37.

Bishop, D. V. (1984) What is semantic-pragmatic disorder? Unpublished lecture, Conference, Dawn House School, Nottingham.

Bishop, D. V. and Rosenbloom, L. (in press) Childhood language disorders: classification and overview. In W. Yule, M. Rutter and M. Bax (eds), *Language Development and Disorders,* London: SIMP/Blackwell Scientific and also Lipincott.

Blank, M. and Franklin, E. (1980) Dialogue with preschoolers. *Applied Psycholinguistics,* 1: 127-50.

Blewitt, P. (1983) *Dog* versus *collie*: vocabulary in speech to young children. *Developmental Psychology,* 19(4): 602-9.

Bloomfield, L. (1933) *Language.* New York: Henry Holt.

Blum, S. and Levenston, E. A. (1978) Universals of lexical simplification. *Language Learning,* 28(2): 399-415.

Bohannon, J. N. and Marquis, A. L. (1977) Children's control of adult speech. *Child Development,* 48: 1002-28.

Bolinger, D. (1980a) Fire in a wooden stove: on being aware in language. In L. Michaels and C. Ricks (eds), *The State of the Language,* London: University of California Press, 379-88.

Bolinger, D. (1980b) *Language the Loaded Weapon.* London: Longman.

Bradbury, M. (1965) *Stepping Westward.* London: Secker and Warburg.

Bradbury, M. (1976) *Who Do You Think You Are?* London: Secker and Warburg.

Brazil, D. (1969) Kinds of English - spoken, written, literary. *Educational Review,* 22(1): 78-92. Reprinted in M. Stubbs and H. Hillier (eds), *Readings on Language, Schools and Classrooms,* London: Methuen, 149-66.

Brazil, D., Coulthard, M. and Johns, K. (1980) *Discourse Intonation and Language Teaching.* London: Longman.

Britton, J., Burgess, T., Martin, N., McLeod, A. and Rosen, H. (1975) *The Development of Writing Abilities (11-18).* London: Macmillan.

Brown, G. (1977) *Listening to Spoken English.* London: Longman.

Brown, G. (1978) Understanding spoken language. *TESOL Quarterly,* 12(3): 271-83. Reprinted in M. Stubbs and H. Hillier (eds), *Readings on Language, Schools and Classrooms,* London: Methuen, 167-84.

Brown, G. (1982) *The Spoken Language*. London: Longman.

Brown, G., Anderson, A., Shillcock, R. and Yule, G. (1984) *Teaching Talk: Strategies for Production and Assessment*. London: Cambridge University Press.

Brown, G., Currie, K. and Kenworthy, J. (1980) *Questions of Intonation*. London: Croom Helm.

Brown, G. and Yule, G. (1983a) *Teaching the Spoken Language*. London: Cambridge University Press.

Brown, G. and Yule, G. (1983b) *Discourse Analysis*. Cambridge: Cambridge University Press.

Brumby, E. and Vaszolyi, E. (eds) (1977) *Language Problems and Aboriginal Education*. Western Australia: Mount Lawley College.

Brumfit, C. J. (1978) The English language, ideology and international communication. In *ELT Documents: English as an International Language*. London: British Council, 15-24.

Brumfit, C. J. and Johnson, K. (eds) (1979) *The Communicative Approach to Language Teaching*. London: Oxford University Press.

Bruner, J. S. (1974) *The Relevance of Education*. Harmondsworth: Penguin.

Bublitz, W. (1978) *Ausdrucksweisen der Sprechereinstellung im Deutschen und im Englischen*. Tuebingen: Niemeyer.

Bugarski, R. (1970) Writing systems and phonological insights. *Papers of the Chicago Linguistic Society*: 453-8.

Burton, D. (1980) *Dialogue and Discourse*. London: Routledge and Kegan Paul.

Byram, M. (1978) 'New objectives' in language teaching. *Modern Languages*, 59(4): 204-7.

Callow, K. (1974) *Discourse Considerations in Translating the Word of God*. Grand Rapids, Michigan: Zondervan.

Campbell-Platt, K. (1976) Distribution of linguistic minorities in Britain. In CILT, *Bilingualism and British Education: the Dimensions of Diversity*, London: Centre for Information on Language Teaching and Research.

Candlin, C. N. (1973) The status of pedagogical grammars. In C. Brumfit and K. Johnson (eds), *The Communicative Approach to Language Teaching*, London: Oxford University Press, 72-81.

Candlin, C. N., Bruton, C. J., Leather, J. L. and Woods, E. (1977) *Doctor-Patient Communication Skills*. Chelmsford: Graves Medical Audiovisual Library.

Carroll, J. B., Davies, P. and Richman, B. (1971) *The American Heritage Word Frequency Book*. New York: Heritage Publishing Co.

Carter, R. (1979) Towards a theory of discourse stylistics. Unpublished Ph.D. thesis, University of Birmingham.

Carter, R. (1980) Linguistics, the teacher and language development: a review of Open University Course PE232. *Educational Review*, 32(2): 223-8.

Carter, R. (1981) Back to basics: assessment, language and the English teacher. *The Times Educational Supplement*, 20 February: 31.

Carter, R. (1982a) A note on core vocabulary. *Nottingham Linguistic Circular*, 11(2): 39-50.

Carter, R. (ed.) (1982b) *Linguistics and the Teacher*. London: Routledge and Kegan Paul.

Carter, R. and Burton, D. (eds) (1982) *Literary Text and Language Study*. London: Edward Arnold.

Cazden, C. B., Johns, V. and Hymes, D. (eds) (1972) *Functions of Language in the Classroom*. New York: Teachers College Press.

Chanan, G. and Delamont, S. (eds) (1975) *Frontiers of Classroom Research*. Slough: National Foundation for Educational Research.

Chapman, R. D. (1976) Bilingualism in Birmingham. In CILT, *Bilingualism and British Education: the Dimensions of Diversity*, London: Centre for Information on Language Teaching and Research, 74-7.

Chomsky, N. (1965) *Aspects of the Theory of Syntax*. Cambridge, Mass: MIT Press.

CILT (1974) *The Space Between: English and Foreign Languages at School*. CILT Reports and Papers 10. London: Centre for Information on Language Teaching and Research.

CILT (1976) *Bilingualism and British Education: the Dimensions of Diversity*, London: Centre for Information on Language Teaching and Research.

Clark, E. V. (1973) What's in a word? In T. Moore (ed.), *Cognitive Development and the Acquisition of Language*, New York: Academic Press, 65-110.

Clarke, D. F. and Nation, I. S. P. (1980) Guessing the meaning of words from context: strategies and techniques. *System*, 8(3): 211-20.

Coates, R. (1982) How standard is standard? In T. Pateman (ed.), *Languages for Life*, Brighton: University of Sussex.

Cochrane, J. (ed.) (1969) *The Penguin Book of American Short Stories*. Harmondsworth: Penguin.

Cole, P. and Morgan, J. L. (eds) (1975) *Syntax and Semantics*, vol. 3, *Speech Acts*. New York: Academic Press.

Comrie, B. (1981) *Language Universals and Linguistic Typology*. Oxford: Blackwell.

Corbett, E. P. J. (1965) *Classical Rhetoric for the Modern Student*. New York: Oxford University Press.

Corder, S. P. (1980) Second language acquisition research and the teaching of grammar. *BAAL Newsletter*, 10: 1-13.

Corder, S. P. and Roulet, E. (eds) (1977) *The Notions of Simplification, Interlanguage and Pidgins and their Relation to Second Language Pedagogy*. University of Neuchatel and Geneva: Librairie Droz.

Coulthard, M. and Ashby, M. C. (1976) A linguistic analysis of doctor-patient interviews. In M. Wadsworth and D. Robinson (eds), *Studies in Everyday Medical Life*, London: Martin Robertson.

Cross, D. (1979) An investigation into the effects of a delayed start in main foreign language learning. *Modern Languages*, 60(2): 92-100.

Cruse, D. A. (1977) The pragmatics of lexical specificity. *Journal of Linguistics*, 13: 153-64.

Crystal, D. (1980) Neglected grammatical factors in conversational English. In S. Greenbaum, G. Leech and J. Svartvik (eds), *Studies in English Linguistics for Randolph Quirk*, London: Longman, 153-66.

Crystal, D. (1982) *Profiling Linguistic Disability*. London: Edward Arnold.

Crystal, D. (1985) How many millions? The statistics of English today. *English Today*, 1: 7-9.

Crystal, D. and Davy, D. (1969) *Investigating English Style*. London: Longman.

Crystal, D. and Davy, D. (1975) *Advanced Conversational English*. London: Longman.

Culler, J. (1975) *Structuralist Poetics*. London: Routledge and Kegan Paul.

Czerniewska, P. (1981) The teacher, language development and linguistics: a response to Carter's review of PE232. *Educational Review*, 33(2): 37-9.

Dalton, P. and Hardcastle, W. D. (1977) *Disorders of Fluency*. London: Edward Arnold.

Darian, S. (1979) The role of redundancy in language and language teaching. *System*, 7(1): 47-59.

Das Gupta, J. (1969) Official language problems and policies in South Asia. In T. A. Sebeok (ed.), *Current Trends in Linguistics*, The Hague: Mouton, vol. 5, 578-96.

Davies, A. (1965) Linguistics and the teaching of spoken English. In A. Wilkinson, A. Davies and D. Atkinson, *Spoken English*. Educational Review Occasional Publications, 2, supplement to 17(2), 17-39.

Davies, A. (ed.) (1968) *Language Testing Symposium*. London: Oxford University Press.

Davies, A. (ed.) (1977) *Language and Learning in Early Childhood*. London: Heinemann.

Davies, A. (1978) Textbook situations and idealized language. *Work in Progress*, 11: 120-33. Department of Linguistics, University of Edinburgh.

DES (1975) *A Language for Life*. Report of the Bullock Committee. London: HMSO.

Dixon, J. (1967) *Growth Through English*. London: Oxford University Press.

Dixon, R. M. W. (1971) A method of semantic description. In D. D. Steinberg and L. A. Jakobovits (eds), *Semantics*, London: Cambridge University Press, 436-70.

Dixon, R. M. W. (1973) The semantics of giving. In M. Gross, M. Halle and M.-P. Schutzenberger (eds), *The Formal Analysis of Natural Languages*, The Hague: Mouton, 205-23.

Dolley, C. (ed.) (1967) *The Penguin Book of English Short Stories*. Harmondsworth: Penguin.

Dressler, W. U. (ed.) (1978) *Current Trends in Text Linguistics*. Berlin: de Gruyter.

Edwards, V. K. (1979) *The West Indian Language Issue in British Schools*. London: Routledge and Kegan Paul.

Edwards, V. K., Trudgill, P. and Weltens, B. (1984) *The Grammar of English Dialect*: *a Survey of Research*. London: Economic and Social Research Council.

Enkvist, N. E. (1981) Some rhetorical aspects of text linguistics. In H. Eichheim and A. Maley (eds), *Fremdsprachenunterricht im Spannungsfeld zwischen Gesellschaft, Schule und Wissenschaften*, Munich: Goethe Institute, 172-206.

Ervin-Tripp, S. and Mitchell-Kernan, C. (eds) (1977) *Child Discourse*. New York: Academic Press.

Exton, R. (1984) The language of literature. In J. Miller (ed.), *Eccentric Propositions: Essays on Literature and the Curriculum*, London: Routledge and Kegan Paul, 70-9.

Eyers, S. and Richmond, J. (eds) (1982) *Becoming our own Experts*. London: ILEA English Centre.

Fasold, R. (1984) *The Sociolinguistics of Society*. Oxford: Blackwell.

Ferguson, C. A. (1962) The language factor in national development. *Anthropological Linguistics*, 4: 23-7.

Ferguson, C. A. (1971a) Contrasting patterns of literacy acquisition in a multilingual nation. In W. H. Whiteley (ed.), *Language Use and Social Change*, London: Oxford University Press, 234-53.

Ferguson, C. A. (1971b) Absence of copula and the notion of simplicity. In D. Hymes (ed.), *Pidginization and Creolization of Languages*. London: Cambridge University Press.

Feyerabend, P. (1975) *Against Method*. London: Verso.

Feyerabend, P. (1978) *Science in a Free Society*. London: New Left Books.

Flanders, N. (1970) *Analysing Teacher Behaviour*. London: Addison Wesley.

Flew, A. (1975) *Thinking about Thinking*. London: Fontana.

Foucault, M. (1972) *The Archaeology of Knowledge*. London: Tavistock.

French, P. and MacLure, M. (eds) (1981a) *Adult-Child Conversation*. London: Croom Helm.

Furlong, V. (1976) Interaction sets in the classroom. In M. Stubbs and S. Delamont (eds), *Explorations in Classroom Observation*, London: Wiley, 23-44.

Gannon, P. and Czerniewska, P. (1980) *Using Linguistics: an Educational Focus*. London: Edward Arnold.

Garfinkel, H. (1967) *Studies in Ethnomethodology*. Englewood Cliffs, NJ: Prentice Hall.

Gazdar, G. (1979) *Pragmatics: Implicature, Presupposition and Logical Form*. New York: Academic Press.

Genette, G. (1980) *Narrative Discourse*. Oxford: Blackwell.

Gimson, A. C. (1984) The RP accent. In P. Trudgill (ed.), *Language in the British Isles*, London: Cambridge University Press, 45-54.

Givón, T. (1978) Negation in language: pragmatics, function and ontology. In P. Cole (ed), *Syntax and Semantics*, vol. 9, *Pragmatics*, New York: Academic Press, 69-112.

Givón, T. (ed.) (1979) *Syntax and Semantics*, vol. 12, *Discourse and Syntax*. New York: Academic Press.

Gleason, H. A. (1968) Contrastive analysis in discourse structure. In J. E. Alatis (ed.), *Contrastive Linguistics and its Pedagogical Implications*, 19th Round Table Meeting, Washington, DC: University of Georgetown Press, 39-63.

Godard, D. (1977) Same setting, different norms: phone call beginnings in France and the United States. *Language in Society*, 6: 209-19.

Goffman, E. (1955) On face work: an analysis of ritual elements in social interaction. In J. Laver and S. Hutcheson (eds), *Face-to-Face Interaction*, Harmondsworth: Penguin, 1972, 319-46.

Goffman, E. (1971) *Relations in Public*. London: Allen Lane.

Goodman, K. (1982) *Language and Literacy*. 2 vols. London: Routledge and Kegan Paul.

Goody, J. (ed.) (1968) *Literacy in Traditional Societies*. London: Cambridge University Press.

Gordon, J. C. B. (1980) A case study in misinterpretation: a note on some dissemi- nations of Bernstein by educationists. *UEA Papers in Linguistics* (University of East Anglia), 12: 45-52.

Gorman, T. (ed.) (1977) *Language and Literacy: Current Issuess and Research*. Tehran: International Institute for Adult Literacy Methods.

Grassby, A. J. (1977) Linguistic genocide. In E. Brumby and E. Vaszolyi (eds), *Language Problems and Aboriginal Education*, Western Australia: Mount Lawley College.

Greenlee, M. (1981) Learning to tell the forest from the trees: unravelling discourse features of a psychotic child. *First Language*, 2: 83-102.

Gregory, G. (1984) Using community-published writing in the classroom. In J. Miller (ed.), *Eccentric Propositions: Essays on Literature and the Curriculum*, London: Routledge and Kegan Paul, 267-78.

Gregory, M. and Carroll, S. (1978) *Language and Situation*. London: Routledge and Kegan Paul.

Grice, H. P. (1975) Logic and conversation. In P. Cole and J. L. Morgan (eds), *Syntax and Semantics*, vol. 3: *Speech Acts*, New York: Academic Press, 41-58.

Gudschinsky, S. C. (1976) *Literacy: the Growing Influence of Linguistics*. The Hague: Mouton.

Gumperz, J. J. (1982a) *Discourse Strategies*. London: Cambridge University Press.

Gumperz, J. J. (ed.) (1982b) *Language and Social Identity.* London: Cambridge University Press.

Gumperz, J. J. and Herasimchuk, E. (1972) The conversational analysis of social meaning. In R. Shuy (ed.), *Sociolinguistics: Current Trends and Prospects,* Washington, DC: Georgetown Monographs on Language and Linguistics.

Habermas, J. (1979) *Communication and the Evolution of Society.* London: Heinemann.

Hale, K. (1971) A note on the Walbiri tradition of antonymy. In D. D. Steinberg and L. A. Jakobovits (eds), *Semantics,* London: Cambridge University Press, 472-83.

Hall, E. T. (1959) *The Silent Language.* New York: Doubleday.

Hall, R. A. Jr (1975) Review of J. Vachek *Written Language. Language,* 51: 461-4.

Halliday, M. A. K. (1961) Categories of the theory of grammar. *Word,* 17(3): 241-92.

Halliday, M. A. K. (1964) Syntax and the consumer. In C. I. J. M. Stewart (ed.), *Report of 15th Annual Round Table Meeting on Linguistics and Language Studies,* Washington, DC: Georgetown University Press, 11-24.

Halliday, M. A. K. (1967) Grammar, society and the noun. Inaugural lecture, University College, London.

Halliday, M. A. K. (1969) Relevant models of language. *Educational Review,* 22: 26-37.

Halliday, M. A. K. (1974) Review of Shuy ed. *Sociolinguistics. Language in Society,* 3: 94-103.

Halliday, M. A. K. (1975) *Learning How to Mean.* London: Edward Arnold.

Halliday, M. A. K. (1978) *Language as Social Semiotic.* London: Edward Arnold.

Halliday, M. A. K. (1982) Linguistics in teacher education. In R. Carter (ed.), *Linguistics and the Teacher,* London: Routledge and Kegan Paul, 10-15.

Halliday, M. A. K. and Hasan, R. (1976) *Cohesion in English.* London: Longman.

Halliday, M. A. K., McIntosh, A. and Strevens, P. (1964) *The Linguistic Sciences and Language Teaching.* London: Longman.

Hamilton, D. (1976) The advent of curriculum integration: paradigm lost or paradigm regained? In M. Stubbs and S. Delamont (eds), *Explorations in Classroom Observation,* London: Wiley, 195-212.

Hammersley, M. (1974) The organization of pupil participation. *Sociological Review,* August.

Hanks, P. (ed.) (1979) *Collins Dictionary of the English Language.* London: Collins.

Hargie, O., Dickson, D. and Saunders, C. (1981) *Social Skills in Interpersonal Communication.* London: Croom Helm.

Harris, S. (1980) Language interaction in magistrates courts. Unpublished Ph.D. thesis, University of Nottingham.

Harrison, C. (1980) *Readability in the Classroom.* London: Cambridge University Press.

Hawkins, E. W. (1979) Language as a curriculum study. In NCLE, *The Mother Tongue and Other Languages in Education,* National Congress on Languages in Education, Papers and Reports, 2, London: Centre for Information on Language Teaching and Research, 61-70.

Hawkins, E. W. (1984) *Awareness of Language: an Introduction.* London: Cambridge University Press.

Hawkins, P. (1969) Social class, the nominal group and reference. *Language and Speech,* 12(2): 125-35.

Hawkins, P. (1977) *Social Class, the Nominal Group and Verbal Strategies.* London: Routledge and Kegan Paul.

Hemingway, E. (1925a) *In Our Time*. New York: Boni and Liveright; also Scribner, 1955.

Hemingway, E. (1925b) Cat in the Rain. In E. Hemingway, *In Our Time*, New York: Boni and Liveright; also Scribner, 1955. Also in *The Essential Hemingway*, London: Jonathan Cape, 1947; also Penguin, 1964; Granada, 1977.

Hemingway, E. (1925c) A very short story. In E. Hemingway, *In Our Time*, New York: Boni and Liveright; also Scribner, 1955. Also in *The Essential Hemingway*, London: Jonathan Cape, 1947; also Penguin, 1964; Granada, 1977.

Hemingway, E. (1947) *The Essential Hemingway*. London: Jonathan Cape; also Penguin, 1964; Granada, 1977.

Hemingway, E. (1968) *By-Line*. London: Collins; also Penguin, 1970.

Hindmarsh, R. (1980) *Cambridge English Lexicon*. Cambridge: Cambridge University Press.

HMSO (1921) *The Teaching of English in England*. The Newbolt Report. London: HMSO.

HMSO (1978) *1981 Census of Population*. London: HMSO.

Holbrook, D. (1973) *English in Australia Now*. London: Cambridge University Press.

Holmes, J. (1983) The structure of teachers' directives: a sociolinguistic analysis. In J. Richards and R. Schmidt (eds), *Communicative Competence*, London: Longman.

Hornby, A. S. (1974) *Oxford Advanced Learner's Dictionary of Current English*. London: Oxford University Press.

Huddleston, R. D. (1980) On Palmer's defence of the distinction between auxiliaries and main verbs. *Lingua*, 50: 101-15.

Hudson, R. A. (1976) *Arguments for a Non-Transformational Grammar*. Chicago: University of Chicago Press.

Hudson, R. A. (1980) *Sociolinguistics*. London: Cambridge University Press.

Hudson, R. A. (1981) Some issues on which linguists can agree. *Journal of Linguistics*, 17: 333-43. Version also in R. Carter (ed.), *Linguistics and the Teacher*, London: Routledge and Kegan Paul.

Hughes, A. and Trudgill, P. (1979) *English Accents and Dialects*. London: Edward Arnold.

Hutchins, W. J. (1977) On the structure of scientific texts. *UEA Papers in Linguistics* (University of East Anglia), 5: 106-28.

Hutchins, W. J. (1978) The concept of 'aboutness' in subject indexing. *Aslib Proceedings*, 30: 172-81.

Hymes, D. (1964) Directions in (ethno)linguistic theory. *American Anthropologist*, 66(3): 2.

Hymes, D. (1972) Introduction. In C. B. Cazden, V. Johns and D. Hymes (eds), *Functions of Language in the Classroom*, New York: Teachers College Press, xi-lvii.

Javal, E. (1897) Essai sur la physiologie de lecture. *Annales d'Oculistique*, 82: 242-53.

Jefferson, G. (1973) A case of precision timing in ordinary conversation. *Semiotica*, 9(1): 47-96.

Jenkins, J. R. and Dixon, R. (1983) Vocabulary learning. *Contemporary Educational Psychology*, 18: 237-60.

Johnson-Laird, P. N. (1983) *Mental Models*. London: Cambridge University Press.

Jones, P. E. (1974) *Education in Australia*. Newton Abbot: David and Charles.

Kachru, B. B. (1969) English in South Asia. In T. A. Sebeok (ed.), *Current Trends in Linguistics*, The Hague: Mouton, vol. 5: 627-78.

Kaplan, R. B. (1967) Contrastive rhetoric and the teaching of composition. *TESOL Quarterly*, 1(4): 10-16.

Kaplan, R. B. (ed.) (1980) *On the Scope of Applied Linguistics*. Rowley, Mass: Newbury House.

Katriel, T. and Dascal, M. (1984) What do indicating devices indicate? *Philosophy and Rhetoric*, 17(1): 1-15.

Keddie, N. (1971) Classroom knowledge. In M. F. D. Young (ed.), *Knowledge and Control*, London: Collier Macmillan.

Keen, J. (1978) *Teaching English: A Linguistic Approach*. London: Methuen.

Kempson, R. (1977) *Semantic Theory*. London: Cambridge University Press.

Kintsch, W., Kozminsky, E., Streby, W. J., McKoon, G. and Keenan, J. M. (1975) Comprehension and recall of text as a function of content variables. *Journal of Verbal Learning and Verbal Behaviour*, 14: 196-214.

Kučera, H. and Francis, W. N. (1967) *Computational Analysis of Present-day American English*. Rhode Island: Brown University Press.

Kuczaj, S. A. (ed.) (1982) *Language Development*, 2 vols. Hillsdale, NJ: Lawrence Erlbaum.

Kuhn, T. S. (1962) *The Structure of Scientific Revolutions*. Chicago: University of Chicago Press.

Labov, W. (1966) *The Social Stratification of English in New York City*. Washington, DC: Center for Applied Linguistics.

Labov, W. (1969) The logic of nonstandard English. In N. Keddie (ed.), *Tinker, Tailor*. Harmondsworth: Penguin, 1974. Also in W. Labov, *Language in the Inner City*, Philadelphia: Pennsylvania University Press, 201-40.

Labov, W. (1970) The study of language in its social context. In W. Labov, *Sociolinguistic Patterns*, Philadelphia: Pennsylvania University Press, 183-259.

Labov, W. (1972a) *Language in the Inner City*. Philadelphia: Pennsylvania University Press.

Labov, W. (1972b) *Sociolinguistic Patterns*. Philadelphia: Pennsylvania University Press.

Labov, W. (1972c) The transformation of experience in narrative syntax. In W. Labov *Language in the Inner City*, Philadelphia: Pennsylvania University Press, 354-96.

Labov, W. (1972d) Some principles of linguistic methodology. *Language in Society*, 1: 1.

Labov, W. (1973) The linguistic consequences of being a lame. *Language in Society*, 2: 81-115. Also in W. Labov, *Language in the Inner City*, Philadelphia: Pennsylvania University Press, 255-92.

Labov, W. (1975) *What is a Linguistic Fact?*. Lisse: Peter de Ridde.

Labov, W. and Fanshel, D. (1977) *Therapeutic Discourse*. New York: Academic Press.

Lakoff, R. (1973) Questionable answers and answerable questions. In B. Kachru et al. (eds), *Papers in Linguistics in Honor of Henry and Renée Kahane*. Urbana: University of Illinois.

Lamb, C. and Lamb, M. (1822) *Tales from Shakespeare*. 4th edn. London: Godwin.

Lawton, D. (1981) *An Introduction to Teaching and Learning*. London: Hodder and Stoughton.

Lawton, D. (1983) *Curriculum Studies and Educational Planning*. London: Hodder and Stoughton.

Leach, E. (1972) Our words. *New Society*, 19 October.

Leech, G. N. and Svartvik, J. (1975) *A Communicative Grammar of English*. London: Longman.

Leeson, R. (1975) *Fluency and Language Teaching*. London: Longman.

Lehmann, W. P. (ed.) (1975) *Language and Linguistics in the People's Republic of China.* Austin: University of Texas Press.

Lehrer, A. (1974) *Semantic Fields and Lexical Structure.* London: North Holland.

Lerman, C. L. (1980) A sociolinguistic study of political discourse: the Nixon Whitehouse conversations. Unpublished Ph.D. thesis, University of Cambridge.

Lester, M. (ed.) (1970) *Readings in Applied Transformational Grammar.* New York: Holt, Rinehart and Winston.

Levine, A. (ed.) (1971) *Penguin English Reader.* Harmondsworth: Penguin.

Levinson, S. C. (1983) *Pragmatics.* Cambridge: Cambridge University Press.

Linguistic Minorities Project (1985) *The Other Languages of England.* London: Routledge and Kegan Paul.

Lipton, J. (1977) *An Exaltation of Larks or the Venereal Game.* Harmondsworth: Penguin.

Livingston, K. R. (1982) Beyond the definition given: on the growth of connotation. In S. A. Kuczaj (ed.), *Language Development,* 2 vols., Hillsdale, NJ: Lawrence Erlbaum, 429-44.

Lodge, D. (1975) *Changing Places.* London: Secker and Warburg.

Lodge, D. (1978) Literary symbolism and Hemingway's 'Cat in the Rain'. University of Birmingham, mimeo.

Longacre, R. E. (1977) Discourse analysis and literacy. In T. Gorman (ed.), *Language and Literacy: Current Issues and Research,* Tehran: International Institute for Adult Literacy Methods, 71-88.

Lunzer, E. and Gardner, K. (eds) (1978) *The Effective Use of Reading.* London: Heinemann.

Lyons, J. (1963) *Structural Semantics.* Oxford: Blackwell.

Lyons, J. (1968) *Introduction to Theoretical Linguistics.* London: Cambridge University Press.

Lyons, J. (1977) *Semantics,* vols 1 and 2. Cambridge: Cambridge University Press.

Lyons, J. (1981) *Language, Meaning and Context.* London: Fontana.

Macaulay, R. K. S. (1977) *Social Class and Education.* Edinburgh: Edinburgh University Press.

McIntosh, A. (1963) Language and style. In J. Pride and J. Holmes (eds), *Socio-linguistics.* Harmondsworth: Penguin, 1972.

Mackay, D., Thompson, B. and Schaub, P. (1970) *Breakthrough to Literacy: Teachers' Manual.* London: Longman.

Mackey, W. and Savard, J.-G. (1967) The indices of coverage: a new dimension in lexicometrics. *International Review of Applied Linguistics,* 2-3: 71-121.

MacKinnon, K. (1977) *Language, Education and Social Process in a Gaelic Community.* London: Routledge and Kegan Paul.

McLuhan, M. (1960) The effect of the printed book on language in the sixteenth century. In E. Carpenter and M. McLuhan (eds), *Explorations in Communication,* London: Cape, 125-35.

McTear, M. F. (1981) The development of conversation in pre-school children. Unpublished Ph.D. thesis, Ulster Polytechnic.

McTear, M. F. (1984) Conversational incompetence: a case study. University of Ulster, mimeo. Revised version in M. F. McTear, *Children's Conversation,* Oxford: Blackwell.

McTear, M. F. (1985) *Children's Conversation.* Oxford: Blackwell.

Malcolm, I. (1979) *Classroom communication and the Aboriginal child.* Unpublished Ph.D. thesis, University of Western Australia.

Maley, A. and Duff. A. (eds) (1976) *Words*. London: Cambridge University Press.

Maley, A. and Duff, A. (1978) *Drama Techniques in Language Learning*. London: Cambridge University Press.

Mandler, J. M. and Johnson, N. S. (1977) Remembrance of things parsed: story structure and recall. *Cognitive Psychology*, 9: 111-51.

Marks, P. M. (1980) Examinations in spoken English for older secondary pupils. Unpublished paper, Assessment of Performance Unit Seminar on Oracy. Cambridge, March.

Meara, P. (1980) Vocabulary acquisition: a neglected aspect of language learning. *Language Teaching and Linguistics Abstracts*, 13(4): 221-46.

Michaels, L. and Ricks, C. (eds) (1980) *The State of the Language*. London: University of California Press.

Michaels, W. B. (1980) Against formalism: chickens and rocks. In L. Michaels and C. Ricks (eds), *The State of the Language*, London: University of California Press, 410-20.

Miller, C. and Swift, K. (1976) *Words and Women*. New York: Anchor/Doubleday; also Harmondsworth: Penguin, 1979.

Miller, J. (ed.) (1984) *Eccentric Propositions: Essays on Literature and the Curriculum*. London: Routledge and Kegan Paul.

Milroy, J. and Milroy, L. (1974) A sociolinguistic project in Belfast. Ulster Polytechnic, mimeo.

Milroy, J. and Milroy, L. (1978) Change and variation in an urban vernacular. In P. Trudgill (ed.), *Sociolinguistic Patterns in British English*, London: Edward Arnold, 19-36.

Milroy, L. (1980) *Language and Social Networks*. Oxford: Blackwell.

Milroy, L. (1984) Urban dialects in the British Isles. In P. Trudgill (ed.), *Language in the British Isles*, London: Cambridge University Press, 199-218.

Milroy, L. and Margrain, S. (1978) Vernacular loyalty and social network. *Language in Society*, 9: 43-71.

Milroy, L. and Milroy, J. (1985) *Authority in Language*. London: Routledge and Kegan Paul.

Mishler, E. (1972) Implications of teacher-strategies for language and cognition. In C. B. Cazden, V. Johns and D. Hymes (eds), *Functions of Language in the Classroom*, New York: Teachers College Press, 267-98.

Montgomery, M. (1977) The structure of lectures. Unpublished M.A. thesis, University of Birmingham.

Moore, T. (ed.) (1973) *Cognitive Development and the Acquisition of Language*. New York: Academic Press.

Morgan, P. (1896) A case of congenital word blindness. *British Medical Journal*, 7 November: 1378.

Moy, B. and Raleigh, M. (1984) Comprehension: bringing it back alive. In J. Miller (ed.), *Eccentric Propositions: Essays on Literature and the Curriculum*, London: Routledge and Kegan Paul, 148-92.

Munby, J. (1978) *Communicative Syllabus Design*. London: Cambridge University Press.

Nash, W. (1980) *Designs in Prose*. London: Longman.

NCLE (1979) *The Mother Tongue and Other Languages in Education*. National Congress on Languages in Education, Papers and Reports 2. London: Centre for Information on Language Teaching and Research.

NCLE (1980) Report of Working Party C: Comparison of English as a foreign language, modern languages and the mother tongue. National Congress on Languages in Education, mimeo.

Nelson, K. (1982) The syntagmatics and paradigmatics of conceptual development. In S. A. Kuczaj (ed.), *Language Development*, Hillsdale, NJ: Lawrence Erlbaum, 335-64.

Newmark, L. (1966) How not to interfere with language learning. *International Journal of American Linguistics*, 32(1): 2. Reprinted in C. J. Brumfit and K. Johnson (eds), *The Communicative Approach to Language Teaching*, London: Oxford University Press, 160-6.

Nida, E. (1975) *The Componential Analysis of Meaning*. The Hague: Mouton.

Nystrand, M. (ed.) (1983a) *What Writers Know*. New York: Academic Press.

Nystrand, M. (1983b) The role of context in written communication. *Nottingham Linguistic Circular*, 12.

Ochs Keenan, E. (1976) The universality of conversational postulates. *Language in Society*, 5: 67-80.

Ochs, E. (1979) Planned and unplanned discourse. In T. Givón (ed.), *Syntax and Semantics*, vol. 12, *Discourse and Syntax*, New York: Academic Press, 51-80.

Ogden, C. K. (1930) *Basic English: A General Introduction with Rules and Grammar*. London: Kegan Paul.

Oller, J. W. Jr. (1979) *Language Tests at School*. London: Longman.

Opie, I. and Opie, P. (1959) *The Lore and Language of Schoolchildren*. London: Oxford University Press.

Orton, H., Sanderson, S. and Widdowson, J. (eds) (1977) *The Linguistic Atlas of England*. London: Croom Helm.

Page, N. (1973) *Speech in the English Novel*. London: Longman.

Palermo, D. S. (1982) Theoretical issues in semantic development. In S. A. Kuczaj (ed.), *Language Development*, 2 vols, Hillsdale, NJ: Lawrence Erlbaum.

Palmer, F. R. (1974) *The English Verb*. London: Longman.

Palmer, F. R. (1979) Why auxiliaries are not main verbs. *Lingua*, 47: 1-26.

Perera, K. (1980) The assessment of linguistic difficulty in reading material. *Educational Review*, 32(2): 151-61. Reprinted in R. Carter (ed.), *Linguistics and the Teacher* (1982b), London: Routledge and Kegan Paul, 101-13.

Perera, K. (1984) *Children's Writing and Reading*. Oxford: Blackwell.

Pirsig, R. (1974) *Zen and the Art of Motorcycle Maintenance*. London: Bodley Head.

Platt, J. T. (1975) The Singapore English speech continuum and its basilect 'singlish' as a creoloid. *Anthropological Linguistics*, 17(7): 363-74.

Potter, S. (1974) English language. *Encyclopaedia Britannica: Macropaedia*, vol. 6. Chicago: William Benton, 874-87.

Powell, J. E. (1980) The language of politics. In L. Michaels and C. Ricks (eds), *The State of the Language*, London: University of California Press, 432-9.

Pratt, M. L. (1977) *Toward a Speech Act Theory of Literary Discourse*. Bloomington: Indiana University Press.

Price-Williams, D. and Sabsay, S. (1979) Communicative competence amongst severely retarded persons. *Semiotica*, 26(1/2): 35-63.

Propp, V. (1928) *Morphology of the Folktale*, trans L. Scott. Bloomington: Indiana University Press.

Pullum, G. K. and Wilson, D. (1977) Autonomous syntax and the analysis of English auxiliaries. *Language*, 53(4): 741-88.

Quirk, R. (1974) Charles Dickens, linguist. In R. Quirk, *The Linguist and the English Language*, London: Edward Arnold, 1-36.

Quirk, R. (1981) International communication and the concept of nuclear English. In L. E. Smith (ed.), *English for Cross-Cultural Communication*, London: Macmillan, 151-65.

Quirk, R. and Greenbaum, S. (1975) *A University Grammar of English*. London: Longman.

Quirk, R., Greenbaum, S., Leech, G. and Svartvik, J. (1972) *A Grammar of Contemporary English*. London: Longman.

Quirk, R., Greenbaum, S., Leech, G. and Svartvik, J. (1985) *A Comprehensive Grammar of the English Language*. London: Longman.

Rapin, I. and Allen, D. (1983) Developmental language disorders. In U. Kirk (ed.), *Neuropsychology of Language, Reading and Spelling*, New York: Academic Press.

Richards, J. (1971) Coverage: what it is and what it isn't. *ITL*, 13: 1-15.

Richmond, J. (1982) Dialect features in children's writing. In S. Eyers and J. Richmond (eds), *Becoming our Own Experts*, London: ILEA English Centre, 98-117.

Rochester, S. and Martin, J. R. (1979) *Crazy Talk: A Study of the Discourse of Schizophrenic Speakers*. New York: Plenum Press.

Roe, P. (1977) The notion of difficulty in scientific text. Unpublished Ph.D. thesis, University of Birmingham.

Roget, P. M. (1852) *Thesaurus of English Words and Phrases*.

Rosch, E. H. (1973) On the internal structure of perceptual and semantic categories. In T. Moore (ed.), *Cognitive Development and the Acquisition of Language*, New York: Academic Press, 111-44.

Rosch, E. H. (1975) Cognitive reference points. *Cognitive Psychology*, 7: 532-47.

Rosen, H. (1978) Signing on. *The New Review*, 4(47): 55-7. Reprinted in *BAAL Newsletter*, 7, June 19.

Rosen, H. (1980) Linguistic diversity in London schools. In A. K. Pugh, V. J. Lee and J. Swann (eds), *Language and Language Use*, London: Heinemann, 46-75.

Rosen, H. and Burgess, T. (1980) *Languages and Dialects of London Schoolchildren*. London: Ward Lock.

Ross, J. (1969) Auxiliaries as main verbs. In W. Todd (ed.), *Studies in Philosophical Linguistics*, vol. 1, Evanston, Ill.: Great Expectations Press.

Rosten, L. (1968) *The Joys of Yiddish*. Harmondsworth: Penguin.

Roulet, E. (1981) L'analyse de conversations authentiques dans une pédagogie intégrée de la langue maternelle et des langues secondes. Paper read to Colloque de Linguistique Appliquée, Berne.

Rubin, A. (1980) A theoretical taxonomy of the differences between oral and written language. In R. J. Spiro, B. C. Bruce and W. F. Brewer (eds), *Theoretical Issues in Reading Comprehension*, Hillsdale, NJ: Lawrence Erlbaum.

Rudzka, B., Channell, J. and Putseys, Y. (1981) *The Words You Need*. London: Macmillan.

Sacks, H. (1970) Unpublished lecture notes. University of California.

Sacks, H. (1972) On the analysability of stories by children. In J. J. Gumperz and D. Hymes (eds), *Directions in Sociolinguistics*, New York: Holt, Rinehart and Winston.

Saifullah Khan, V. (1976) Provision by minorities for language maintenance. In CILT, *Bilingualism and British Education: the Dimensions of Diversity*, London: Centre for Information on Language Teaching and Research, 31-47.

Saifullah Khan, V. (1978) *Bilingualism and Linguistic Minorities in Britain*. London: Runnymede Trust.

Saifullah Khan, V. (1980) The 'mother tongue' of linguistic minorities in multicultural England. *Journal of Multilingual and Multicultural Development*, 1: 71-88.

Sampson, G. (1975) Theory choice in a two-level science. *British Journal for the Philosophy of Science*, 26: 303-18.

Sampson, G. (1980) *Schools of Linguistics*. London: Hutchinson.

Saunders, C. (1978) *Census 1981 - Question on Racial and Ethnic Origin*. London: Runnymede Trust.

Schegloff, E. A. and Sacks, H. (1973) Opening up closings. *Semiotica*, 8: 289-327.

Searle, J. R. (1975) The logical status of fictional discourse. *New Literary History*, 6(2).

Sebeok, T. A. (1963-76) *Current Trends in Linguistics*, vols 1-14. The Hague: Mouton.

Sheppard, N. (1975) *Alitjinya Ngura Tjukurtarangka*. (Alice in the Dreamtime.) South Australia: University of Adelaide.

Shipley, E. F., Kuhn, J. F. and Madden, E. C. (1983) Mother's use of superordinate category terms. *Journal of Child Language*, 10: 571-88.

Short, M. H. (1981) Discourse analysis and the analysis of drama. *Applied Linguistics*, 2(2): 180-202.

Sinclair, J. McH. (1972) *A Course in Spoken English*, vol. 3: *Grammar*. London: Oxford University Press.

Sinclair, J. McH. (1978) Issues in current ESP project design and management. *MALS Journal* (Midlands Association for Linguistic Study), Summer: 104-25.

Sinclair, J. McH. (ed.) (1980) *Applied Discourse Analysis*. Thematic issue of *Applied Linguistics*, 1(3).

Sinclair, J. McH. (1981) Planes of discourse in literature. University of Birmingham, mimeo.

Sinclair, J. McH. (1982) Linguistics and the teacher. In R. Carter (ed.), *Linguistics and the Teacher*, London: Routledge and Kegan Paul, 16-30.

Sinclair, J. McH. and Coulthard, R. M. (1975) *Towards an Analysis of Discourse*. London: Oxford University Press.

Smith, F. (1973) *Psycholinguistics and Reading*. London: Holt, Rinehart and Winston.

Smith, L. E. (ed.) (1981) *English for Cross-Cultural Communication*. London: Macmillan.

Smith, N. and Wilson, D. (1979) *Modern Linguistics: the Results of Chomsky's Revolution*. Harmondsworth: Penguin.

Snow, C. E. and Ferguson, C. A. (eds) (1977) *Talking to Children: Language Input and Acquisition*. Cambridge: Cambridge University Press.

Spencer, J. (1966) The Anglo-Indians and their speech: a sociolinguistic essay. *Lingua*, 16: 57-70.

Spencer, J. (ed.) (1971) *The English Language in West Africa*. London: Longman.

Sperber, D. and Wilson, D. (1983) Irony and the use-mention distinction. In P. Cole (ed.), *Radical Pragmatics*, New York: Academic Press.

Spiro, R. J., Bruce, B. C. and Brewer, W. F. (eds) (1980) *Theoretical Issues in Reading Comprehension*. Hillsdale, NJ: Lawrence Erlbaum.

Stein, G. (1978) Nuclear English: reflections on the structure of its vocabulary. *Poetica*, 10: 64-76.

Stein, N. L. and Glenn, C. G. (1979) An analysis of story comprehension in elementary school children. In R. Freedle (ed.), *Discourse Processing*, Norwood, NJ: Ablex.

Steinberg, D. D. and Jakobovits, L. A. (eds) (1971) *Semantics*. London: Cambridge University Press.

Stoppard, T. (1980) *Dogg's Hamlet, Cahoot's Macbeth*. London: Faber and Faber.

Strang, B. M. H. (1970) *A History of English*. London: Methuen.

Stratta, L., Dixon, J. and Wilkinson, A. (1973) *Patterns of Language: Explorations in the Teaching of English*. London: Heinemann.

Street, B. V. (1985) *Literacy in Theory and Practice*. London: Cambridge University Press.

Strunk, W. Jr. and White, E. B. (1979) *The Elements of Style*. 3rd edn. New York: Macmillan.

Stubbs, M. (1975) Teaching and talking: a sociolinguistic approach to classroom interaction. In G. Chanan and S. Delamont (eds), *Frontiers of Classroom Research*, Slough: National Foundation for Educational Research, 233-46.

Stubbs, M. (1976) Keeping in touch: some functions of teacher-talk. In M. Stubbs and S. Delamont (eds), *Explorations in Classroom Observation*, London: Wiley, 151-72.

Stubbs, M. (1978) Review of Hawkins *Social Class, the Nominal Group and Verbal Strategies*. *British Journal of Educational Studies*, 26(2).

Stubbs, M. (1980) *Language and Literacy: The Sociolinguistics of Reading and Writing*. London: Routledge and Kegan Paul.

Stubbs, M. (1983a) *Language, Schools and Classrooms*. 2nd edn. London: Methuen.

Stubbs, M. (1983b) *Discourse Analysis: the Sociolinguistic Analysis of Natural Language*. Oxford: Blackwell.

Stubbs, M. (1986) A matter of prolonged fieldwork: notes towards a modal grammar of English. *Applied Linguistics*, 7(1): 1-25.

Stubbs, M. and Berry, M. (1980) The Duke of Wellington's gambit: notes on the English verbal group. *Nottingham Linguistic Circular*, 9(2): 143-62.

Stubbs, M. and Delamont, S. (eds) (1976) *Explorations in Classroom Observation*. London: Wiley.

Stubbs, M. and Hillier, H. (eds) (1983) *Readings on Language, Schools and Classrooms*. London: Methuen.

Stubbs, M. and Robinson, B. (1979) Analysing classroom language. In M. Stubbs, B. Robinson, and S. Twite, *Observing Classroom Language*, Block 5, PE232, Milton Keynes: Open University Press.

Sutcliffe, D. (1982) *British Black English*. Oxford: Blackwell.

Svartvik, J., Eeg-Olofsson, M., Forsheden, O., Orestrom, B. and Thavenius, C. (1982) *Survey of Spoken English: Report on Research 1975-81*. Lund Studies in English 63.

Svartvik, J. and Quirk, R. (eds) (1979) *A Corpus of English Conversation*. Lund: Gleerup.

Tadros, A. (1980) Prediction in economics text. *ELR Journal* (English Language Research), 1: 42-59. University of Birmingham, mimeo.

Tang, Xiaoping and Chen Kaixin (1979) *Shiyong yingyu huihua*. (Practical English Dialogues.) Guangxi.

Thomson, D. (1976) *Gaelic in Scotland. [Gaidhlig ann an Albainn]*. Ed. R. MacThomais. Glasgow: Gairm.

Thorndike, E. (1921) *The Teacher's Wordbook*. New York: Columbia Teachers College.

Thorndike, E. and Lorge, I. (1944) *Teacher's Wordbook of 30,000 Words*. New York: Columbia Teachers College.

Tinkel, T. (1979) A proposal for the teaching of linguistics at the secondary school level. *MALS Journal* (Midlands Association for Linguistic Studies), 4: 79-100.

Tizard, B. and Hughes, M. (1984) *Young Children Learning. Talking and Thinking at Home and at School*. London: Fontana.

Todorov, T. (1969) *Grammaire du Decameron*. The Hague: Mouton.

Torode, B. (1976) Teachers' talk and classroom discipline. In M. Stubbs and S. Delamont (eds), *Explorations in Classroom Observation*, London: Wiley, 173–92.

Trier, J. (1931) *Der Deutsche Wortschatz im Sinnbezirk des Verstandes*. Heidelberg: Winter.

Trudgill, P. (1974) *Sociolinguistics*. Harmondsworth: Penguin. 2nd edn, 1983.

Trudgill, P. (1975) *Accent, Dialect and the School*. London: Edward Arnold.

Trudgill, P. (ed.) (1978) *Sociolinguistic Patterns in British English*. London: Edward Arnold.

Trudgill, P. (1979) Standard and non-standard dialects of English in the United Kingdom. *International Journal of the Sociology of Language*, 21: 9–24. In P. Trudgill, *On Dialect*, Oxford: Blackwell, 1983, 50–69. Also in M. Stubbs and H. Hillier (eds), *Readings on Language, Schools and Classrooms*, London: Methuen, 1983, 186–200.

Trudgill, P. (1983) *On Dialect*. Oxford: Blackwell.

Trudgill, P. (1984a) Standard English in England. In P. Trudgill (ed.), *Language in the British Isles*, London: Cambridge University Press, 32–44.

Trudgill, P. (ed.) (1984b) *Language in the British Isles*. London: Cambridge University Press.

Trudgill, P. and Hannah, J. (1982) *International English: a Guide to Varieties of Standard English*. London: Edward Arnold.

Turner, G. W. (1966) *The English Language in Australia and New Zealand*. London: Longman.

Unwin, S. and Dewar, R. (1961) *The Miscillian Manuscript*. London: Cassel.

Vachek, J. (1973) *Written Language: General Problems and Problems of English*. The Hague: Mouton.

Valkhoff, M. F. (1971) Descriptive bibliography of the linguistics of Afrikaans. In T. A. Sebeok (ed.), *Current Trends in Linguistics*, The Hague: Mouton, vol. 7: 455–500.

Van Dijk, T. A. (1981) Discourse studies and education. *Applied Linguistics*, 2(1): 1–26.

Van Dijk, T. A. and Kintsch, W. (1978) Cognitive psychology and discourse: recalling and summarizing stories. In W. U. Dressler (ed.), *Current Trends in Text Linguistics*, Berlin: de Gruyter, 61–80.

Van Ek, J. A. (1975) *The Threshold Level*. Strasbourg: Council of Europe.

Van Ek, J. A. and Alexander, L. G. (1977) *Threshold Level English*. Oxford: Pergamon.

Venezky, R. L. (1970) *The Structure of English Orthography*. The Hague: Mouton.

Von Faber, H. and Heid, M. (eds) (1981) *Lesen in der Fremdsprache*. Munich: Goethe Institute.

Walker, R. and Adelman, C. (1972) Towards a sociography of the classroom. Report to Social Science Research Council, mimeo, HR/1142/1.

Walker, R. and Adelman, C. (1976) Strawberries. In M. Stubbs and S. Delamont (eds), *Explorations in Classroom Observation*, London: Wiley, 133–50.

Waters, H. S. (1980) 'Class news': a single subject longitudinal study of prose production and schema formation during childhood. *Journal of Verbal Learning and Verbal Behaviour*, 19: 152–67.

Wells, C. G. (1984) *Language Development in the Pre-School Years*. London: Cambridge University Press.

Wells, J. C. (1982) *Accents of English*, 3 vols. London: Cambridge University Press.

West, M. (1953) *A General Service List of English Words*. London: Longman.

Whiteley, W. H. (ed.) (1971) *Language Use and Social Change*. London: Oxford University Press.

Widdowson, H. G. (1975a) *Stylistics and the Teaching of Literature*. London: Longman.

Widdowson, H. G. (1975b) An applied linguistic approach to discourse analysis. Unpublished Ph.D. thesis, University of Edinburgh.

Widdowson, H. G. (1978) *Teaching Language as Communication*. London: Oxford University Press.

Widdowson, H. G. (1979a) *Explorations in Applied Linguistics*. Oxford: Oxford University Press.

Widdowson, H. G. (1979b) Linguistic insights and language teaching principles. In H. G. Widdowson, *Explorations in Applied Linguistics*, Oxford: Oxford University Press, 215-33.

Widdowson, H. G. (1979c) The partiality and relevance of linguistic descriptions. In H. G. Widdowson, *Explorations in Applied Linguistics*, Oxford: Oxford University Press, 234-45.

Widdowson, H. G. (1979d) Notional syllabuses. In H. G. Widdowson, *Explorations in Applied Linguistics*, Oxford: Oxford University Press, 247-50.

Widdowson, H. G. (1980a) Applied linguistics: the pursuit of relevance. In R. B. Kaplan (ed.), *On the Scope of Applied Linguistics*, Rowley, Mass: Newbury House, 74-87.

Widdowson, H. G. (1980b) Models and fictions. *Applied Linguistics*, 1(2): 165-70.

Wight, J. (1974) The space between. In CILT, *The Space Between: English and Foreign Languages at School*, CILT Reports and Papers 10, London: Centre for Information on Language Teaching and Research, 101-10.

Wiles, S. (1979) The multilingual classroom. *Language Development*, PE232. Milton Keynes: Open University Press.

Wilkins, D. A. (1976) *Notional Syllabuses*. London: Oxford University Press.

Wilkinson, A. (1965a) *Some Aspects of Oracy*. National Association for the Teaching English. Bulletin, 11(2).

Wilkinson, A. (1965b) Research in listening comprehension. *Educational Research*, 12(2): 140-4.

Wilkinson, A. (1968a) The testing of oracy. In A. Davies (ed.), *Language Testing Symposium*, London: Oxford University Press, 117-32.

Wilkinson, A. (1968b) The implications of oracy. *Educational Review*, 20(2): 125-35.

Wilkinson, A., Davies, A. and Atkinson, D. (1965) *Spoken English*. Educational Review Occasional Publications, 2, supplement to 17(2).

Wilkinson, A. and Stratta, L. (1970) Listening comprehension at 13 plus. *Educational Review*, 22(3): 228-42.

Wilkinson, A. and Stratta, L. (1972) Listening and language. *Educational Review*, 25(1).

Wilkinson, A., Stratta, L. and Dudley, P. (1974) *The Quality of Listening*. London: Macmillan.

Wilkinson, A. and Wilkinson, E. (1968) The development of language in the middle years. *English in Education*, 12(1): 42-52.

Willes, M. J. (1978) Early lessons learned too well. Supplementary reading to *Language Development*, PE232. Milton Keynes: Open University Press.

Willes, M. J. (1981) Learning to take part in classroom interaction. In P. French and M. MacLure (eds), *Adult-Child Conversation*, London: Croom Helm, 73-90.

Willes, M. J. (1983) *Children into Pupils: a Study of Language in Early Schooling*. London: Routledge and Kegan Paul.

Williams, R. (1976) *Keywords*. London: Fontana.

Wolfson, N. (1979) The conversational historical present alteration. *Language*, 55(1): 168-82.

Young, M. F. D. (ed.) (1971) *Knowledge and Control*. London: Collier Macmillan.

Name index

Subject index

The index of this book is organized around several sets of concepts which are explicitly proposed in the book itself, in its attempt to define the components of an educational theory of language (e.g. see pp. 1, 29). I propose (pp. 9, 80-1, 84, 132) that such a theory must consist of: *descriptions* of language in use; and discussions of language *variation* and of language *planning and policy*. Such a theory inevitably involves *cultural*, *institutional* and *ideological* analysis. An educational theory must also have a *developmental* dimension. I also propose that linguistic description must involve a *model of language* itself (p. 10), including a representation of different *levels of language* (pp. 20-1): *phonetics and phonology, morphology, lexis, syntax, semantics* and *discourse*. The concept of the inherent variability of language is discussed mainly in terms of *dialects* and *diatypes*, and in terms of *speaking, listening, writing* and *reading*.

These categories provide the main structure of the index. (Other index entries are mainly for varieties of *English* and *other languages*, branches of *linguistics*, and technical terms.)

The book exemplifies these categories, but also makes them problematic in its discursive detail, as the book itself indexes other books and articles in a web of intertextuality. Nevertheless, an explicit structure is useful, since its provisional categories, with their inevitable biases, are thereby more visible. A refusal to be explicit is a way of concealing ideology.